Drawing Closer to

GOD

MW00389134

Drawing Closer to GOD

365 Daily Meditations
on Questions from Scripture

Dianne Neal Matthews

BakerBooks
a division of Baker Publishing Group
Grand Rapids, Michigan

© 2010 by Dianne Neal Matthews

Published by Baker Books
a division of Baker Publishing Group
P.O. Box 6287, Grand Rapids, MI 49516-6287
www.bakerbooks.com

Printed in the United States of America

All rights reserved. No part of this publication may be reproduced, stored in a retrieval system, or transmitted in any form or by any means—for example, electronic, photocopy, recording—without the prior written permission of the publisher. The only exception is brief quotations in printed reviews.

Library of Congress Cataloging-in-Publication Data
Matthews, Dianne Neal.
Drawing closer to God : 365 daily meditations on questions from Scripture / Dianne Neal Matthews.
p. cm.
ISBN 978-0-8010-7272-7 (pbk.)
1. Devotional calendars. I. Title.
BV4811.M339 2010
242′.2—dc22 2010021085

Unless otherwise indicated, Scripture is taken from GOD'S WORD®, a copyrighted work of God's Word to the Nations. Quotations are used by permission. Copyright 1995 by God's Word to the Nations. All rights reserved.

Scripture marked NASB is taken from the New American Standard Bible®, Copyright © 1960, 1962, 1963, 1968, 1971, 1972, 1973, 1975, 1977, 1995 by The Lockman Foundation. Used by permission.

Scripture marked NIV is taken from the HOLY BIBLE, NEW INTERNATIONAL VERSION®. NIV®. Copyright © 1973, 1978, 1984 by International Bible Society. Used by permission of Zondervan. All rights reserved.

Scripture marked NKJV is taken from the New King James Version. Copyright © 1982 by Thomas Nelson, Inc. Used by permission. All rights reserved.

Scripture marked NLT is taken from the *Holy Bible*, New Living Translation, copyright © 1996, 2004. Used by permission of Tyndale House Publishers, Inc., Wheaton, Illinois 60189. All rights reserved.

Scripture marked TLB is taken from *The Living Bible*, copyright © 1971. Used by permission of Tyndale House Publishers, Inc., Wheaton, Illinois 60189. All rights reserved.

Published in association with MacGregor Literary Agency.

10 11 12 13 14 15 16 7 6 5 4 3 2 1

In keeping with biblical principles of creation stewardship, Baker Publishing Group advocates the responsible use of our natural resources. As a member of the Green Press Initiative, our company uses recycled paper when possible. The text paper of this book is comprised of 30% post-consumer waste.

green press INITIATIVE

Dedicated with love and appreciation to Richard,
for his support and willingness to put up with the craziness
of being married to a writer.

Thank you to everyone who helped make this book a reality:
my patient, persevering agent, Chip MacGregor;
the staff at Baker Books, including Bob Hosack and Lindsey Spoolstra;
Mark Veldheer, who did the beautiful cover design;
and my prayer support team, who held me up when I needed it the most.

Glory belongs to God, whose power is at work in us. By this power he can do infinitely more than we can ask or imagine. Glory belongs to God in the church and in Christ Jesus for all time and eternity! Amen.

Ephesians 3:20–21

Introduction

I've been full of questions ever since I was a little girl; after writing this book, I've decided that's okay. After all, the Bible is full of questions—asked by God, his followers, his enemies, seekers, Jesus, Satan, and even a donkey. Some express doubts and struggles most of us wrestle with at some point but may be reluctant to verbalize. David cried out, "Why are you so distant, Lord? Why do you hide yourself in times of trouble?" (Ps. 10:1). Gideon asked an angel, "If the Lord is with us, why has all this happened to us?" (Judg. 6:13).

As Jesus taught, he used questions that I can easily relate to: "Can any of you add an hour to your life by worrying?" (Luke 12:25). "Why do you see the piece of sawdust in another believer's eye and not notice the wooden beam in your own eye?" (Matt. 7:3). So did the New Testament writers: "What good does it do if someone claims to have faith but doesn't do any good things?" (James 2:14).

As we read the Bible, God's Holy Spirit uses questions to encourage us: "Is anything too hard for the Lord?" (Gen. 18:14), comfort us: "If God is for us, who can be against us?" (Rom. 8:31), and convict us: "Why do you call me Lord but don't do what I tell you?" (Luke 6:46). If we read carefully, we'll see that God has already answered many of our questions before we could think of them. Before Pilate asked the universal question, "What is truth?" (John 18:38), Jesus had already answered it as he prayed: "Your words are truth" (John 17:17).

The process of studying for this book strengthened my conviction that God is never offended by honest questions. Since our human understanding is limited, there are some things we'll never fully understand during our earthly life. But we can know the One who is the answer to all our questions. I hope these meditations will encourage you as you draw closer to him.

JANUARY

1

“Can you say that anything is new?”

Ecclesiastes 1:8–11

Karla did a double-take when she saw the price tags on the clothes her teenage daughter had just picked out. “Why spend this money?” she asked. “I’ve got stuff just like this up in the attic.” Bethany rolled her eyes. “Oh, Mom.” Later that evening, Karla modeled clothes from her own teen years, including an embroidered peasant top, bell-bottom jeans, and a sweater dress. “You know the old saying,” Karla said. “Everything old is new again.” Bethany smiled. “Well, that old saying is new to me.”

In Ecclesiastes, Solomon compared the seasons and repetitive cycles in nature to people’s lives. Nothing happens that hasn’t happened before. No one can do anything that is really new. “There is nothing new under the sun,” he wrote. “Can you say that anything is new? It has already been here long before us.” Solomon’s comments about the monotony of life underscored his message: true meaning can only be found in a personal relationship with our Creator.

God is called the Ancient of Days, but he delights in doing new things. When we place our faith in Christ and become part of the new covenant, God makes us into a new creation. We have a new nature and a new way of living. As we grow in our faith, God shows us new ways to use our gifts for him and reveals fresh insights from his Word.

Even as a Christian, there may be times when our life seems monotonous—just more of the “same old, same old.” That feeling of dissatisfaction may be our spirit yearning for the future that awaits us. When God makes a new heaven and earth, we’ll fit right in because he’ll renew us, too. As we go to live with our Savior, we’ll be perfect like him—and that will *really* be something new.

The one sitting on the throne said,
“I am making everything new.”
Revelation 21:5

Ask God **what new things he wants to do in your life.**

JANUARY

2

"Did God really say . . . ?"

Genesis 2:15–17; 3:1–8

As I strolled over to watch my husband replace a light switch, he launched into a mini-lecture on the dangers of touching live wires. I felt that my intelligence had been insulted—until I reached out to brush away some dust under the wires and got a jolt up my arm. My husband shook his head, wondering why I hadn't taken him at his word.

The first question recorded in God's Word is designed to question his words. When Satan struck up a conversation with Eve, he slightly altered the wording of God's command to Adam and Eve: "Did God really say, 'You must not eat from *any* tree in the garden'?" Eve responded with her own variation: they must not *touch* the tree of knowledge of good and evil. Satan contradicted God by assuring Eve they would not die if they ate from it. Then he hinted that God had given the command out of jealousy, because he didn't want Adam and Eve to become like him.

Satan still uses the same strategy. He encourages us to question God's Word ("Did God *really* say that all sex outside of marriage is wrong?") and God's character ("Why would a loving God allow so much suffering in the world?"). Unlike Eve, we enjoy the blessing of God's Word in written form, but that doesn't guarantee we'll avoid Satan's traps.

If we have only a superficial knowledge of the Scriptures, Satan can easily substitute a lie for God's truth. God gave us the Bible for daily study, meditation, and application. Once our minds are saturated with the Scriptures, we'll recognize when Satan—or anyone else—is distorting God's Word.

Never stop reciting these teachings. You must think about them night and day so that you will faithfully do everything written in them.

Joshua 1:8

Ask God **to give you a renewed passion for his Word and a commitment to spend time in it every day.**

"Where are you?"

Genesis 3:8–10

I always had fun playing hide-and-seek with my toddlers. How hilarious to see them crouching behind some small object, with their heads covered but the lower halves of their bodies sticking out. It was hard to keep from laughing, knowing they seriously believed I couldn't see *them* since they couldn't see *me*.

Adam and Eve acted a bit like toddlers, but this was no game. They ate the forbidden fruit to gain knowledge and wisdom, yet were foolish enough to think they could hide among the trees from an all-seeing God. Instead of enjoying intimate fellowship with God as before, their first instinct was to avoid him. Adam and Eve didn't become like God; they became alienated from him.

Since we all suffer from the effects of Adam and Eve's fall into sin, we still try to hide from God. Some people hide behind manmade philosophies, a set of rules and regulations, or their own idea of "goodness." Christians usually play a more subtle game, using church activities or spiritual busyness to avoid total openness and honesty with the Lord we claim to serve.

There is nothing we can do to hide our guilt or shame from God; there is nothing we can confess that will shock him. Thankfully, there is also nothing we can do that will make our heavenly Father withdraw his love from us. God sent a Savior to take the penalty for our sins so that we can stand before him unashamed.

His call of "Where are you?" represents an invitation to be transparent before him and discover the joy of being fully accepted by our Creator. We never need to hide from God if we've taken off the "fig leaves" we've gathered and stand before him in the covering he has provided.

So we can go confidently to the throne of God's kindness to receive mercy and find kindness.

Hebrews 4:16

Ask yourself: **Is there any area of my life where I'm trying to hide from God?**

JANUARY
4

"What have you done?"

Genesis 3:11–19

In August of 2009, a man in Florida was charged with possession of child pornography, but he blamed it on his cat. The man told investigators that he left the room while downloading music and his cat jumped up on the keyboard, causing the pictures to download. What a busy cat—the police found more than a thousand pornographic images on the man's computer.

God must have found Adam and Eve's attempts to pass the buck just as ludicrous. He knew exactly what Adam and Eve had been up to, but he gave them each a chance to clear their conscience. When God asked Adam if he had eaten from the forbidden tree, Adam tried to lay the blame on Eve, reminding God that he was the one who'd given him the woman in the first place. When God questioned Eve, she tried to pass the blame on to the serpent who had tricked her.

Our human tendency is to make excuses for our mistakes. We blame other people, our childhood, difficult circumstances, our environment—anything except our own sinful nature. Other people may accept our explanations, but we can't rationalize our behavior to God. While many factors do influence our attitudes and behavior, God holds us accountable for our choices. We can never explain away our sin to him.

Part of the Holy Spirit's role in our life is to sharpen our awareness of personal sins. A guilty conscience can be a blessing by prompting us to make things right in our relationship with God. Our loving Father promises that if we will admit our sins, he will forgive and cleanse us. When we sense his Spirit asking, "What have you done?" we're much better off with honest confession rather than lame attempts to pass the buck.

If we confess our sins, he forgives them and
cleanses us from everything we've done wrong.

1 John 1:9

Ask God to show you any sins in your life you need to confess and turn away from.

"What have we done?"

Jeremiah 8:4–9

What happens if the Holy Spirit pricks our conscience over a sin we commit, but we refuse to confess and turn away from it? David, Israel's poet-king, gives us a clear picture of this scenario. After committing adultery with Bathsheba, David refused to admit his sin for a year. Finally, he broke down and begged for God's forgiveness, recording his prayer in Psalm 51.

In Psalm 32, David described his experience and celebrated God's mercy. As long as he refused to acknowledge his sin, he sensed God's heavy hand on him. The burden of guilt triggered physical and mental consequences, with David suffering from weakness, lack of energy, and severe anxiety. Once he freely confessed his sin to God and received forgiveness, his joy and strength returned.

Feeling miserable isn't always enough to make people change their ways. In Jeremiah 8, God described Judah's spiritual condition after continually refusing to return to him. Instead of admitting any wrongdoing, the people downplayed their sins. They never stopped to reflect on their behavior and ask, "What have we done?" Rather than changing the direction they were headed, they charged full speed ahead like a horse going into battle. As a result, they became spiritually confused, living under self-deception and no longer able to discern God's will.

Ignoring God's conviction of sin in our life is an extremely dangerous habit. It hinders our relationship with God, clouds our judgment, and makes us vulnerable to temptations that lead to poor choices. It also leaves us open to Satan's deception. First Timothy 4:2 refers to false teachers whose "consciences have been scarred as if branded by a red-hot iron." Why would we risk becoming spiritually insensitive when we can confess our sins and receive forgiveness and joy as David did?

Finally, I confessed all my sins to you and
stopped trying to hide my guilt.

Psalm 32:5 NLT

Ask God **to keep your conscience sensitive to his Spirit's promptings.**

JANUARY
6

“Am I trying to please people?”

Galatians 1:6–10

An Aesop’s fable tells of a father and son walking with their donkey to market until a man calls them fools for not riding. The son rides the donkey until someone criticizes him for being lazy and making his father walk; when they switch places, the father gets the same criticism. So they both ride, until townspeople scoff at them for overloading the poor animal. Finally, the man and boy tie the donkey’s feet to a pole and carry him. As they cross a bridge amidst jeers and laughter, the struggling donkey falls into the water and drowns.

The father and son went to ridiculous lengths to try to please everybody they met, but Paul wrote that we should focus on pleasing God alone. Paul made no apologies for his harsh letter addressing the false teachings the Galatian Christians had accepted. He denied the accusation from his Jewish critics that he taught salvation by grace in order to win the favor of Gentile Christians.

“Am I saying this now to win the approval of people or God?” he asked. “Am I trying to please people? If I were still trying to please people, I would not be Christ’s servant.” Paul knew that he had to choose between pleasing people or his Lord; he couldn’t do both. He cared little for what others thought about him as long as it didn’t damage his ministry or the message he proclaimed.

We may be people-pleasers by nature, or maybe we’ve been trained to let others’ opinions dictate our behavior. But believers need to focus on pleasing God first and foremost. If we examine the true motives for our actions, we may find that we’re more interested in courting other people’s favor than in pleasing the One whose opinion counts the most.

We don’t try to please people but God, who tests our motives.

1 Thessalonians 2:4

Ask yourself: **In what areas am I more concerned with pleasing people than God?**

"Which of you wants a full life?"

Psalm 34

"Live well, laugh often, love much." I've seen this quotation on plaques, posters, coasters, bookmarks—anything that can have words printed on it.[1] Each time I see these popular lines, I think about how the last two phrases are self-explanatory, but the first one is wide open to interpretation.

God gives direction on how to "live well" in Psalm 34. "Which of you wants a full life?" David asks. "Who would like to live long enough to enjoy good things?" God promises those who fear him a life rich with his blessings, but many of these blessings require action on our part. We are to refrain from lying, turn from evil, do good, pursue peace, keep our heart humble, and call out to God in times of need.

Living a full life doesn't mean that we'll have everything we want. It doesn't necessarily mean that we won't go through times of disappointment, hardship, and poverty. But if we do our best to live a righteous life as described in the Bible, and learn to depend on God, we can be sure that we'll have a full life.

Jesus didn't come to earth, suffer, and die so that we could merely exist. His sacrificial death made it possible for us to enjoy a personal relationship with God and eternal life that begins the moment we place our faith in him. If we honor God and his Word and treat other people as we should, our life will overflow with things that satisfy the soul, such as love, joy, and peace. The best way to live well is to obey God's instructions, which ensures a life full of spiritual blessings.

[Jesus said] "I have come that they may have life, and have it to the full."

John 10:10 NIV

Ask God **to show you any habits, attitudes, or behaviors that hold you back from living a full life.**

1. Taken from Bessie Anderson Stanley, "Success," 1904.

JANUARY
8

"Are these all the sons you have?"

1 Samuel 16:1–13

Shana couldn't believe that she'd managed to finagle her way into this party. Now all she had to do was zero in on the company's owner and convince him to give her one of the few coveted internships. *That's got to be him*, she thought. Shana marched up to the man in the designer suit who seemed to command everyone's attention and started her spiel. A few minutes later, red faced, she approached the unassuming man in the corner.

Samuel had trouble zeroing in on the right man when God sent him to anoint Israel's next king. *That's got to be him*, Samuel thought, impressed by the appearance of Jesse's oldest son. But one by one, six of Jesse's sons passed before Samuel; one by one, God eliminated them all. "Are these all the sons you have?" Samuel asked. Jesse sent someone to bring in his youngest son from tending the sheep. As soon as David walked in, God told Samuel, "Go ahead, anoint him. He is the one."

Since we tend to judge others by what we see, we often discount a person who strikes us as boring, frumpy, or just plain ordinary. But just because someone doesn't stand out from the crowd doesn't mean they're not outstanding. Only God can see what's on the inside, where a person's true quality lies. How many rewarding relationships have we missed out on because we wrote someone off when their appearance didn't impress us?

We shouldn't write ourselves off, either. The incident with Jesse's sons reminds us that we don't have to be the biggest, the smartest, the strongest, or the best for God to use us in a special way. What impresses him is a heart that desires to serve him above everything else. And that's what we want him to see when he looks at us.

Humans look at outward appearances,
but the LORD *looks into the heart.*

1 Samuel 16:7

Ask yourself: **Is there someone in my life whom I've written off because of outward appearance?**

"Why aren't you repairing the damage in the temple?"

2 Kings 12:1–15

When Joash came to the throne in Jerusalem, the temple was rundown. It had suffered years of neglect and deliberate damage during the reign of earlier rulers who had worshiped other gods. Joash ordered the priests to make the needed repairs by using part of the regular offerings the people brought in. But years passed and the work had not been done. Joash sent for the priests and asked them, "Why aren't you repairing the damage in the temple?"

The temple represented the priests' lifework, but apparently they lacked either the commitment, money, or time needed to take care of repairing it. So Joash set up a way to collect funds for the restoration work and keep it separate from money for the priests' support and temple upkeep. This money was given to trusted overseers who moved the renovation project forward.

According to the New Testament, each individual believer's body is a temple where God's Holy Spirit lives. Many of these temples have suffered neglect or damage from unhealthy habits such as poor nutrition, smoking, not enough exercise, or too much drinking. If we've let our temple get rundown due to our own actions, its condition is a reflection on our Creator.

Since God owns our body, the way we treat it either honors or dishonors him. Plus, taking good care of ourselves makes us better able to carry out his work. It's never too late to start a renovation project and make changes that will benefit our health. These steps will require commitment, time, and maybe money, but God will be pleased with our efforts. And we won't have to hear him ask, "Why aren't you repairing the damage in the temple?"

The Holy Spirit, whom you received from God, lives in you. You don't belong to yourselves. You were bought for a price. So bring glory to God in the way you use your body.

1 Corinthians 6:19–20

Ask yourself: **Do I honor God in the way I treat my body?**

JANUARY

10

"Can any of you add a single hour to your life by worrying?"

Matthew 6:25–34

If there's one thing I'm good at, it's worrying. I worry about everything from the noise that my washing machine makes to global terrorism. I worry when I watch news reports about crime and when I read articles about cancer rates. I worry about how I handled things in the past and what might happen in the future. And I worry about how all this worrying is affecting me.

Jesus asked, "Can any of you add a single hour to your life by worrying?" He pointed out that God knows exactly what we need. He promises to provide for us as long as we focus on loving him and doing his will. If he feeds the birds, how can we doubt that he will take care of us? Although this doesn't mean we shouldn't be concerned or plan for the future, it does remind us that a child of God has no reason to be eaten up by worry when we know our loving God is in control.

According to current research linking stress and anxiety to many diseases, worrying can apparently shorten our life. God understands our tendency to worry and shares the antidote in Philippians 4:6–7. He wants us to talk to him about everything that concerns us—not with wimpy, hurried, or memorized prayers that we occasionally shoot up but with ongoing, honest, heart-to-heart conversation.

What a comfort to know that God desires to hear about everything that worries me. What security to know that he promises to meet all my needs if I give him first priority. When I'm spending my time in Philippians 4:6 prayer, then I won't have time to worry about things that I can't control anyway. And I just may live longer.

Never worry about anything. But in every situation let God know what you need in prayers and requests while giving thanks.

Philippians 4:6

Ask yourself: **Do I spend more time worrying or praying?**

JANUARY
11

"Does not wisdom call out?"

Proverbs 8:1–11

Sometimes when a person in a cartoon or television sitcom has a choice to make, they have two miniature versions of themselves sitting on their shoulders. On one side, the little person is dressed in white and wearing a halo, trying to talk the character into doing the right thing. The other shoulder holds a tiny person dressed in red, holding a pitchfork and trying to persuade the character into doing something against their better judgment.

We find this scenario amusing, but according to Proverbs we all face that situation every day. Chapter 7 describes a loud, brash, immoral woman calling out to a naïve young man. With her seductive dress and smooth talk, she tempts him to come with her, and finally seduces him. The young man has no idea that this path leads to destruction.

In chapter 8, another voice calls out. Wisdom is portrayed as a virtuous woman offering an open, honest invitation to anyone wanting to acquire understanding and instruction for wise living. The words that wisdom speaks are true, noble, and of infinite value. Listening to this voice leads to a life blessed by God's favor.

Every day, moment by moment, we have different voices calling out to us. Our decision about which one we listen to affects every area of our life. It determines whether we follow God's way or whether we go down a different path—and end up where we don't really want to be.

It's not always easy to distinguish between the voices. Satan's subtle lies can mimic truth, and so can the voice of the culture around us. And we can mistake our own ideas for God's leading. It's important to stay familiar with God's voice through prayer and Bible study. That's the only way to make sure we listen to the right voice and stay on the path of wisdom.

Blessed is the person who listens to me, watches at my door day after day, and waits by my doorposts.

Proverbs 8:34

Ask yourself: **Which voice will I listen to and obey today?**

JANUARY

12

"Where are all the miracles?"

Judges 6:11–14

Amber smiled to herself as the doctor left the room. She'd been scheduled for surgery to remove the cancerous tumor from her abdomen, but pre-op X-rays showed no traces of the mass. The doctor had been dumbfounded but Amber accepted it as a miracle. Now she couldn't wait to see Jeff's reaction. As prayer chains were activated on Amber's behalf, her skeptical husband had scoffed at the idea that God might heal her. *Let's see how he explains this away*, Amber thought.

Gideon revealed a skeptical attitude about God's dealings with Israel. When the messenger of the Lord appeared to him, Gideon questioned God's involvement with his nation. "Where are all the miracles our ancestors have told us about?" he asked. "Didn't they say, 'The LORD brought us out of Egypt'?" Gideon had heard about God's miraculous deliverance and provision for his ancestors, but now he saw no visible evidence that God still worked on Israel's behalf.

Some people scoff at the idea that God ever performed miracles, labeling people who believe such "nonsense" as unenlightened. Yet many scientists come to believe in God when they see his hand in the majesty of outer space or in the mysterious, complex workings of the human body. Every day we're surrounded by God's miraculous involvement in his creation, from the tiniest atoms in our bodies to the activity of heavenly bodies.

Just as in biblical times, God is intimately involved in the lives of his children. We don't always see visible evidence of it, but he still performs miracles to protect us, guide us, and provide for us. A cynical attitude dulls our recognition of his working on our behalf. But whether behind the scenes or in plain sight, we can be sure that our God still performs miracles today.

He does great things that we cannot understand
and miracles that we cannot count.

Job 5:9

Ask God to open your eyes to the miracles he performs in your life and in the world.

"Why are you discouraged, my soul?"

Psalm 42

The deer staggered through the brush, his sides heaving in the hot, oppressive air. White flecks of foam gathered in the corners of his mouth; his eyes looked wild and hollow. At last he stepped into the clearing. Plunging his head into the rippling stream, he drank long and deeply.

The writer of Psalm 42 illustrated his need for God with the picture of a deer desperately panting for water. Because the psalmist had an acute awareness of his dependence on God, he knew how to handle times of sadness and despondency. The psalm describes an Israelite in exile, far away from his homeland. Surrounded by enemies who mocked his faith, his situation made him feel separated from God.

"Why are you discouraged, my soul?" he cried out. "Why are you so restless?" Even while freely expressing his sadness, the psalmist made the deliberate choice to meditate on God's goodness, power, and mercy. He remembered the joy he found in worshiping in the temple in Jerusalem. He reminded himself that he could trust God, ending on a positive note: "Put your hope in God, because I will still praise him. He is my savior and my God."

We can all identify with feelings of discouragement and sadness. Some of us give in to these emotions until we can't see anything else; others respond by hiding their feelings and pretending that nothing is wrong. The psalmist shows us a healthy way to manage these emotions. We can freely express negative feelings to God, then deliberately turn our thoughts to him, meditating on his goodness as recorded in the Bible and revealed in our personal life. When we end our conversations with him on a positive note, it's amazing how that change in focus can affect our mood.

Put your hope in God, because I will still praise him. He is my savior and my God.

Psalm 42:11

Ask yourself: **When I feel discouraged or despondent, do I focus on myself or do I choose to meditate on God's goodness?**

JANUARY

14

"Who is there to be afraid of?"

Psalm 27

Marla grabbed the remote and changed the channel as fast as she could. The last thing she needed to do was watch a horror movie, especially with her husband out of town. It didn't take much to trigger Marla's vivid imagination—even the nightly news could do a number on her brain. Whenever she was home alone, she lay awake half the night, jumping at every little creak and noise. Friends recommended sleeping pills, but Marla worried that they would keep her from hearing a prowler break in.

David encountered many reasons to be afraid during his life. As a boy, he guarded his father's sheep from wild animals, including an occasional lion or bear. Later he spent years being chased by the jealous King Saul and his men. Once, the Philistines captured him. Near the end of his reign, he had to flee for his life when his son led a rebellion against him. But David learned to place his confidence in God even during the most fearful times. He called God his "light" and his "life's fortress." "Who is there to fear?" he wrote. "Who is there to be afraid of?"

We live in a dangerous world, but no one can touch us without God's permission. We can either let our fears control us or we can learn to put our confidence in God. Focusing on God instead of what might happen helps, along with rehearsing past experiences of his protection and deliverance. We can meditate on verses that refer to God's ever-present protection. And whenever we sense fear creeping in, we can turn to God in prayer, verbally affirming our trust in his care. Each of us can think of reasons to feel afraid, but they all dwindle in the light of our one reason to feel safe.

Whenever I am afraid, I will trust in You.

Psalm 56:3 NKJV

Ask yourself: **How can I replace my fears with faith and trust in God?**

"Why are you pretending to be someone else?"

1 Kings 14:1–6

The queen set out for the trip to Shiloh, confident that no one recognized her. Following her husband's instructions, she had removed her queenly robes and jewels and dressed as an ordinary woman. Although King Jeroboam had set up idols for the people to worship, now he wanted to consult a prophet of the Lord. Jeroboam remembered Ahijah's prediction of his kingship; now he hoped to receive word from the prophet that his sick son would recover.

Ahijah may have been blind and old, but God told him who was coming to visit him and what to say to her. As soon as the queen entered the room, the prophet said, "You're Jeroboam's wife. Why are you pretending to be someone else?" He then delivered God's message of judgment on Jeroboam's family and the nation of Israel for their sin and idolatry.

Many people go through life wearing a disguise of some sort, either consciously or subconsciously. Maybe we try to project an image of being smarter or more virtuous than we are. Or maybe we pattern our speech, behavior, or lifestyle after someone else who seems superior to us. Are we trying to win other people's approval? Do we fear that others won't like us if they see the "real me"? If we feel insecure, it can be hard to let down our guard with our friends, our family, and even our spouse.

Sadly, we often carry this tendency into our relationship with God. Our prayer life becomes shallow if we hold back from discussing our deepest needs, hurts, and struggles with sin out of fear that God will think less of us. What a comfort to know that the One who knows us better than we know ourselves loves us more than we can imagine. There's never a need to pretend to be someone else with him.

Yet, you desire truth and sincerity.

Psalm 51:6

Ask yourself: **Do I ever wear a disguise in front of God?**

JANUARY

16

“What kind of man is this?”

Matthew 8:23–27

A painting by Jack E. Dawson depicts torrents of water rushing over jagged rocks on a mountainside. A handful of scrub trees are bent over by the wind and rain, and veins of lightning pierce the dark sky. At first glance, a person might wonder why the artist titled this painting “Peace in the Midst of the Storm.” A closer look reveals a small dove resting peacefully in a cleft in the rock.

Jesus displayed that same kind of peace in the middle of a storm that terrified his disciples. These experienced fishermen were used to the sudden violent onslaughts of wind and waves that struck the Sea of Galilee. But this storm made them fear for their lives. How could Jesus be sleeping through this?

The disciples woke their leader, crying out, “Lord! Save us!” Jesus rebuked them for their weak faith and ordered the wind and waves to be still. Instantly, the sea became calm. The amazed disciples asked each other, “What kind of man is this? Even the wind and the sea obey him!”

When life’s storms hit, one of the hardest things to do is to be still and let God do his job. When the terrified Israelites found themselves caught between the Egyptian army and the Red Sea, Moses told them, “The LORD is fighting for you! So be still!” (Exod. 14:14).

Even when things around us are calm, human nature can whip up some terrific turbulence. The same God who has authority over weather and nature can help us control our violent emotions. He wants to give us a peace that withstands both external and internal storms. If only we could learn to obey him as well as the wind and sea do.

Then he got up, ordered the wind to stop, and said to the sea, “Be still, absolutely still!” The wind stopped blowing, and the sea became very calm.

Mark 4:39

Ask yourself: **Is God telling me to “be still” right now and let him take control of a situation?**

"Aren't you discriminating against people?"

James 2:1–13

Jonas walked out onto the sales floor. "What happened with that man who just left the store?" The salesman shrugged. "Guess he got tired of waiting. No big deal—did you see his clothes? He couldn't have afforded anything in here anyway." Jonas frowned. "Would you like to know who it was you just snubbed?" The salesman's face blanched as Jonas explained how the owner of the chain liked to visit his stores incognito to see how the staff treated people.

James described another hypothetical situation to show the importance of not favoring one person over another. His example included two men visiting a worship service, one dressed in fine clothes and the other shabbily dressed. The rich man was given the best seat while the poor man was told to stand or sit on the floor. "Aren't you discriminating against people and using a corrupt standard to make judgments?" James asked. He labeled such preferential treatment as sin.

Anyone who claims to be completely free of prejudice is kidding themselves. We all react to people on the basis of preconceived notions and our first impressions. It's human nature to identify with some people more than others based on ethnicity, mannerisms, dress, our perceptions of their intelligence, or any number of other things. But that doesn't give us an excuse to treat some people better than others.

Such behavior is incompatible with faith in Jesus Christ. God wants us to do our best to treat everyone with dignity, respect, and compassion. Rather than act on the basis of our impressions, we can remember that each person we meet is someone whom God created and Jesus died for. Since God went to such lengths to offer his favor to everyone, how can we favor one person over another?

If you favor one person over another, you're sinning.

James 2:9

Ask yourself: **Do I do my best not to let preconceived notions or first impressions affect how I treat people?**

JANUARY

18

"Why do you spend money on what cannot nourish you?"

Isaiah 55:1–7

Junk food is big business in America. It's not easy to choose fruits and vegetables when we're surrounded by an endless array of ready-to-eat foods like pastries, chips, and candy. Such snacks may please our taste buds and give an immediate energy boost, but they fail to satisfy our hunger in the long run. A love affair with unhealthy, processed foods results in a host of health problems.

In Isaiah 55, God issues an invitation for people to find true nourishment for their souls. "Why do you spend money on what cannot nourish you and your wages on what does not satisfy you?" he asks. He urges people to receive his free gift of salvation, the only way to find lasting fulfillment.

Jesus identified himself as the "bread of life." While there are other sources of "bread" we can feed on, only Jesus offers eternal life. Many philosophies and false religions appeal to our intellect and emotions; in reality they are junk that can never truly satisfy. Other worldly pursuits that seem so wholesome are nothing more than cotton candy for the mind and eventually prove to be disastrous for our spiritual health.

Even believers sometimes starve themselves. If we fail to guard our mind, we may substitute worldly thinking for God's truth. Then we can fall into attitudes, relationships, and behaviors that displease God. Or we may spend time on personal pleasures and neglect daily nourishment from God's Word and prayer.

Just as it doesn't make sense to spend money on food that doesn't offer any benefits, it's also a waste of time and energy to search for satisfaction in sources other than the only One who can offer lasting fulfillment. Why snack on spiritual junk food when we can feast on the truth?

Jesus told them, "I am the bread of life. Whoever comes to me will never become hungry."

John 6:35

Ask yourself: **What am I feeding on to provide satisfaction and nourishment for my soul?**

"Which commandment is the most important of them all?"

Mark 12:28–34

No one can say how many laws are on the books in the United States. Each level of government has authority to make laws, but city, county, and state laws all fall under the umbrella of federal law. Each day new laws are drafted, and sometimes laws have to be passed just to get rid of old and sometimes ridiculous laws still on record.

In Jesus's day, Jewish scribes had identified more than six hundred commands in the Mosaic law. These were a source of much debate, as the religious leaders argued over how to rank the commands according to importance, or tried to come up with a single command to sum up the entire law. After hearing Jesus's discussion with the Sadducees, one of the scribes brought his own burning question to Jesus: Which commandment was the most important?

Jesus answered that the most important commandment is to love God with all our heart, soul, mind, and strength. Then he added its counterpart: to love others as we love ourselves. With his answer, Jesus distilled everything in the Law and Prophets into two simple principles for living that everybody can understand. The scribes' lofty debates seemed silly once Jesus pointed out that anyone who obeyed those two commands would fulfill all of the law.

Wholeheartedly loving God and caring for other people as we care for ourselves are much more important than rituals or external shows of faith. Bible study, church activities, ministry to others, and prayer are all important, but if we're not growing in our love for God and others, then there's a problem somewhere. What we *do* can't make up for a lack of love in our heart. As Jesus pointed out, true obedience to God means a commitment to love him and the people around us with all of our heart.

[Jesus said] "No other commandment is greater than these."

Mark 12:31

Ask yourself: **Am I daily growing in my love for God and other people?**

JANUARY
20

"Can any of you convict me of committing a sin?"

John 8:42–48

In a discussion with the Pharisees about sin, Jesus rebuked them for refusing to believe the truth. "Can any of you convict me of committing a sin?" he challenged. Since his enemies had no reasonable answer, they resorted to verbal abuse. Later, during Jesus's trials, the chief priests and Jewish council searched for evidence against Jesus but found nothing. Many people gave false testimony, but their statements didn't line up (see Mark 14:55–56).

How would people today answer Jesus's question? According to recent survey results released by the Barna Group, only 40 percent of American adults are convinced that Jesus lived a sinless life while on earth. Within the population subset described as born again, less than two-thirds strongly believe he was sinless.[2]

Does the Bible teach that Jesus lived a sinless life? First Peter 2:22 and 1 John 3:5 state unequivocally that Jesus committed no sin. Second Corinthians 5:21 explains that God had Christ, who was sinless, take our sins upon himself so that we could be made right with God. This is a foundational truth of our faith. Since Jesus never sinned, his sacrifice of himself paid the price for the sins of all who choose to believe in him. Only the perfect Lamb of God could abolish the need for animal sacrifices that only temporarily removed a person's sins.

Not only did his perfection secure our salvation, but it impacts our day-by-day life. Hebrews 4 teaches that although Jesus never sinned, he experienced the same temptations that we do. We have a God who can sympathize and identify with whatever we face. And the only perfect human being who ever lived wants to help us imperfect people resist sin's pull.

He was tempted in every way that we are, but he didn't sin.

Hebrews 4:15

Ask God **to help you understand more fully what Jesus's sinless life means to you personally.**

2. "Barna Survey Examines Changes in Worldview Among Christians over the Past 13 Years," March 6, 2009. www.barna.org.

"What do people gain from all their hard work under the sun?"

Ecclesiastes 1:3; 2:4–11

The man reached for his cane and rose stiffly from the bench. It was pleasant out here, but he preferred to spend visiting hours in his room. He couldn't remember the last time someone had stopped by to see *him*, but what else could he expect? At last he understood why his ex-wife had accused him of being "married to his job," and why his kids treated him like a stranger. He didn't have a lot to show for his "successful" career, but he'd trade it all for the chance to go back in time and do things over.

The writer of Ecclesiastes pointed out the foolishness of expecting work to be the basis of our fulfillment. "What do people gain from all their hard work under the sun?" he wrote. If Solomon is the author, as many scholars believe, his negative attitude is especially poignant. With his prosperous reign, worldwide fame, and staggering list of achievements, Solomon seemed to have more reason than most to take pride in his career. But he shared his discovery that no human endeavor has lasting value in and of itself.

Our society's emphasis on career and material success shapes many people into workaholics. Workers who are overcommitted to their job often claim the "future good" of their family as their motivation. But they may find the future to be empty and meaningless once it arrives. No career advancement is worth the sacrifice of our family relationships, our friends, or our spiritual growth. God designed us to take time off for rest, worship, and family time. He even set an example for us by taking a day off after the creation process. If our priorities are in the right order, work won't be at the top of the list.

On the seventh day he stopped the work he had been doing.

Genesis 2:2

Ask yourself: **Do I neglect my relationships with God and other people because of workaholic tendencies?**

JANUARY
22

"What does pleasure accomplish?"

Ecclesiastes 2:1–11

Nick stared at the ceiling and thanked his lucky stars he didn't have many sleepless nights like this. He hated that vague sense of uneasiness that crept inside his brain. *Maybe this is why I don't usually sleep alone*, he thought. Thinking about the coming weekend, Nick pondered his options. In a few hours, he'd call around and see if he couldn't scare up a party. Or maybe he'd plan an outing on his boat. And he just might treat himself to that bigger-screen TV. After all, he deserved to live the good life, didn't he?

Solomon knew about living "the good life." When he decided to see if life's meaning could be found by pursuing pleasure, he threw all his resources into the experiment. And Solomon had a lot of resources. He could buy anything he wanted to possess, add as many women as he desired to his harem, and have all the servants he wanted at his beck and call. Although Solomon did enjoy himself sometimes, he found no lasting satisfaction. "What does pleasure accomplish?" he concluded.

Our pleasure-obsessed culture tries to convince us that the purpose of life is to have a good time. We're bombarded with entertainment options and commercials for the latest "toys" and gadgets. Most of us would be shocked if we knew how much time and money we spend just to amuse ourselves. But it's not amusing when our chasing after fun covers up spiritual needs.

What society calls "the good life" is a pitiful substitute for a life spent loving and serving God. Even worthwhile pleasures will disappoint if they're an end in themselves. God likes to see us enjoy ourselves, but he created us for so much more. If our priorities are in the right order, pleasure won't be at the top of the list.

But even this was pointless.
Ecclesiastes 2:1

Ask yourself: **How much of my time, money, and energy do I devote to seeking pleasure?**

"Where, now, is the one who is supposed to save you?"

Hosea 13:9–14

As election day neared, the candidate's promises grew more extravagant while his supporters grew more deeply devoted to his campaign. They seemed convinced that once he was president, he would solve all the problems facing our country and improve everyone's life. Several months after his inauguration, however, polls revealed that the number of people satisfied with his performance had plunged.

God mocked Israel for depending on political leaders rather than him. During Samuel's tenure as judge, Israel's leaders demanded he appoint a king to rule them. The people wanted to be like the other nations around them, but they were rejecting God's kingship. God reluctantly granted their request, and Israel was later blessed by David's reign. But when the nation split under Solomon, the northern kingdom suffered from a succession of evil kings.

After Israel continued to ignore God's calls for repentance, God warned of coming judgment. "Where, now, is your king, the one who is supposed to save you?" God asked. "Where in all your cities are your judges?" Israel had gotten their wish for a king, but what good had it done them? Nothing could save them from punishment, since they had rejected their only real Savior.

Too often we look around for someone to fix our life, while ignoring the only One who can truly make a difference. Only God can deal with our sin, the root cause of our personal—and national—problems. On a personal level, we can repent of any disobedience and commit to living life according to God's standards. On a national level, we have the responsibility to vote according to our conscience and then pray for our leaders. But we should always remember that human leaders are limited in what they can accomplish; they can never replace the only One who can be our Savior.

There is no savior except me.

Hosea 13:4

Ask yourself: **Am I putting my trust in anything or anyone other than my Savior?**

JANUARY

24

"How can you say, 'Show us the Father'?"

John 14:8–17

I hated feeling skeptical as I listened to my friend's enraptured description of her latest experience with God. She showed no interest in Bible study or learning about the Christian life; her church attendance was sporadic. Instead, she constantly looked for God to reveal himself to her through some dramatic way. However, her "supernatural experiences" usually sounded like natural events that she had interpreted as something more.

Philip expressed a universal longing of the human race when he asked for an appearance of God. "Lord, show us the Father, and that will satisfy us," he said. Philip may have been thinking of Moses or Isaiah, who each had a limited vision of God's glory. Or he might have remembered a time from Israel's history when God had visibly manifested himself as a cloud or pillar of fire.

Jesus wanted the disciples to understand that they had seen something far better over the past three years. "The person who has seen me has seen the Father," he answered. "So how can you say, 'Show us the Father'?" Jesus explained that the Son is the visible image of God the Father, whom no human being has ever seen (see John 1:18). The words Jesus spoke came from the Father; the miracles he performed represented God working through him.

God revealed his presence through his creation; he revealed his mind through his written Word. In Jesus, we have a living, breathing revelation of what our heavenly Father is like. God still chooses sometimes to give tangible proofs of his presence, but we can miss the most obvious example by only looking for dramatic experiences. God has shown himself through Jesus, and that tells us what we need to know. The more we know Jesus, the more clearly we see God.

[Jesus said] "The Father and I are one."

John 10:30

Ask yourself: **Am I getting to know Jesus more intimately as time passes?**

JANUARY
25

"Why isn't this bush burning up?"

Exodus 3:1–6

As Moses tended his father-in-law's sheep in a remote desert area, a strange sight grabbed his attention. There on Mount Horeb, Moses saw a bush that was on fire, yet not burning up. How could such a thing be possible? Moses's curiosity drew him over to investigate, just as God had planned. When Moses came close, God called out to him from among the flames. He told Moses to remove his sandals as an act of worship, and then identified himself as the God of Moses's ancestors Abraham, Isaac, and Jacob.

In the Old Testament, God often appeared to his followers in visible form. When he made a covenant with Abraham, God revealed himself as a flaming torch and a smoking oven. As the Israelites journeyed through the wilderness to the Promised Land, God led them as a column of smoke by day and a column of fire at night. Today, God can reveal himself to us in a more personal, intimate way because of Jesus's death and resurrection.

Every believer now has God's Holy Spirit living within them, giving discernment for decisions and guidance on living a life pleasing to him. Through his Spirit, God talks to us as we read his Word and pray. He also communicates with us in unexpected ways—through other people, unusual experiences, or circumstances that defy logic.

If we stay tuned in to the Holy Spirit, we won't miss his unmistakable nudges and promptings. But some people expect God to reveal himself only through dramatic miracles and "lightning bolt" experiences. They have no interest in listening for God to speak through prayer, Bible study, or other believers. Any time God communicates with us, it's a supernatural experience. But if we're only looking around for burning bushes, we may miss what he wants to say.

Be careful that you do not refuse to listen when God speaks.

Hebrews 12:25

Ask God **to make you more sensitive to his Holy Spirit's leading in your life.**

JANUARY
26

"Who am I that I should go to Pharaoh?"

Exodus 3:7–22

While working as a volunteer in a prison ministry, Laurie Jackson felt shocked when she sensed God telling her to develop a new organization. Public speaking had always made Laurie nauseated—how could she oversee a ministry? Today, Open Heart Prison Ministries reaches out to female prisoners in east central Illinois. Laurie serves as executive director, teaches Bible studies—and speaks at churches and fundraising banquets.

Moses felt inadequate for the assignment God had in mind for him. God wanted to send him to confront the powerful ruler of Egypt who had held the Hebrews in cruel slavery for hundreds of years. Moses would demand their release, then lead them toward a new land. Moses could hardly believe his ears. "Who am I that I should go to Pharaoh and bring the people of Israel out of Egypt?" he protested.

Raised as the son of an Egyptian princess, Moses had fled the country after killing an Egyptian he saw beating a Hebrew slave. Even though he had been protecting one of his own people, the Israelites rejected him. When Pharaoh heard of the incident, he tried to have Moses killed. Now Moses had spent forty years in the wilderness, living the life of a nomadic shepherd, an occupation despised by the Egyptians. How could he possibly be the one for this job?

Sometimes God gives us assignments that seem far beyond our ability. We immediately start thinking about our inadequacies and how impossible the goal looks. But when God calls us to do something, he doesn't plan to let us fail. He will provide the resources, skills, wisdom, and strength we need to carry out his work. Most importantly, he promises to go along with us. Instead of questioning "Who am I?" we'd be better off concentrating on who God is.

God answered, "I will be with you."

Exodus 3:12

Ask yourself: **Am I letting feelings of inadequacy hold me back from accomplishing something for God?**

"What's that in your hand?"

Exodus 4:1–9

Dan walked past the Missions Sunday display tables and sat down in the sanctuary. He enjoyed hearing stories about the various trips, but what could a foreman of a roofing company do? He struggled with learning languages, had no medical skills or teaching experience, and couldn't see himself witnessing in the streets. Later that morning, however, his heartbeat quickened as the pastor described an upcoming trip to restore homes ravaged by a recent hurricane.

God often uses common, ordinary things to accomplish his purposes. When Moses doubted that the Israelites would listen to him, God asked, "What's that in your hand?" God told him to throw his shepherd's staff on the ground. The staff turned into a snake. Then God had Moses pick up the snake by the tail, and it turned back into a staff.

The message was clear: Snakes symbolized power to the Egyptians; their power would be no match for Moses with God at his side. Moses used his simple wooden staff to perform miracles before Pharaoh as God directed. Later, during the wilderness journey, he used the staff to strike a rock and provide water for the thirsty Israelites.

Right now, at this very moment, our hands hold something that can be used for God. When we become a follower of Christ, God gives us spiritual gifts chosen just for us. In addition, each one of us has a unique mix of natural talents, learned skills, material resources, experiences, and social connections. All of these represent opportunities for God to display his power.

After he points out what we hold in our hand, God's second question is, "Will you dedicate it to me?" Then it's time to stand back and watch him work. God used a wooden stick in Moses's hand; he can also use our hammer, or pen, or needle and thread, or whisk, or . . .

God in his kindness gave each of us different gifts.

Romans 12:6

Ask yourself: **What am I holding on to that God wants to use for his glory?**

JANUARY

28

“Who gave humans their mouths?”

Exodus 4:10–17

Moses still had one more excuse left. God had promised to go with him to confront the ruler of Egypt. He’d assured Moses that the Israelites would listen to him and that the mission would succeed; Pharaoh would eventually free the slaves. God had even given Moses a sample of the miracles he would perform through him. “But I’m not a good speaker,” Moses protested. “I speak slowly and get tongue-tied easily.”

God’s patience began to wear thin as he pointed out the obvious. “Who gave humans their mouths?” he asked. Since he created Moses’s mouth, didn’t he have the right to use it for his purposes? God graciously promised to help Moses speak and teach him what to say. Still, Moses balked at his God-given assignment. In anger, God finally appointed Moses’s brother Aaron to do the talking. Aaron would be the spokesman and Moses would tell him what to say.

Public speaking is one of the most common fears people express, and for Christians, talking to others about God is often a weak area. Sharing our faith with close family and friends can be especially intimidating. Yet God calls each one of us to tell others about his message of love and forgiveness.

We may be afraid of how others will react, but our responsibility is to obey God, not worry about their response. We may think we have to be a smooth, persuasive speaker or a Bible expert to share God’s truth. But whenever God prompts us to witness to anyone, he promises to teach us the words to say. We don’t have to be a professional orator or debater; we only need a mouth willing to obey the One who made it.

[God said] “I will help you speak and will teach you what to say.”

Exodus 4:12

Ask yourself: **Who around me needs to hear the gospel?**

Ask God **to give you the right words to say.**

JANUARY
29

"Who would be able to stand if you kept a record of sins?"

Psalm 130

Joel laid his briefcase on the table and introduced himself. As a public defender assigned to this case, he wanted to do the best he could for his client. But this guy had a rap sheet as long as his arm—an assortment of petty crimes over the past twelve years. Joel began the conversation by trying to give a realistic picture of how the young man's record might affect the outcome of the case. The man grunted. "So you think they might hold that against me?"

Fortunately for us, God doesn't keep a record of our crimes. The writer of Psalm 130 cried out in despair over sin. "O Lord, who would be able to stand if you kept a record of sins?" he asked. The psalmist knew the answer: no one. He also knew that God stands ready to offer mercy whenever there is true repentance and confession. "But with you there is forgiveness," he affirmed.

Another psalmist wrote that God's love and mercy for us are as great as the height between the heavens and the earth. When we admit our sins and come to him for forgiveness, he removes them as far as the east is from the west. We might keep dredging up the past, but God doesn't. He not only forgives us; he chooses not to remember our sins. If God kept all of our mistakes, failures, and transgressions on file, none of us would have much of a case. But once we confess and repent of sin, God gives us a clean slate instead of a rap sheet.

As far as the east is from the west—that is how far he has removed our rebellious acts from himself.

Psalm 103:12

Ask yourself: **Do I have trouble believing that God has completely forgiven me of a specific sin?**

Ask God **to help you trust his promise to remove that sin.**

JANUARY

30

"Why are you coming to me now when you're in trouble?"

Judges 11:1–11

Chad caught his breath as he recognized the voice on the other end of the line. He hadn't heard from his son in almost a year, not since Derek had stormed out of the house vowing to never come back. Chad's phone calls and letters had gone unanswered; holidays and birthdays had passed without any contact. *He must be in some kind of trouble*, Chad thought grimly. "Dad, I need some bail money," his son began.

Jephthah was surprised when his countrymen contacted him after so much time had passed. As the son of a prostitute, he still remembered the stinging names and insults. He hadn't forgotten how his half brothers had chased him off. But since then he'd gained a following, of sorts, and apparently a reputation.

Now that Israel had been invaded, the leaders of Gilead came to ask for his help with waging war against Ammon. Jephthah wasn't about to let them off that easy. "Didn't you throw me out of my father's house?" he reminded them. "So why are you coming to me now when you're in trouble?"

Sometimes God must feel like asking that same question. We're told that prayer has no place in public life—until a national crisis hits. Many people sail through life without giving a thought to their Creator—until they face a serious problem they can't handle on their own. Even Christians may neglect regular communion with God while things seem to be going smoothly. Then when trouble strikes, we suddenly regain our interest in prayer. God always has his ear tuned to his children, but it's an insult to treat him like a crisis hotline. He deserves to hear from us not just because we're in trouble but because we're in love with him.

I will call on him as long as I live because
he turns his ear toward me.

Psalm 116:2

Ask yourself: **Do I neglect my prayer life until I find myself in trouble?**

"Shouldn't we take everything our God took for us?"

Judges 11:12–24

Once he assumed leadership over Gilead, Jephthah tried to negotiate a peaceful resolution to the conflict with Ammon. He sent messengers to ask the king why he had invaded and made war against Gilead. The king falsely accused Israel of stealing part of his land when they came out of slavery in Egypt a few hundred years earlier.

Jephthah outlined the history of the land in question and explained why Israel had a legitimate claim to it. The bottom line: God had given the land to Israel. "So what right do you have to take it back?" Jephthah reasoned. "Shouldn't you take possession of what your god Chemosh took for you? Shouldn't we take everything the LORD our God took for us?"

Sometimes we need a history lesson, just as the king of Ammon did. God won a great victory for us through Jesus's death on the cross. Once we believe in Christ, God can lead us to our Promised Land—a life of godly living through his power and strength, bearing fruit for his kingdom. But Satan constantly tries to steal our rightful inheritance out from under us. He bombards us with temptations and plants fear and doubt in our mind. Each time we give in to him, we lose ground.

Our lives often fall far short of what God intends for us. Christ paid a high price for us to live in victory over sin; yet we often settle for a mediocre life. We fight the same battles over and over in our own puny strength, instead of relying on the power of God's Spirit within us. A rich Promised Land is within our reach. Shouldn't we take everything the Lord took for us?

"This is the inheritance of the LORD's servants. Their victory comes from me," declares the LORD.

Isaiah 54:17

Ask yourself: **Does my life reflect the victory that Christ won for me, or am I giving up ground to my enemy?**

FEBRUARY

1

"Why should I wait any longer for the Lord to help us?"

2 Kings 6:24–33

Severe famine spread through Samaria as the siege against the capital city dragged on. When King Joram heard about a starving mother who had eaten her child, he ripped his clothes as an expression of grief. But Joram didn't admit that Israel had brought this punishment on herself by idolatry. He didn't repent that he had allowed Baal worship to continue. Instead, he became angry and blamed Elisha, God's messenger, who had warned of these events if Israel refused to return to God.

The king vowed to have Elisha executed that very day. As Joram stormed into the prophet's house, he blurted out, "Why should I wait any longer for the Lord to help us?" Evidently, Elisha had earlier delivered God's message that the king should wait for God to free the city instead of surrendering to the Arameans. But Joram had had enough. Even though he acknowledged that the famine came "from the Lord's hand," he was ready to disobey and give up.

"Do something—even if it's wrong!" This may be a familiar cliché, but it's not good advice. When our troubles drag on with no end in sight, it's hard to think straight. It's also hard to remember that God has everything under his loving control. Sometimes God calls us to action and shows us how to handle a problem; other times, he tells us to wait for him to work things out in his own way.

When we're suffering, waiting for God's timing can stretch our faith to its limits. Will we wait for him to resolve the situation, or will we give up and take matters into our own hands? If God instructs us to wait for his deliverance, surrendering to the temptation to handle things in our way is inviting disaster.

Be strong, all who wait with hope for the LORD, and let your heart be courageous.

Psalm 31:24

Ask yourself: **Is there a situation in which God is calling me to wait for his intervention?**

"Could this happen even if the Lord poured rain through windows in the sky?"

2 Kings 7

The king of Israel was tired of waiting for God to deliver the besieged city of Samaria as he had promised. Wouldn't it be better to surrender to the Arameans than to let the people die of starvation? But Elisha delivered a startling prophecy: within twenty-four hours, the siege would end and there would be plenty of food.

This prediction proved too much for the king's officer to believe. He'd seen people paying exorbitant prices for donkeys' heads; he'd heard about women eating their children. How could such an extreme situation be reversed in one day? "Could this happen even if the Lord poured rain through windows in the sky?" he blurted out. His comment prompted Elisha to give a second prophecy: the man would see the miracle happen, but he would not eat any of the food.

Later that day, God tricked the Aramean army into retreating in such a hurry that they left behind supplies and animals. Once this news reached the city, people rushed out in droves to loot the army camp. The earliest arrivals sold food at the exact prices that God had predicted through Elisha. But the king's officer who had scoffed at the prophecy didn't get to enjoy the bounty. As he stood guard at the city gates, the crowd trampled him to death.

When we're facing a dismal situation, it's easy to become cynical. We may even scoff at the idea that God can correct the situation. Through prayer and meditation on God's past miracles, we can hold on to an attitude of expectancy as we wait for him to act. God will always keep his promises. We don't want to miss out on blessings by letting our hopes get trampled to death by our cynicism.

God faithfully keeps his promises.

1 Corinthians 1:9

Ask yourself: **Am I having trouble believing one of God's promises right now? Why?**

FEBRUARY
3

"Doesn't he leave the 99 and look for the lost sheep?"

Luke 15:1–7

Michelle watched her little boy's beaming face as he carefully placed the Matchbox car with the rest of his collection. As soon as he'd noticed the empty spot on his shelf, he'd started combing the house, looking in every nook and cranny. "Jared," Michelle asked, "are you so excited because you've found your favorite car?" "No, Mommy," Jared answered. "Because I found the one that was lost."

Jesus told a parable about a shepherd who noticed one of his sheep missing. "Doesn't he leave the 99 sheep grazing in the pasture and look for the lost sheep until he finds it?" asked Jesus. When the shepherd found the one that had wandered off, he put it on his shoulders and called for his friends and neighbors to help celebrate his joy.

Just as each sheep was valuable to the shepherd, every individual is precious to God. With billions of people in the world, it can sometimes feel as though we're just another face in the crowd. But God loves each one of us so much that he sent a Shepherd to tenderly search for those who are lost and bring them to God. Each time a lost person comes to God, there is a joyful celebration in heaven.

Some people seem so far from God that we may be tempted to consider them hopeless cases. But no one is out of God's reach, no matter how far they've wandered. God gives us the privilege of praying that lost people will respond to his message of love and forgiveness. He doesn't give up on people and neither should we. Then we can share in the Shepherd's joy when a lost sheep is found.

Indeed, the Son of Man has come to seek
and to save people who are lost.

Luke 19:10

Ask God **to give you his heart for people who are lost.**

FEBRUARY

4

"Do we have anything to brag about?"

Romans 3:21–28

In any gathering, people try their best to avoid Pam and Roger. It's obvious that this couple has one thing in common: they both like to brag. He brags about his work promotions, smart investments, and the newest addition to his car collection. She brags about her latest redecorating project, the vacations they take, and their superior children. Sometimes their bragging is obvious, and sometimes it's subtle. But even when they're not talking, they wear an air of boastfulness.

The Bible has advice for such people. Paul points out in Romans 3 that from a spiritual standpoint, no one has any right to boast. "So, do we have anything to brag about?" he asks. His answer is that bragging has been eliminated on the basis of faith. We all receive salvation as a gift, not through any merit or efforts of our own. We come to God as helpless sinners, and as his children, we remain dependent on his mercy and power to live a godly life.

We can't brag about our possessions, wisdom, or abilities because they're all gifts from God. It makes no sense to brag about what we plan to do, because we don't know what the future holds. And it's foolish to brag about sins we've never committed because each one of us could fall at any time.

God does allow one type of boasting, however: " 'If they want to brag, they should brag that they understand and know me. They should brag that I, the Lord, act out of love, righteousness, and justice on the earth. This kind of bragging pleases me,' declares the LORD" (Jer. 9:24). How gracious of God to encourage us to brag about the most precious thing in our life.

It's unthinkable that I could ever brag about anything except the cross of our Lord Jesus Christ.

Galatians 6:14

Ask God **to help you examine your attitudes and identify any boastful tendencies.**

FEBRUARY

5

"What have I done to you to make you hit me three times?"

Numbers 22:21–33

The light turned green and Janice moved her foot from the brake to the accelerator. The car refused to budge. Irritation instantly washed over her. *What the . . . I just had this car tuned up! I'm already running late. . . .* Just then, another car streaked across the intersection, ignoring the red light. When Janice pressed the accelerator a second time, her car moved forward as if nothing had happened.

Balaam felt more than irritation when his donkey wouldn't budge. Each time the animal turned aside from the road or lay down, he beat her. Finally, the donkey spoke: "What have I done to you to make you hit me three times?" Balaam fumed that he would kill her if he had a sword. Then God opened Balaam's eyes to see the angel of the Lord standing in the road with a drawn sword. Balaam understood that his donkey had saved his life by refusing to go where he wanted her to go.

It's easy to acknowledge that God is in control of our lives when things run smoothly. But when we don't get what we want, that's a different story. How can events that thwart our plans or desires come from the hand of a loving God? While our choices and behavior influence our circumstances, God holds ultimate control. Everything he allows to touch us has a purpose even when we can't see it.

Whether we're frustrated over little details or major events, remembering who is in control curbs our aggravation. Balaam couldn't see the danger his donkey protected him from; we can't always see how our situation fits into God's plan. But we can trust him to use everything that happens to us for our good and for his glory.

We know that all things work together for
the good of those who love God.

Romans 8:28

Ask yourself: **What is the greatest source of frustration in my life at this moment?**

Ask God **to open your eyes so you see his hand even in that area.**

"How can I find the right words to speak with him?"

Job 9:14–18

After a wave of disasters swept through his life, Job wasn't sure what he wanted to say to God. "How can I possibly answer God?" he asked his friends. "How can I find the right words to speak with him?" With a sense of God's majesty, Job imagined himself speechless in God's presence. His grief over his losses probably made it hard to believe God even listened to him.

We don't have to go through calamity to be at a loss for words in prayer. Sometimes our emotions make it hard to crystallize our thoughts into words. Perhaps we've grown weary of praying for the same thing over and over. Sometimes we just have a difficult time verbalizing our needs or concerns. God understands, and has provided two indispensable resources for times like these.

The Bible does more than teach us *about* prayer; it also offers words *of* prayer. We can use passages, verses, or even phrases as starting points for our own conversations with God. Prayers of biblical characters like Hannah, Solomon, Hezekiah, or Paul offer guidelines as we communicate our needs and feelings. The book of Psalms is filled with heartfelt prayers expressing a wide range of emotions. We can turn psalms into powerful prayers by adapting them to fit our specific situations.

Even when we can't manage any words at all, God's Spirit intercedes for us in prayer. And we can trust the Spirit to always pray in accordance with God's will. With the Bible and the Holy Spirit as prayer support, we never need to worry about finding the right words to say.

At the same time the Spirit also helps us in our weakness, because we don't know how to pray for what we need. But the Spirit intercedes along with our groans that cannot be expressed in words.

Romans 8:26

Ask God **to lead you to Scriptures you can use as prayers for your specific needs.**

FEBRUARY

7

"Who can enjoy themselves without God?"

Ecclesiastes 2:24–26

Television commercials and glossy magazine ads try to convince us there's something out there that will vastly improve our life—and for a measly $19.95 (plus shipping and handling, of course). Before that man inserted those gel pads in his shoes, he looked sad. That woman wore a frown before she bought that new, improved duster. But now, they flash smiles that nearly blind us (which we can also have for $19.95 plus shipping and handling).

Solomon discovered that only one thing can truly improve our life. After searching for life's meaning through pursuit of work, pleasure, personal achievements, and man's wisdom, he discovered that everything is meaningless apart from God. "Who can eat or enjoy themselves without God?" he wrote. Solomon concluded that those who truly enjoy life are the ones who serve and obey God while accepting everything as a gift from his hand.

Christians are often portrayed as people who don't get much enjoyment out of life, but what could be more absurd? How could anyone enjoy life more than someone who intimately knows their Creator? Our past sins are forgiven and we have a glorious future ahead of us. We live each day knowing that God loves us unconditionally and watches over every detail of our life.

Knowing God makes everything in life better. Sunsets look more spectacular because we know the One who paints them. We appreciate the beauty and intricacy in nature more because we understand who planned each detail. Our food tastes better and our home feels more comfortable because we know who provides it. Every day is a gift from our heavenly Father, and he loves to see his children enjoying what he gives them.

They should place their confidence in God who richly provides us with everything to enjoy.

1 Timothy 6:17

Ask yourself: **How is my attitude toward God affecting my enjoyment of life?**

"Why are you crying?"

1 Samuel 1:1–20

Wendy bit her lip as the baby dedication service started, determined not to embarrass Trevor during church. Her husband had been attentive and loving after the miscarriage, but he thought she should be over it by now. It didn't help her to hear Trevor list the reasons why the timing had been off for having a baby anyway. Wendy cast a sideways glance at Trevor. *There's just no way he can understand how I feel*, she thought.

Hannah knew how it felt to be misunderstood. She lived in a culture that considered barrenness a curse, and she had to share her husband with a woman who ridiculed her for being childless. Elkanah did his best to comfort her. "Hannah, why are you crying?" he asked. "Don't I mean more to you than ten sons?" Hannah's husband seemed unable to understand her grief. When she poured out her heartache to God, the priest accused her of being drunk. But Hannah trusted that God knew her heart's desire and would grant it.

We never have to worry about God not understanding us. He knows every thought before it enters our mind and he's already aware of our needs before we ask him. God sees every worry that we can't shake, and he understands our deepest heartaches and pain. Why should we hold back from pouring out our heart to the One who created us and then died for us?

Even our family members and friends won't always comprehend our feelings or be able to empathize with our suffering. But God knows us better than we know ourselves, and he loves us more than anyone else possibly can. We can take comfort in knowing that God sees what others can't see, and he understands.

> *I will rejoice and be glad because of your mercy. You have seen my misery. You have known the troubles in my soul.*
>
> Psalm 31:7

Ask yourself: **What heartache do I have that no one can understand except God?**

FEBRUARY
9

"Who can find a wife with a strong character?"

Proverbs 31:10–12

I had a sick feeling as I looked at the television program my friend was watching. For cash prizes and trophies, little girls paraded across the stage wearing full makeup, false eyelashes, massive wigs, and sometimes even blindingly white removable teeth. Backstage, mothers coached girls as young as preschoolers as they practiced their plastered grins and lilting walks; some even rehearsed sensual movements.

Our society may be obsessed with physical appearance, but the book of Proverbs describes something far more valuable than outward beauty. "Who can find a wife with a strong character?" the writer asks. "She is worth far more than jewels." The passage goes on to list the character traits of an ideal woman, but they could also be adapted to fit the ideal man: wise, hardworking, compassionate, and trustworthy. All of these desirable traits stem from a reverence for God and a commitment to live according to his standards.

Just because a woman has a beautiful face and figure doesn't mean she'll be a good wife. Bulging biceps and washboard abs don't make a man husband material. While the world tends to judge a person by external appearance, true beauty lies on the inside. A person's character will determine the quality of a relationship *and* the quality of their life by the standards that truly count.

It's hard to resist our culture's pressure to focus on physical appearance, especially when we have so many magazines and television shows demonstrating "extreme makeovers." There's nothing wrong with wanting to look our best, except when that desire pushes us to become so preoccupied with the external that we neglect to cultivate a strong character. Our main focus needs to be on the kind of beauty that never fades away.

Beauty is something internal that can't be destroyed.

1 Peter 3:4

Ask yourself: **Am I more concerned with improving my physical appearance or developing godly character traits?**

"Why should water flow out of your spring?"

Proverbs 5:15–22

A politician's affair is exposed by the media. A pastor's wife leaves him to run away with a church deacon. A Hollywood couple cheats on each other, even though they left their former spouses to get married. Adultery has become so commonplace that it's often viewed as a reasonable response when a marriage grows stale. Movies and television sometimes portray infidelity as a beautiful thing, because the person has supposedly found their true "soul mate."

God takes marriage seriously. Proverbs warns against unfaithfulness in marriage by using a word picture of a well or cistern, a precious possession in desert lands. "Drink water out of your own cistern," the writer advises. "Why should water flow out of your spring? Why should your streams flow into the streets?" Chapter 6 uses a different image: "Can anyone walk on red-hot coals without burning his feet?" (v. 28).

God made marital faithfulness one of the Ten Commandments. It's clear that he created marriage to be a sacred covenant relationship. But our society has watered it down into a casual choice that can be easily broken if one or both partners decide the union doesn't make them happy. Now a battle rages to redefine marriage to please those who practice homosexuality.

Married believers have the responsibility to treat each other with honor and respect, to guard their relationship as something precious, and to stay faithful in their body and their mind. Single believers also have responsibilities to honor marriage. They can uphold the biblical definition of marriage and they can support, encourage, and pray for married couples within their circle of acquaintances. If everyone respected marital faithfulness as God intended, we would notice a world of difference in our families and our culture.

Marriage is honorable in every way, so husbands and wives should be faithful to each other.

Hebrews 13:4

Ask yourself: **Do I honor marriage by upholding God's perspective about it?**

FEBRUARY
11

"How can God's love be in that person if he doesn't bother to help?"

1 John 3:11–18

Shelley thought back over the past year and wondered how she'd come through it with her sanity intact. First, she'd been laid off, then her husband was injured at work. As they adjusted to that change, a fire destroyed their kitchen. During the repairs, Shelley tripped and broke her ankle. She felt grateful for the many cards, phone calls, and promised prayers. But what Shelley most remembered were the people who showed up in person—bringing meals, cleaning up, or driving her and her husband to appointments.

John wrote that the proof God lives in us can be seen in our love and care for other believers. He illustrated this action-oriented love with an example of someone who has plenty and sees a fellow believer in need. "How can God's love be in that person if he doesn't bother to help the other believer?" he asked. God doesn't measure our love by our words or good intentions but by how willing we are to help other believers.

Jesus said that the world would recognize his followers by their love for each other (see John 13:35). He provided the model for Christian love by willingly laying down his life for us. Because of his sacrifice, God asks us to give our life in service to others without expecting to get paid back. He wants us to put aside our own interests and desires and share our money, time, and other resources with fellow believers in need.

We miss the point when we treat love like a sentimental feeling and pass up practical ways to meet someone's needs. There are times we can bless someone with verbal encouragement, but when it comes to love, actions speak much louder than words.

Dear children, we must show love through actions
that are sincere, not through empty words.

1 John 3:18

Ask yourself: **Do I demonstrate my love for fellow believers through actions, not just words?**

"How can you say that you love me when your heart isn't mine?"

Judges 16:4–17

Delilah swallowed her anger. Three times she had asked Samson the source of his extraordinary strength; three times he had given her a false answer. But she wasn't about to give up that easily. The Philistine rulers had offered big bucks for Samson's secret. "How can you say that you love me when your heart isn't mine?" she lashed out. "You've made fun of me three times now, but you still haven't told me what makes you so strong." Day after day Delilah badgered Samson. Her pestering made his life so miserable that he finally gave in.

People react in different ways when they don't get what they want. Some are like Delilah, whining and nagging the person who frustrates their desires. Proverbs 27:15 compares this type of response with the steady dripping of rain. Others react with pouting, resentment, or the silent treatment. When a man refused to sell a vineyard to Ahab, the king "lay on the couch, turned his face from everyone, and refused to eat" (1 Kings 21:4).

These negative patterns of communication can infiltrate our attitudes toward God if we're not careful. When we get tired of waiting for God to grant our request, our prayers can take on a whiny tone. If God answers with a clear no, we may start to question his motives: "How can you say you love me when . . ." Or we may stop talking to him altogether.

What's the best response when we don't get what we ask for in prayer? We can examine the request to make sure it's reasonable, and then honestly communicate our feelings to God. After that, we need to accept that if he denies a request, it's because he wants what is best for us.

Constantly dripping water on a rainy
day is like a quarreling woman.

Proverbs 27:15

Ask yourself: **How do I react when I don't get what I want?**

"If you love those who love you, do you deserve a reward?"

Matthew 5:38–48

The people in the courtroom sat in stunned silence as the man in the wheelchair finished speaking. A year earlier, the teenager on trial had been arrested for the burglary of the elderly couple's home. In the process, the wife had been killed and the husband seriously injured. Now, the man had come to deliver a simple message to the offender: "I forgive you."

Jesus's teaching in Matthew 5 must have stunned the Jewish people listening to him. They were familiar with the principle, "An eye for an eye and a tooth for a tooth." Although this law had been given to judges to ensure that punishments fit the crimes without going too far, some people used it to excuse their desire for personal revenge. They interpreted the mandate to "love your neighbor" as permission to hate their enemies. But Jesus gave new guidelines.

"If you love those who love you, do you deserve a reward?" he asked. "Even the tax collectors do that!" In other words, it's no big deal when we love those who treat us well. But God calls us to go way beyond that. We're to give up our personal rights, go the extra mile, show love to those who hate us, and pray for people who persecute us. How can we fill such a tall order?

Following God often means fighting our natural impulses. Will we respond to others based on our feelings toward them, or will we show love to people simply because they are someone created by God? When we choose to obey Jesus's instructions in Matthew 5, we prove that we're God's children, because the only way someone can love like that is with his help.

Love your enemies, and pray for those who persecute you.

Matthew 5:44

Ask yourself: **Do I show love based on how other people treat me or out of obedience to God's command?**

"What will separate us from the love Christ has for us?"

Romans 8:31–39

Love is a popular topic for movies, plays, songs, television programs, and greeting cards. Bookstores and library shelves are filled with romance novels and romantic poetry. Shakespeare's work alone includes hundreds of love sonnets. But nothing has ever been written that compares with Paul's rapture-filled tribute to God's love found in Romans 8.

"What will separate us from the love Christ has for us?" Paul asked. Then he listed seven things that would become realities for his listeners as the Church faced increasing persecution from a hostile world. Paul stressed that instead of coming between the believer and God, these afflictions demonstrated God's power to the world as he enabled believers to be victorious.

After asserting his conviction that nothing can separate us from God's love, Paul added to his list. Whether we live or die, we remain in his love. Neither angels nor demonic rulers have the power to sever our relationship. Nothing in the present or the future can do it. Nothing in the sky above, the earth below, or anything in all of creation will ever be able to divide us from God's love or his presence.

These verses serve as a beautiful reminder of God's deep, profound love for his children. Nothing that happens to us can undo our relationship with him. Nothing that we do ourselves can break the bond of love that connects us. Our soul is completely, utterly safe in the hands of the One who took on the form of a human being and suffered a horrible death to pay the penalty for our sins—all because he wanted to have a personal relationship with us. Would a God like that ever allow anything to come between us?

I am convinced that nothing can ever separate us from God's love which Christ Jesus our Lord shows us.

Romans 8:38

Ask God **to give you a deeper understanding of his immeasurable love for you.**

FEBRUARY

15

"What are you doing here?"

Judges 18:1–10

During the time of Israel's judges, the nation had rejected God's standards and the people did whatever seemed right to them. In Ephraim a man named Micah hired a young Levite named Jonathan (see v. 30) to serve as a priest to his household, contrary to God's law. There Jonathan "ministered" among Micah's shrine and idols, which God also had forbidden.

Meanwhile, the tribe of Dan needed more living space. They had failed to conquer all of their allotted territory in the Promised Land. So they sent five men to search for an area that would be easy to capture. At Micah's house, the spies recognized the Levite's accent and bombarded him with questions. "Who brought you here?" they asked. "What are you doing here? Why are you here?"

If Jonathan thought he was serving God, he was sadly deceived. He pretended to be a priest, and he even delivered a supposed message from the Lord to the spies. But his actions encouraged the idolatry of a family and later spread it to an entire tribe.

Sometimes we may think that we're involved in ministry when we're really not where God wants us to be. God says the only way to discern his will is to let him change the way we think. If we're not transformed by his Word, we'll be influenced by the world's thinking, which can lead to self-deception. Whenever we wander away from God's will, we risk ending up in the wrong place at the wrong time. Before that happens, we may need to stop and ask ourselves, "What in the world am I doing here?"

Don't copy the behavior and customs of this world, but let God transform you into a new person by changing the way you think. Then you will learn to know God's will for you, which is good and pleasing and perfect.

Romans 12:2 NLT

Ask yourself: **How can I make sure that I stay in the center of God's will?**

"If your child asks for bread, would you give him a stone?"

Matthew 7:7–11

I couldn't wait for my daughter to get home from school and find the surprise in her room. We'd had a discussion about jeans in THAT BRAND being way overpriced, and Holly had reluctantly agreed. But while running errands that morning, I'd noticed a store that had marked them down to a reasonable price. Now a pair of special jeans lay across Holly's bed, and I waited to hear her reaction.

As Jesus taught about prayer, he described God as a loving Father who delights in giving gifts to his children. "If your child asks you for bread, would any of you give him a stone?" he asked. "Or if your child asks for a fish, would you give him a snake?" Jesus explained that, since even imperfect earthly parents provide for their children, how much more our heavenly Father would give good things to us if we ask him.

But sometimes children ask for something that's not good for them. In the same way, we don't always pray the way we should. God may deny our request altogether, or he may answer in a different way than we expected. Can we accept that this job is his will, even though we prayed to get the other one? If our problem doesn't work out the way we hoped, can we trust that our Father knows best?

God may allow something in our life that certainly doesn't look like a gift at first, but as time passes we see the value of it. He always answers our prayers in ways that will bring him glory and help us grow more Christlike. When we understand that, we can joyfully accept whatever gift comes from our Father's hand—even if it's not what we asked for.

Every good present and every perfect gift comes from above.

James 1:17

Ask God **to help you trust that he will provide for you as a loving heavenly Father.**

FEBRUARY

19

"Why do you let others tell you how to live?"

Colossians 2:8–23

As Renee thinks back to her former life, she wonders what in the world she could have been thinking. The people in the small, informal house church had seemed so godly. Their leader delivered powerful messages and expressed deep concern for his "little flock." But as the years passed and the membership grew, he laid down increasingly stringent rules. Members were told how to dress and act, even whom to marry. Renee reacted in shock when the leader was arrested and newspapers labeled the group a cult. She didn't understand—until she started studying the Bible for herself.

The Colossian Christians were being pulled away from the truth by false philosophies based on human reasoning. Among other things, these teachers promoted harsh self-denial of the body and tried to impose legalistic rules on the believers. Paul reminded the believers they were no longer obligated to obey worldly rules.

"If you have died with Christ to the world's way of doing things, why do you let others tell you how to live?" he asked. Christ's death had freed them to live by the Spirit's power instead of trying to follow rules and rituals that merely give the appearance of wisdom and godliness.

If we have a personal relationship with Jesus, we don't need human philosophies or mystical revelations. We don't need lists of rules and prohibitions that lack any real power against the temptation of sin. We have the Holy Spirit, the Bible, and prayer to guide us in living a godly life. If we let anything pull us away from focusing on Jesus, we'll lose spiritual blessings and rewards. Since we died with Christ, only he can show us how to live.

We know that people don't receive God's approval because of their own efforts to live according to a set of standards, but only by believing in Jesus Christ.

Galatians 2:16

Ask God **to reveal any tendencies toward legalism in your thinking and attitudes.**

"Why should my freedom be judged by someone else's conscience?"

1 Corinthians 10:23–33

As the server gathered the menus and walked away, Tyler felt puzzled. "How come you guys didn't order wine with your dinner?" he asked. "You always do that when we eat here." His dad leaned forward. "Remember that couple from church who waved to us as they were seated across the room? They have very strong feelings that drinking alcohol is wrong," he explained. Tyler frowned. "So? How is that *your* problem?"

Dealing with a hot topic for Corinthian believers, Paul explained that we need to be sensitive to other people's feelings on issues not forbidden in Scripture. He confirmed that eating meat initially offered to idols and then sold in the market was perfectly acceptable. But believers should not do it in the presence of someone who thought the practice was wrong.

Paul imagined his readers protesting: "Why should my freedom be judged by someone else's conscience?" He further explained that we don't have to change our personal convictions, just adapt our behavior so we don't risk offending someone or prompting them to do something against their own conscience (see Rom. 14:14).

This wonderful freedom we have in Christ is to be governed by love. We may feel free to enjoy certain activities, but in the presence of someone who thinks those activities are sinful, God wants us to defer to the other person. Such an attitude clashes with our human nature and with our culture's "me-first" attitude. But no personal liberty is worth hurting someone or causing them to lose faith. When it comes to gray areas, our behavior is to be guided by a desire to glorify God in all that we do, and by love and concern for others.

People should be concerned about others
and not just about themselves.

1 Corinthians 10:24

Ask yourself: **Do I make an effort to be sensitive to how my behavior affects others who think differently from me?**

FEBRUARY
21

"Who will accuse those whom God has chosen?"

Romans 8

Thad breathed in the fresh air as he walked out of the jail with his dad. He couldn't blame the person who had called the police; after all, the school had been broken into twice already this fall. But Thad hadn't been able to convince the officers that he was there helping his dad, especially since he'd wandered off so far by himself. Finally, Thad's father came to the station, explained that he worked as the school custodian, and identified his son.

As Paul outlined the wonderful truths of our identity as God's children, he explained what Christ's sacrifice accomplished for us. "Who will accuse those whom God has chosen?" he asked. "God has approved of them. Who will condemn them?" Paul had already declared that believers in Jesus Christ can no longer be condemned because the law of the Spirit of life has freed them from the law of sin and death (see Rom. 8:1–2).

According to Revelation 12:10, Satan accuses believers day and night in God's presence. Satan may build a good case based on our struggles with our old sinful nature, but God is the judge. Based on our faith in Jesus, God has already acquitted us and removed the guilt of our sin. The charges against us have been dropped.

Satan also likes to fill our thoughts with accusations concerning past sins or imagined failures. The burden of a guilty conscience can hinder our relationship with God and paralyze our spiritual growth. At those times, we need to remember who is on our side. Jesus Christ sits at God's right hand interceding for us. Once he identifies us as his own, no charges against us can stand up in that court.

Christ has the highest position in heaven.
Christ also intercedes for us.

Romans 8:34

Ask God **to remind you that he has declared you "not guilty" the next time Satan tries to make you feel condemned.**

FEBRUARY
22

"Why do you call me Lord but don't do what I tell you?"

Luke 6:46–49

The famous singer writhed and gyrated in her skimpy clothing and five-inch heels. The suggestive words of her songs contrasted sharply with her recent interview in which she and her father proclaimed to be followers of Christ. Last week she seemed to be promoting God; on the concert stage she was obviously promoting sin.

Jesus had similar "followers" when he lived on the earth. He taught that calling him "Lord" means nothing if we don't also obey him. Jesus used a parable to demonstrate the importance of obedience versus mere outward expression. The person who hears Jesus's words and obeys them is like someone who lays the foundation of his home on bedrock. When floodwaters come, the house stands because of its solid foundation.

In contrast, the person who hears Jesus's words but refuses to obey them is compared to someone who builds his house without a foundation. It may look as solid as the first house, but it collapses when a flood comes. Only God can see whether we've built our life on a solid foundation—until life's storms and crises come along and test that foundation.

It's much easier to talk about being a Christian than it is to live a life of commitment and faith. But God is more interested in obedience than external expressions of love. We may wear a big gold cross around our neck or sport a fish symbol on our car, but that means nothing to God if we don't try to live according to his commands. God wants more than hollow words; he wants us to live a lifestyle that proves who our Lord is.

These people honor me with their lips,
but their hearts are far from me.

Matthew 15:8

Ask God **to reveal any areas where your lifestyle doesn't match your claim to be his follower.**

FEBRUARY

23

"When will you comfort me?"

Psalm 119:81–86

The little boy fell off the swing and started wailing. Fortunately, the wood chips cushioned his fall, so I felt sure he was more scared than hurt. I longed to reach out and comfort him, but he had already stumbled toward his mom. She scooped him up and within seconds the crying stopped. The little boy quietly snuggled against his mother as she stroked his hair and murmured soothing words in his ear.

Isaiah 66:13 compares God to a mother comforting her child, but sometimes we don't sense that. In Psalm 119, the writer admitted that he was tired of waiting for God to reach out to him. "My eyes have become strained from looking for your promise," he confessed. "I ask, 'When will you comfort me?'" The psalmist felt so beaten down by adversity and his enemies that he compared himself to a shriveled, dried-out wineskin. Yet he still clung to God's Word and found reassurance there.

God never promised to make all our troubles go away, but he does promise to always be there to comfort us. Sometimes when we're hurting it's hard to sense his presence, especially if we're angry or bitter. If we're receptive and open to his consolation, God will speak soothing words to us through prayer, his Word, his Holy Spirit, or other believers.

The solace we receive from God is not for our benefit alone; God wants us to turn around and comfort others. When we've gone through a severe trial, part of our healing process is to use what we've learned to minister to others facing similar circumstances. Whenever we're hurt, we can run to our heavenly Father, knowing that he'll not only comfort us but others through us.

He is the Father who is compassionate and the God who gives comfort. He comforts us whenever we suffer.

2 Corinthians 1:3–4

Ask yourself: **How has God's comfort prepared me to reach out to others who are hurting?**

FEBRUARY

24

"How could it be a body if it only had one part?"

1 Corinthians 12:12–27

Pitcher Dizzy Dean was one of the few baseball players in history to play for both the St. Louis Cardinals and their rivals, the Chicago Cubs. For several years, Dean racked up impressive titles and records, but his career was cut short when a line drive broke his big toe. When Dean altered his pitching style to compensate for the hurt toe, his throwing arm also suffered injury.

Just as each part of the human body influences its overall functioning, the body of Christ is made up of many members all performing vital roles. Paul used this illustration when he addressed problems in the church at Corinth. The people had allowed their differences to divide them instead of working together. Some had elevated the more "showy" spiritual gifts above other roles, resulting in pride and jealousy.

Paul painted an absurd image of a body that was nothing but an eye or an ear. Such a "body" certainly wouldn't be very effective. "How could it be a body if it only had one part?" he asked. In a similar way, Christ's body will only be effective when all of its members perform the various functions assigned to them by God.

God arranged the parts of his body just the way he wanted. With our different backgrounds, personalities, abilities, and spiritual gifts, each one of us brings something unique to God's family. Some of us have highly visible roles while others function quietly behind the scenes. But every person's part helps the body function; every role should be treated as valuable as we work together toward the common goal of spreading the Good News. Whether we're a pitching arm or a big toe, we all have an important part to play in Christ's body.

God put each and every part of the body together as he wanted it.

1 Corinthians 12:18

Ask yourself: **How has God equipped me to fulfill my role in the body of Christ?**

FEBRUARY
25

"What do you want to tell me?"

Joshua 5:13–15

So much for my big announcement, Tanya thought as she snapped her cell phone shut. Her daughter had responded to the voicemail asking her to call so she could "hear some exciting news." But between Valorie gushing over her great deals at the mall, complaining about the weather, and asking Tanya to babysit that night, both women forgot the real reason for the call. Suddenly, a familiar beep signaled a text message: *sorry mom, i 4got. what did u want 2 tell me?*

When the stranger facing Joshua identified himself as the "commander of the LORD's army," Joshua bowed with his face to the ground in worship. "Sir, what do you want to tell me?" he asked. His visitor told him to remove his sandals as a gesture of respect and reverence. At some point following this encounter, God told Joshua about his highly unconventional plan for Israel's conquest of Jericho.

Sometimes we miss what God wants to say to us because we forget that prayer is a two-way conversation. Our mind may be filled with all that we want to say to him—our requests and needs, maybe a complaint or two. If we don't make time to quiet our minds and listen for his voice, we can miss so much. Maybe God wants to offer comfort or encouragement, conviction of sin, a new assignment, or guidance about a decision.

When Samuel was a little boy serving in the tabernacle, God called to him during the night. Samuel thought that the voice belonged to Eli the priest until Eli explained that it was God. We probably won't hear an audible voice as Samuel did, but we can take a cue from his response. Our prayer time won't be complete unless we approach it with an attitude of, "Speak, Lord, for your servant is listening."

Then Samuel said, "Speak, for your servant is listening."

1 Samuel 3:10 NIV

Ask yourself: **During prayer, do I make time to listen for what God wants to tell me?**

“How can anyone be born when he’s an old man?”

John 3:1–12

I stamped the snow off my feet and walked into the church for the memorial service. Although I’d never met my friend’s father, I knew that he had become a Christian during his final months on earth. The beautiful arrangement on the altar seemed appropriate—brilliant red roses scattered among snow-white flowers. Like roses blooming in winter, this elderly man’s faith had blossomed in the winter of his life.

Nicodemus may have been an old man when he visited Jesus to learn more about his identity. Although he was a Pharisee, Nicodemus believed that Jesus had been sent from God because of the miracles he performed. Jesus immediately challenged Nicodemus with the declaration that no one can see God’s kingdom without being born again, or born from above.

Nicodemus struggled to make sense of Jesus’s words. “How can anyone be born when he’s an old man?” he asked. “He can’t go back inside his mother a second time to be born, can he?” Jesus explained that entrance into God’s kingdom requires that a person be spiritually reborn, which can be accomplished only through the Holy Spirit.

When we place our faith in Christ and his death on our behalf, God re-creates us. We aren’t just a reconfigured model of our former self but a brand-new person. That means each one of us starts our spiritual journey as a baby, having to “grow into” our new life with its transformed desires, attitudes, goals, and behavior. Just as in the physical realm, we all mature at different rates, but if we nurture our relationship with God, we will be making progress. Regardless of our chronological age, all of us are trying to grow up to be just like our Father.

Whoever is a believer in Christ is a new creation.

2 Corinthians 5:17

Ask yourself: **How does my life show that I have been reborn?**

FEBRUARY
27

"Why are you thinking evil things?"

Matthew 9:1–8

"Boy, have I got a bag for you!" the airline worker called out as she stared at the X-ray machine. *Uh-oh, somebody's in trouble!* I thought smugly as I removed my shoes. The next minute, I stood in front of two big men looking inside my small purse. My jaw dropped as one of them said, "What do we have here?" and pulled out my Swiss army knife. Sure, it was only an inch and a half long, and I mainly used it for the tiny scissors, but it was still a forbidden item. And I'd completely forgotten it was in the bottom of my purse.

Jesus often revealed what lay hidden in people's hearts. Before healing the paralyzed man, he addressed his spiritual needs and told him that his sins were forgiven. Some of the religious leaders were shocked at what they considered blasphemy. Jesus knew their thoughts and confronted them. "Why are you thinking evil things?" He asked them which would be easier: to tell the man his sins were forgiven, or to tell him to get up and walk. Then Jesus demonstrated his authority by healing the man's physical condition as well.

We may claim we have no control over our thought life, but the Bible teaches that we're responsible for what we allow to stay in our minds. God instructs us to evaluate every thought expressed by others as well as our own thoughts. Does it contradict God's truth? Would it dishonor my Lord? Could it lead to unhealthy attitudes, desires, or habits?

With the help of God's Word and his Holy Spirit, we can learn to recognize and get rid of thoughts that aren't worthy of a child of God. When we submit our thought life to God's inspection, we may be surprised at what lies at the bottom of our heart.

We take every thought captive so that it is obedient to Christ.

2 Corinthians 10:5

Ask God **to make you immediately aware of any thought that is displeasing to him.**

"Don't you realize that everyone runs to win, but only one gets the prize?"

1 Corinthians 9:24–27

The gunshot rang out and the crowd surged forward. As Melissa jostled for a better spot, she thought about the past ten months of training. She'd gotten expert advice on which shoes to buy. She'd mapped out a running schedule of two hours a day, although sometimes she had skipped sessions. Now, Melissa couldn't help wondering—was it enough for a marathon? How would she feel in two hours—in three hours?

Paul used the concept of a long-distance race to illustrate the Christian life. "Don't you realize that everyone who runs in a race runs to win, but only one runner gets the prize?" he asked. "Run like them, so that you can win." Just like athletes in the Greek games, Paul submitted himself to strict training, mastering his body and mind so he wouldn't be disqualified from the privilege of sharing the Good News of Jesus Christ. And he always looked ahead to the joy of receiving rewards in heaven.

The Christian life is not an easy path. It calls for ongoing training through Bible study, prayer, and fellowship with other believers. We have to constantly be on guard for habits and behaviors that could make us stumble, and discipline our body and mind to resist our sinful nature's attempts to get us sidelined. We need to be careful to run the course marked out for us by God and not drift into someone else's lane.

Along with training and discipline, perseverance is needed to help us stay the course. The Bible gives examples of people who started out committed to God but ended up getting off track. If we stay close to God, he will give us the endurance to finish our race well.

We must run the race that lies ahead of us and never give up.

Hebrews 12:1

Ask God **to help you develop the self-discipline and endurance you need to finish your race well.**

MARCH
1

“Does anyone bring a lamp into a room to put it under a basket?”

Matthew 5:14–16; Mark 4:21–25

Ramona had the UPS man bring the package inside. With trembling hands, she slit the box open and gently removed the bubble wrap. Ramona had wanted a Tiffany lamp ever since she could remember. On her last birthday, her father had taken her into a store to pick out the one she wanted. And now, it was hers. Ramona found the perfect spot for the lamp in her living room, plugged it in, and flipped the switch. She gasped. *It's even more beautiful than I remembered.* Then Ramona found her thickest blanket and draped it over her new lamp.

None of us would do such a dumb thing, but Jesus had to warn us not to act that way with our faith. “Does anyone bring a lamp into a room to put it under a basket or under a bed?” he asked. Jesus called his followers “light for the world.” He pointed out that when a Jewish family lit a lamp, they put it on a stand so its light would shine on everyone. In the same way, believers are to live such a godly lifestyle that others recognize the light of God's truth and love.

Jesus said, “As long as I'm in the world, I'm light for the world” (John 9:5). Now it's our responsibility to reflect his light to everyone around us. By living for Christ, we show how dark life is without him, shed light on God's Word, and direct others to the path to find him. We want to be careful not to let timidity, sin, or a reluctance to share our faith dim our light. Wherever we go, our Father wants us to shine so brightly that others will see him.

In the same way let your light shine in front of people. Then they will see the good that you do and praise your Father in heaven.

Matthew 5:16

Ask yourself: **What can I do to help my light shine more brightly?**

"How long will you try to have it both ways?"

1 Kings 18:20–40

The speaker walked away from the stage to lukewarm applause. He had spoken with skill and passion, engaging the audience with stories and anecdotes. But many people left the auditorium feeling confused. After 45 minutes of listening to the politician try to appeal to both conservative and liberal voters, they still had no clue as to where he stood on the issues that concerned them.

The people in Elijah's day were reluctant to take a stand, wavering between worshiping Yahweh or Baal. "How long will you try to have it both ways?" Elijah demanded. He challenged the Israelites to follow either the Lord or Baal as the only true God, and forget about the false one. When they responded with silence, Elijah set up a contest between himself and 450 of Baal's prophets. On Mount Carmel, God revealed his power in a dramatic way. Fire from heaven streaked down and consumed the offering and stones that had been drenched with water. The crowd burst out crying, "The Lord is God!"

We might get away with not taking a stand on political issues, but when it comes to spiritual matters, a middle-of-the-road approach doesn't work. In appreciation for diversity, many people try to accept all belief systems. Others sample different philosophies to see which one works for them. Some people even attempt to mesh elements of other religions with their Christian beliefs.

God calls us to make a clear-cut choice: Will we love and serve him, or someone or something else? Following Christ means committing every aspect of our life to his control. In God's eyes, there's no such thing as a "moderate" Christian. Just as in Elijah's day, we can't have it both ways.

Choose today whom you will serve.

Joshua 24:15

Ask yourself: **Is there any area of my life where I avoid taking a stand for God?**

MARCH
3

"O God, who is like you?"

Psalm 71:15–19

The late Dr. S. M. Lockridge served as pastor of Calvary Baptist Church from 1952 until 1993. After his retirement, he remained a popular guest lecturer and public speaker. Dr. Lockridge is perhaps best known for a portion of a rousing sermon often referred to as "That's My King" in which he spends several minutes describing Jesus Christ:

> He's enduringly strong. He's entirely sincere. He's eternally steadfast. He's immortally graceful. He's imperially powerful. He's impartially merciful. . . . He's the sinner's savior. He's the centerpiece of civilization. . . . His promise is sure. His light is matchless. His goodness is limitless. His mercy is everlasting. His love never changes. His Word is enough. His grace is sufficient. His reign is righteous. . . . I wish I could describe Him to you . . . but He's indescribable. That's my King.

In Psalm 71, David burst out in wonder and amazement as he looked back at how God had worked in his life. "Your righteousness reaches to the heavens, O God. You have done great things. O God, who is like you?" he exclaimed. Whenever David meditated on God's unique qualities, he found words inadequate to describe him. But thankfully he never stopped trying, and as a result we are blessed by many psalms that remind us of God's goodness, power, and mercy.

Learning biblical facts is important, but we receive more blessing from knowing God's character. Meditating on his character traits builds up our faith and helps us trust in him. And we just might be tempted to burst out in adoration and worship as David and Dr. Lockridge did. We may not understand everything about Christianity or the Bible, but we know the answer to the question in Psalm 71: "O God, who is like you?" Absolutely no one.

No one compares to you!

Psalm 40:5

Ask yourself: **How often do I express adoration and worship on the basis of God's character?**

"What can I give you?"

1 Kings 3:5–15

I sat by my four-year-old granddaughter and wondered how many times she'd watched this same movie over the past few months. Lacey seemed mesmerized as the genie popped out of the magic lamp and offered to grant Aladdin three wishes. The familiar storyline caused my own mind to wander. *If I had three wishes, what would I ask for? And how could I hold my list down to only three?*

Soon after Solomon became king of Israel, God appeared to him in a dream and offered to grant him a wish. "What can I give you?" God asked. Solomon requested understanding and discernment to help him govern the people effectively and tell the difference between right and wrong. Solomon's answer pleased God so much that he promised to also give the young king what he didn't ask for: riches and honor never seen before in Israel, and also a long life if he remained obedient to God's commands.

If someone offered to grant a wish for us, our answer would say a lot about our values. Would our first thought be for wealth, fame, or perfect health? Would we request something to benefit a loved one? Or would our answer reflect an interest in spiritual matters? Solomon's concern wasn't for his personal gain but for the ability to carry out his God-ordained role as Israel's leader. His request revealed his heart for following God.

David wrote that we can have our heart's desires granted—if we make the conscious decision to look for our happiness in the right place. As we grow closer to God, we can learn to find our joy and delight in him. Then we will have desires that line up with his will. And any wish we make will be something that he wants to give us.

Be happy with the Lord, and he will give you the desires of your heart.

Psalm 37:4

Ask yourself: **What would I ask for if God offered to grant the deepest desire of my heart?**

MARCH
5

"Wasn't it because of marriages like these that Solomon sinned?"

Nehemiah 13:23–29

For all his wisdom, Solomon made a dumb move when he broke God's command forbidding intermarriage with pagan people. Solomon let his love of foreign women get out of control and accumulated seven hundred wives of royal birth and three hundred concubines. Eventually, his harem influenced him to worship other gods that had once been detestable to him.

Centuries later, Nehemiah pointed to Solomon's example when he confronted the people of Judah. Returning to Jerusalem after a long absence, Nehemiah discovered they had been intermarrying with pagan people even though they had promised not to when they reaffirmed their covenant with God. Many of the children spoke their mother's language instead of Hebrew. Even the high priest's son was guilty of intermarriage.

"Wasn't it because of marriages like these that King Solomon of Israel sinned?" Nehemiah reminded them. If one of Israel's greatest kings had been led into sin by pagan wives, shouldn't they learn from his example? Solomon had tried to combine his worship of Yahweh with worship of other gods—and his idolatry brought tragedy to the entire nation of Israel, as God had warned would happen.

Influenced by our culture's obsession with diversity, some Christians try to mix their faith with elements of other belief systems. The concepts of karma, reincarnation, astrology, and certain meditation techniques may seem harmless, even sometimes beneficial. But any time we intermarry our faith with nonbiblical principles, we risk weakening our commitment to God. We open ourselves up to the danger of being led into idolatry. If we're smart, we'll learn from the sad example of the wisest man who ever lived.

Never worship any other god, because the Lord
is a God who does not tolerate rivals.

Exodus 34:14

Ask yourself: **Am I mingling my Christian faith with elements of other belief systems?**

"How many of my father's hired men have more food than they can eat, while I'm starving?"

Luke 15:11–32

The young man's stomach growled as he watched the pigs gobbling up their feed. *It wasn't supposed to turn out like this*, he told himself for the hundredth time. When he'd demanded his inheritance from his father, the young man had imagined a life of freedom and pleasure. And that's just what he had—until the money ran out. Then his new friends disappeared and he understood how much he had wasted.

A famine had forced him to take a job tending pigs, animals that Jewish people would not even touch. He figured he couldn't sink any lower—until the morning he found himself drooling over the pigs' food. Suddenly, a light bulb went on in his head. "How many of my father's hired men have more food than they can eat, while I'm starving to death here?" he asked. The man decided to go home and ask to be his father's hired man since he no longer deserved to be a son.

The story of the prodigal son is constantly played out in people's lives. Husbands and wives leave their spouse for a more exciting relationship. Children rebel against parents who seem too strict. Christians reject God's standards to choose their own lifestyle. But the thrill of such "freedom" is usually short-lived.

The prodigal son had to hit bottom before he came to his senses. He finally understood that the fleeting pleasures of sin were nothing compared with what he'd walked away from. How much pain and suffering could we avoid if we figured that out sooner rather than later? Once we make the choice to turn away from our rebellious lifestyle, we'll find what the prodigal son found: a loving Father waiting and watching for our return.

I'll go at once to my father.

Luke 15:18

Ask yourself: **Is there any area of my life where I'm acting like a prodigal?**

MARCH
7

"Can it be that I have become your enemy for telling you the truth?"

Galatians 4:12–20

Lisa took a deep breath as she saw her friend step into the coffee shop. *This is going to be tough*, she thought. She'd debated for months over whether or not to confront Debbie with her drinking problem—until the dinner party proved that the situation had spiraled out of control. *How can I be a true friend without trying to convince Debbie of how she's hurting herself and her family?*

Paul had to share some tough words with the Christians in Galatia. Even though they knew the truth, they were allowing themselves to be influenced by false teachers. A faction within the church had convinced them that Gentiles had to obey Jewish laws in addition to believing in Christ for salvation.

As a result of his correction, the Galatians' attitude toward Paul had drastically changed. He reminded them of their former devotion to him and wondered why they no longer looked forward to his visits. "What happened to your positive attitude?" he asked. "Can it be that I have become your enemy for telling you the truth?"

It's not easy to confront someone with a truth they don't want to face. We worry about their response; we may even wonder if the relationship will survive. But being a friend means caring enough to say what the other person needs to hear instead of helping them deny the problem.

It's not any easier being on the receiving end of constructive criticism. Our natural response is to get defensive or angry. Instead, we need to consider the source. Is this someone who wants the best for us? If so, then we need to prayerfully and honestly evaluate their words. When our best friend tells us something for our own good, we don't want to treat them like our worst enemy.

Wounds made by a friend are intended to help.

Proverbs 27:6

Ask yourself: **How do I react when someone I trust corrects me?**

"Who touched my clothes?"

Mark 5:25–34

The desperate woman pushed her way through the crowd. *This is my last hope*, she thought. After twelve years of searching for a cure, her money had disappeared and her condition had worsened. Besides being a serious health problem, her chronic bleeding made her continuously unclean, shut out from normal social contact.

She'd heard about Jesus and his miracles. So many people had been healed, but how could she bear the shame of approaching him with such an embarrassing problem? *If I can just touch his clothes, I'll get well*, she assured herself. The instant she stretched out a timid hand and touched Jesus's robe, the woman felt her bleeding stop.

Suddenly Jesus turned around. "Who touched my clothes?" he asked. The woman's heart stopped. How would he react if he knew who had touched him and why? Trembling, she bowed in front of Jesus and spilled out her story. Jesus addressed her with a term of affection and assured her that her healing was permanent.

Jesus didn't need to ask who had touched his clothes; he knew exactly what had happened. He also knew that this woman needed to confess her shame in order to be fully healed of her painful past. He knew she needed more than a physical touch of his robe; she needed a personal relationship with him.

No one has such a shameful history that God will not forgive them on the basis of faith in Jesus. And once we become God's child, there's nothing that should make us timid about approaching him. We already have his acceptance and unconditional love. Why would we ever feel too ashamed to come before him face-to-face?

We can go to God with bold confidence
through faith in Christ.

Ephesians 3:12

Ask yourself: **Is there something in my life that makes me feel ashamed to come before God in prayer?**

MARCH
9

"Why bother the teacher anymore?"

Mark 5:21–24, 35–43

The synagogue ruler stood by Jesus's side, frustrated at the interruption. As Jesus spoke with the woman in the crowd, Jairus wanted to scream. *We're wasting precious time—time my little girl might not have!* He believed that his daughter would get well if Jesus laid his hands on her—if they could only get there before it was too late.

The young father's heart sank as he turned to see a familiar face and heard the dreaded words: "Your daughter has died. Why bother the teacher anymore?" But the next instant, Jairus heard a different voice. "Don't be afraid! Just believe," Jesus told him. Jairus held on to those words as he walked home with Jesus, toward the loud sounds of wailing and weeping.

It's impossible to imagine the emotions that flooded Jairus as Jesus agreed to heal his daughter but allowed the trip to his house to be halted by the encounter with the woman in the crowd—and then heard the news that his girl had died. But we can all relate to the feeling that it's time to give up.

Why bother praying when we haven't seen an answer? Why keep fighting that same temptation when we always give in? Why should we keep trying to live by God's standards when we keep failing? Some days we may even wonder why we should bother getting out of bed.

Whether we struggle with a relationship, a habit, or day-to-day living, giving up is never the answer. Jesus walked through a crowd of mourners and raised Jairus's daughter to life. We never know when he will step into our situation and give new life to hopes and dreams that seem dead. When we hear a voice whispering, "Why bother?" we can read God's Word and hear a different voice urging us to "just believe."

We're frustrated, but we don't give up.
2 Corinthians 4:8

Ask yourself: **What struggles or problems make me feel like giving up?**

"Where is the evidence of your mercy, Lord?"

Psalm 89:49–52

Does any of this sound familiar?

> "If God exists, why is there so much evil in the world?"
> "How could a loving God allow such great suffering and injustice?"
> "God, why did you let this happen to me?"

The writer of Psalm 89 cried out to God in a similar way during a time when the Jewish people could see no proof of God's love. Despite God's covenant promises, the nation had been defeated and suffered mockery from her enemies. The psalmist called for God to remember his relationship with Israel and asked, "Where is the evidence of your mercy, Lord?"

A little child is kidnapped from her home and brutally murdered. A crazed gunman takes the lives of an entire family. An oppressive regime commits genocide on a native population. As we look at the horrible things happening around the globe, it's tempting to question God's love and mercy. We forget that we live on a planet distorted by sin and under the temporary control of Satan (see 1 John 5:19). We don't remember that God will one day right all wrongs and rid the world of sin and suffering. We just want to see some proof that he still cares.

Whether we're depressed by global events or oppressed by troubles in our personal life, we can honestly cry out to God. He understands our anger and grief over sin, and he feels the same way. But he doesn't want us to focus on the evil in the world and miss the obvious proofs of his love. Because of God's care, the sun rises and sets, rain waters the ground, flowers bloom, and crops grow. He keeps our planet spinning in space and our hearts pumping blood. He provides everything we enjoy. Whether we realize it or not, every breath we take is evidence of God's mercy.

> *He gives everyone life, breath, and everything they have.*
> Acts 17:25

Ask God **to make you more aware of daily evidence of his love and care.**

MARCH
11

"Won't you ever learn your lesson and obey my words?"

Jeremiah 35:1–19

Maria quietly slipped through the door of her husband's workshop. She was anxious to get a peek at the new entertainment center Tony had almost finished. What she saw nauseated her. *Well, he's done it again*, Maria thought. Tony always tackled a woodworking project by studying how-to books. But then he had a habit of ignoring steps in the instructions, taking shortcuts, and doing things his own way. *When will he ever learn his lesson?* Maria wondered.

God wondered the same thing about the people of Judah. He used the family of Rechab to emphasize the Israelites' disobedience. For two hundred years, this family had faithfully obeyed their ancestor's command to abstain from wine and to live a nomadic lifestyle. In contrast, Israel had consistently broken her covenant with God and disobeyed his laws, ignoring the warnings he sent through prophets again and again. "Won't you ever learn your lesson and obey my words?" God asked.

God's commands are designed to protect us physically, emotionally, and spiritually. His Word provides the guidelines for enjoying a personal relationship with him and healthy relationships with other people. By faithfully obeying his Word, we can avoid a lot of pain and heartache. But when we ignore God's instructions and do things our own way, our life won't turn out right.

Despite God's gift of his Word, sometimes we choose to learn things the hard way by experiencing the consequences of disobedience. We may even repeat the same mistakes over and over, making us wonder, "When will we ever learn?" Faithfully obeying God's commands is hard, but in the long run it's easier and safer to follow his how-to instructions than to do things our way.

It is the result of their own plots, because
they won't pay attention to my words.

Jeremiah 6:19

Ask yourself: **What lessons have I learned the hard way because of disobedience to God's Word?**

MARCH
12

"What credit do you deserve if you endure a beating for doing wrong?"

1 Peter 2:19–25

When Jay offended neighbors with his sarcastic humor, they excluded him from their annual Christmas party. He called it "being persecuted for my faith." After he missed a few deadlines at work, he referred to his irate boss as "the cross I have to bear." Finally, a friend explained to Jay that suffering for Christ is not the same thing as suffering for being a jerk.

Some people think of themselves as a martyr whenever they undergo any kind of mistreatment or censure, even when it results from their own foolish actions. But God says that's nothing to be commended for. "What credit do you deserve if you endure a beating for doing something wrong?" Paul wrote. "But if you endure suffering for doing something good, God is pleased with you."

This is a difficult passage to embrace. Whenever we're treated unfairly, our first instinct is to scream out, "That's not fair!" We want to strike back at our persecutor, or at least demand that God rectify the situation—immediately. Instead, God tells us to follow Christ's example of patient submission in the face of unjust suffering. Such a demonstration of trust may stretch our faith to its limits, but it pleases God.

Even though Jesus was without sin, he suffered insults, false accusations, abuse, and injury of the worst kind. He could have ended it at any moment, yet he accepted and bore everything for our sake. Remembering all that Jesus went through will help us patiently endure unfair treatment. We know that God will either intervene in the situation or reward us in the future. Since suffering is inevitable in this world, it's better by far to accept mistreatment we don't deserve, rather than be punished for doing something wrong.

God called you to endure suffering
because Christ suffered for you.

1 Peter 2:21

Ask yourself: **Am I prepared to patiently endure unfair treatment as Jesus did?**

MARCH
13

"Is it legal for you to whip a Roman citizen who hasn't had a trial?"

Acts 22:22–30

The mob listened to Paul's personal testimony—until he proclaimed that God had appointed him to share the gospel with Gentiles. These words ignited the crowd into a fury. They screamed and flung dust in the air to express their rage and contempt. Since the Roman commander didn't understand Hebrew, he had no idea what had set off the crowd. He decided to examine Paul under scourging.

As the soldiers stretched Paul out, he asked a question that stopped them in their tracks. "Is it legal for you to whip a Roman citizen who hasn't had a trial?" This terrified the officer in charge, who could face serious consequences for violating the law. What's more, this prisoner was born a Roman citizen, instead of having a purchased citizenship like the officer. The commander released Paul and arranged a hearing before the Jewish council.

Paul never shied away from hardship. During his ministry, he received the Jewish punishment of thirty-nine lashes on five occasions; three times the Romans beat him with clubs. But the Roman scourging, done with whips embedded with metal or bone, often left a man permanently maimed or dead. Paul would have gladly given his life for Christ, but he wasn't about to throw it away needlessly. He knew that his work on earth wasn't finished yet, so he used his citizenship to escape the torture.

The Bible tells us to imitate Jesus in the face of persecution or abuse, but this incident shows that sometimes we need to speak up in our own defense. How can we know which approach to take? We'll know only by staying in tune with God's Spirit and letting him show us when to speak up and when to quietly submit.

[There is] a time to keep quiet and a time to speak out.

Ecclesiastes 3:7

Ask God **to give you the wisdom to know when to speak out on your own behalf and when to submit to unjust treatment.**

"But what does it matter?"

Philippians 1:12–18

All morning I stayed busy, sending business emails, paying bills, taking phone calls, corresponding with an editor and a fellow author, and squeezing in all the household chores I could manage. At lunchtime, I realized that I hadn't made any progress on the article with the approaching deadline. Instead, I had fallen prey to what Charles Hummel called the "tyranny of the urgent" in his 1967 essay by the same name.[3] I had allowed things that seemed urgent to crowd out what was most important.

The apostle Paul never let anything interfere with his number one priority: spreading the Good News. To him, imprisonment in Rome meant a chance to share the gospel with the guards. The fact that some people who opposed his ministry used his absence to build a following for themselves didn't bother him. "But what does it matter?" he asked. "Nothing matters except that, in one way or another, people are told the message about Christ."

Paul kept his focus on the job God had given him and didn't worry about things that lacked eternal value. If we want to accomplish our God-ordained role in his kingdom, it's important to order our priorities. Once we list what's most important, we can concentrate on the items at the top. But we need to be prepared for those seemingly "urgent" things that bombard us daily and sidetrack us from our real purpose.

Often we think we have a shortage of time when the problem may actually be a matter of priorities. Whenever something demands our attention, we can evaluate it by asking, "But what does it matter from an eternal perspective?" We can also meditate on these lines by missionary Charles T. Studd: "Just one life, 'twill soon be past. Only what's done for Christ will last."

Everything else is worthless when compared with the infinite value of knowing Christ Jesus my Lord.

Philippians 3:8 NLT

Ask yourself: **Do I spend my time and energy on things that really matter?**

3. Charles E. Hummel, *Tyranny of the Urgent*, rev. ed. (Downers Grove, IL: InterVarsity, 1994).

MARCH
15

"Do you think I came to bring peace to earth?"

Luke 12:49–53

Sachar sighed as he hung up the phone. Two years had passed, and his parents still refused to answer his calls. The last words they'd spoken to Sachar replayed in his mind: "If you do this, you will become dead to us." Sachar missed his parents and five siblings, but he knew he had made the right choice. After secretly reading the New Testament, Sachar had found the Messiah. How could he let anything stop him from following Christ? But he couldn't help wondering, *Will they ever accept me as part of the family again?*

Jesus warned that his ministry would often bring conflict instead of peace. These words sound strange coming from one who was called "Prince of Peace" before his birth (see Isa. 9:6). But today, the gospel message still sparks disagreements, conflicts, and even family splits, as some decide to follow Christ and others choose to reject him. God calls us to place our loyalty to Christ above all earthly relationships. We may have people in our life who find that hard to accept.

Even if we're not ostracized, becoming a Christian will impact all of our relationships to some degree. It may lead to conflicts with our boss or coworkers. Old friends may avoid us. Relatives may ignore us or even make fun of our newfound faith. But hopefully, the witness of our changed life will eventually lead them to discover the Savior for themselves.

Even as we're surrounded by discord, we can rest in the deep sense of peace that comes from being in a right relationship with God. We can trust him with every area of our life. No matter what happens in our earthly relationships, we've been reconciled with God. And that brings a peace on the inside that lasts forever.

I'm giving you my peace.
John 14:27

Ask yourself: **Do I put any earthly relationship above following Christ?**

MARCH
16

"What good will it do for people to win the whole world and lose their lives?"

Matthew 16:24–28

The news report sounded sad but all too familiar. On the surface, the Hollywood star seemed to have it all—loaded bank accounts, lavish houses in several locations, a private jet, a troop of people at his beck and call, and the adoration of countless fans. But in reality, his dream lifestyle had morphed into a nightmare. His attempts to fill the emptiness in his spirit led him down a self-destructive path, and a household name became a newspaper obituary.

Chasing worldly security, wealth, or fame can never bring meaning or lasting joy to our life. If our main goal is to get as many earthly comforts as possible during our brief lifespan, we're missing the big picture. Jesus taught that following him means giving up our worldly view of things and adopting an eternal perspective. "What good will it do for people to win the whole world and lose their lives?" he asked. We can appear to "have it all" and yet miss out on a worthwhile life—and more importantly, eternal life.

Jesus pointed out the irony of having the wrong priorities. By focusing solely on preserving our physical life, we put ourselves in danger. But the more we give up to follow Christ, the more we gain. Each time we give ourselves to love and service to God, we invest in the life we will spend in eternity. But whenever we put worldly goals or pleasures above following God's will, we miss out on something spiritually. It's only when we lose ourselves in him that we find the true meaning of life. And that's worth more than owning the whole world.

[Jesus said]"But those who lose their lives for me will find them."

Matthew 16:25

Ask God **to help you stay focused on giving your life to him rather than to worldly pursuits.**

MARCH
17

"How have I displeased you that you put the burden of all these people on me?"

Numbers 11:1–17

Number two hundred, all finished! I felt like celebrating. I'd been working on the new one-year devotional practically every day for three months, putting in ten or eleven hours each weekday. Then it dawned on me—a year has 365 days. I still had 165 devotions to write! Suddenly, I didn't feel like celebrating; I just felt weary. But later that week, God renewed my sense of what a privilege it is to spend time studying and writing about his Word. And once again I felt gratitude for the blessing of a book contract.

My struggle reminded me of a plaque I once saw of a smiling woman surrounded by several small children pulling at her clothes and vying for her attention. The caption read: "Lord, give me the patience to bear my blessings." Moses could have related to that. When the Israelites got tired of manna, they complained and cried for meat. Poor Moses felt like he couldn't take it anymore.

"LORD, why have you brought me this trouble?" Moses prayed. "How have I displeased you that you put the burden of all these people on me?" Moses said that leading Israel was too much work for him and suggested that God just kill him. God didn't kill Moses or remove him as leader; instead he instructed Moses to choose men who could share the responsibilities.

Sometimes our God-given responsibilities can start to feel like burdens. We lose the sense of wonder that the God of heaven allows us to share in his work. During those times, God wants us to honestly share our feelings with him as Moses did. He may send people to help us carry our load or he may give us his supernatural strength. But we can trust him to give us the ability to do whatever task he assigns us. When stress takes away the joy of serving, we can ask God to help us see what a blessing our responsibilities are.

I can do everything through Christ who strengthens me.

Philippians 4:13

Ask yourself: **Do I have any blessings in my life that seem more like burdens right now?**

"Don't you know that if you offer to be someone's slave, you must obey that master?"

Romans 6:15–20

Thomas braced himself as he saw his master raise his hand. For six years he'd worked for this man to pay off his debt. According to the law, his master must now set him free after generously providing him with livestock, grain, and wine. But Thomas didn't want to leave. He'd found a good home, working for a God-fearing family who treated him with kindness. The master's hand came down. With a single stroke, the awl pierced Thomas's earlobe. Now he was bound to his master for life.

Voluntary slavery sounds like an oxymoron to our modern ears (see Deut. 15:12–17). But the Bible teaches that, spiritually speaking, we're all slaves to a master of our own choosing. We will either serve sin by gratifying the desires of our human nature, or we will serve God. In Romans 6 Paul acknowledged that he used the illustration of slavery so they could understand his point. He knew the analogy was imperfect, since God doesn't treat his children as slaves. He gives us the power to do his will, but leaves us the choice of whether to obey or not.

Even though Christians have been set free from the penalty and power of sin by Christ's death, choosing to disobey God is serious business. The more we give in to temptations, the more we give sin authority to control us. With each compromise, sinning becomes easier. On the other hand, if we commit our body and mind to making godly choices, living a holy life will become easier. Still, the struggle will never end while we live on earth. Day by day, moment by moment, we have to make a choice: Will I give in to my old sinful nature or obey my new Master's call to live a godly life?

A person is a slave to whatever he gives in to.

2 Peter 2:19

Ask yourself: **Which master will I choose to serve today?**

MARCH
19

“What should I do to inherit eternal life?”

Mark 10:17–27

The young man’s actions took the onlookers by surprise. This wealthy, prominent community leader rushed out to the road like a little boy when he saw Jesus coming. Kneeling before Jesus, he spoke with deep respect. “Good Teacher, what should I do to inherit eternal life?” When Jesus recited several commandments relating to human relationships, the man declared that he had kept them all since his childhood.

Jesus looked into the man’s heart and lovingly pointed out the one thing missing. The rich man’s love of money and pride in his achievements had created a wall between himself and God. By loving his wealth more than God, he broke the first commandment: “Never have any other god” (Exod. 20:3). Jesus exposed the man’s flaw with a two-part challenge. He told him to sell everything he owned and give the money to the poor, and then to follow him. Hearing these words, the man’s face fell and he walked away.

Jesus doesn’t ask all of his followers to sell everything they own, but he does ask us to get rid of any obstacle that keeps us from loving and serving him fully. Those barriers differ from person to person—material possessions, popularity, career success, certain relationships, anything we devote ourselves to more than God.

We can’t “do” anything to inherit eternal life, because salvation is based on a relationship with God through faith in Jesus Christ. But God sometimes has to lovingly confront us with the condition of our heart and challenge us to give up something we love. How will we respond? Will we obey the most important commandment, or walk away sad like the rich young man?

Love the LORD your God with all your heart, with all your soul, and with all your strength.

Deuteronomy 6:5

Ask yourself: **Is God calling me to give up something so I can love him with my whole heart?**

"What is the purpose of the laws given to Moses?"

Galatians 3:15–29

The news frequently includes stories of battles over the privilege of hanging the Ten Commandments in public places. Why such strong feelings about these ancient words that God carved into stone and gave to Moses? Are they still applicable to us today, three thousand years later? According to the Bible, the answer is yes.

In Galatians 3, Paul mainly addressed a group of people who claimed it was necessary to obey the Mosaic laws in order to be saved. He explained that the law was given to show people how God wanted them to live, and to point out their sins. Since no one could keep all the laws perfectly, the Ten Commandments proved that it's impossible to please God on our own. This paved the way for the gospel by revealing our need for a Savior.

Jesus taught that he did not come to set aside Moses's teachings but to bring them to fulfillment. The Old Testament laws restrained sin at a time when God's Spirit didn't live inside his followers, except when it was given for a specific time and purpose. Jesus's death and resurrection made it possible for every believer to be led by the Holy Spirit on a daily basis, receiving guidance in how to live according to God's standards.

As believers, we are free from the ceremonial and civil laws given to Israel, but God's moral law still stands. The Ten Commandments contain God's guidelines for a lifestyle that is healthy, purposeful, and most importantly, pleasing to him. Just like the Old Testament Jews, we can't be saved by following any set of rules—even if we could pull it off. But with God's Holy Spirit and his timeless commandments, we have the perfect tools for a spiritual checkup.

I wouldn't have recognized sin if those laws hadn't shown it to me.

Romans 7:7

Ask God **to use his Ten Commandments to pinpoint areas of your life that need attention.**

MARCH
21

"Don't you care that my sister has left me to do the work all by myself?"

Luke 10:38–42

The guest speaker quietly excused himself from the family gathering. "I have a 4:30 a.m. appointment with God," he explained to his hostess. "4:30 a.m.!" she exclaimed. "But you have such a full day tomorrow with the church services, afternoon luncheon, and evening meetings." "Exactly." He smiled. "That makes it even more important for me to have my time with God in the morning."

When Jesus visited Martha's home in Bethany, she let her busy schedule interfere with the chance to spend precious time with him during his last week on earth. As hostess, she wanted everything to be just right for her guests, but her sister Mary only seemed interested in sitting and listening to Jesus. Finally, the stress of all the dinner preparations made Martha irritable.

"Lord, don't you care that my sister has left me to do the work all by myself?" she asked Jesus. "Tell her to help me." Instead of rebuking Mary, Jesus lovingly corrected Martha. "You worry and fuss about a lot of things. There's only one thing you need." Jesus pointed out that Martha's work paled in comparison to what Mary had chosen. Time spent in fellowship with Jesus reaps more eternal rewards than any earthly project or endeavor.

As Christians, we want to do all we can to serve God and our family, church, and community. It's easy to get so busy doing things *for* God that we neglect to spend time *with* him. We can end up with a full schedule and an empty heart, wondering what happened to the joy we once felt. A daily time of prayer and quiet communion helps us grow closer to God and strengthens us for whatever life holds in store. The busier we are, the more desperately we need that one thing.

[Jesus said] "There's only one thing you need."
Luke 10:42

Ask yourself: **Do I ever let busyness keep me from spending time at Jesus's feet?**

MARCH

22

"Why are you, the king's son, so worn out morning after morning?"

2 Samuel 13:2–4; 1 Corinthians 13:4–7

Amnon may have thought he was in love with Tamar, but what he felt for her turned out to be something quite different. He allowed his thoughts of her physical beauty to grow into an obsession, to the point that he looked haggard and dejected. His cousin noticed something different about him and asked why he looked worn out every morning.

After Amnon raped his half sister, he was filled with loathing for the woman he had claimed to love. Instead of feeling remorse, Amnon shamed Tamar further by making it appear that she was bothering him. His selfish actions not only ruined Tamar's life, they set off a destructive chain of events that led to his murder by his half brother Absalom, a bloody rebellion against King David, and Absalom's death. Not exactly the ending we expect from a love story.

Similar scenarios play out every day, as people confuse love with something else. Living in a society obsessed with pleasure and sex makes it especially hard to distinguish between love and lust or infatuation. The media constantly bombards us with images that encourage people to act on their impulses, leaving a trail of destroyed lives behind. Many people never experience the healthy expression of sexual desire within a marriage relationship as God intended.

First Corinthians 13 gives a description of true love that fits any context. Love is patient, kind, and enduring. It is not arrogant, rude, or jealous. Above all, love doesn't demand its own way but always has the other person's best interests in mind. When genuine love is the foundation of a relationship, neither person will end up feeling used. With God's help, we can resist unhealthy impulses and learn to love in a way that delights in doing good for others.

[Love] doesn't think about itself.

1 Corinthians 13:5

Ask yourself: **How does my love for others measure up to the guidelines in 1 Corinthians 13?**

MARCH
23

"Where could I go in my disgrace?"

2 Samuel 13:1–20

Many girls and women in Darfur have become victims of brutal rape during the country's civil war. Besides suffering the devastating effects of sexual violence, most of them were subsequently rejected by their husbands. Their futures look bleak in a culture where a woman's well-being usually depends on men.

King David's beautiful daughter Tamar also faced a future with the stigma of rape. When Amnon became obsessed with his half sister, his cousin concocted a scheme to get Tamar away from the protection of the palace. Pretending to be sick, Amnon asked his father to send Tamar to prepare a meal for him. After he got rid of the servants, Amnon grabbed Tamar and demanded that she go to bed with him.

Tamar begged Amnon to reconsider. "Don't do this godless act! Where could I go in my disgrace?" After Amnon satisfied his lust, he hated Tamar and sent her away. Tamar's brother Absalom urged her to keep quiet about the crime, and David chose not to punish Amnon. Tamar lived in Absalom's house, a desolate woman considered unfit for marriage by her culture.

Many people go through life feeling disgraced. Sometimes we feel that way because of what someone did to us. Even though we were innocent of any guilt in the situation, we still carry the shame. Other times, we feel we have disgraced ourselves by our own poor choices. We can also feel shamed by the behavior of our children or other family members.

No matter what stigma we carry around, God wants to help us. If someone has wronged us, he can help us forgive them. He also offers forgiveness for wrongs we have committed. Through his grace, we can leave our disgrace behind us and move on with a new attitude.

You will never again be ashamed or disgraced.

Isaiah 45:17

Ask God to help you turn your feelings of shame and disgrace over to him.

"Who is really wise?"

Ecclesiastes 8:1; Proverbs 2:1–11

According to Mensa's website, the organization was formed in 1946 to provide cultural and social activities for people with high IQs. Membership is open to anyone who achieves a score within the top 2 percent of the population on an approved and supervised intelligence test. Aside from the test scores, this diverse group has little in common. Ages range from four to ninety-four. Some members are high school dropouts, while others hold multiple degrees. Some members are on welfare; some are millionaires. Mensa describes the range of its members' occupations as "staggering."

It's obvious that having a high IQ doesn't guarantee a successful life. We all know people who test high but don't seem very smart. The Bible has a lot to say about true wisdom, which has nothing to do with scores or credentials. Proverbs explains that the foundation of wisdom is a correct attitude toward God, giving him the respect and honor he deserves. The more we get to know God and honor him, the more understanding and insight he gives us.

Although wisdom is a gift from God, he expects us to seek it like valuable treasure, and make the effort to cultivate it as a habit. As we study his Word, obey his commands, and fellowship with other believers, our life will be marked by godly living that brings peace, joy, and security.

The writer of Ecclesiastes asked, "Who is really wise?" and then noted that wisdom makes a person's face shine. More importantly, the wisdom that leads to godly choices makes a person's life shine. Once we experience a close relationship with God and the rewards of an obedient lifestyle, we'll understand that anything less is just plain dumb.

The fear of the Lord is the beginning of wisdom. The knowledge of the Holy One is understanding.

Proverbs 9:10

Ask yourself: **Am I growing in the wisdom that comes from God?**

MARCH
25

"Could you tell us these new ideas that you're teaching?"

Acts 17:16–23

As Paul looked around Athens, he grieved to see it filled with statues of idols. The city represented the world's intellectual center, yet for all their education and thirst for knowledge, they knew nothing of the true God. So Paul looked for ways to share the Good News about Jesus Christ. Since the people in Athens loved nothing better than discussing the latest ideas, he found plenty of opportunities. He threw himself into discussions in the synagogue and marketplace and debated the Greek philosophers.

Eventually Paul landed in front of the Areopagus, the city's high council. "Could you tell us these new ideas that you're teaching?" they asked. Paul's first thought was surely, *I'm glad you asked that*. Rather than begin by reviewing Jewish history as he usually did, Paul looked for examples his audience would understand. He found the perfect starting point in an inscription he'd noticed in the city. In their fear of missing some deity they didn't know about, they had dedicated an altar "To an unknown god." Now, Paul offered to introduce them to the one true God they had missed.

The Bible urges us to always be prepared to talk about our hope for eternal life through Jesus's death and resurrection. We don't have to be a highly educated man like Paul to share the gospel, but we can take some cues from his approach. Our witness will be more effective if we answer people with gentleness and respect, never mocking or demeaning their erroneous beliefs. We can look for examples our audience can relate to and find some common ground as a starting point. With God's help, we can be prepared to think, *I'm glad you asked that*.

Always be ready to defend your confidence in God when anyone asks you to explain it.

1 Peter 3:15

Ask yourself: **Am I prepared to share the Good News about Jesus when someone asks me what I believe?**

"Can a human be of any use to God?"

Job 22:1–2; Acts 17:24–31

This question asked by Job's so-called friend sounds insensitive and inappropriate. Eliphaz hinted that Job thought his goodness and upright behavior gave God some kind of benefit. What Eliphaz implied didn't apply to Job's thinking, but it expresses an unconscious attitude of some Christians. After we've been serving God for a while, we may begin to think we're really helping him out, making a vital contribution to his kingdom work.

When Paul spoke to the city council in Athens, he stressed how the one true God differed from the various idols worshiped in Greece. The Creator doesn't live in a shrine made by human hands. He doesn't need offerings of food to sustain him or numerous attendants to work in his temple, as they believed their gods did. God is self-sufficient, and humans can't serve his needs because he has none. Instead, he is the One who meets the needs of every living thing on earth, sustaining our life and breath.

This aspect of God's character gives us a hint of his great love for us. He didn't create humans because he needed our company but because he desired it. We may wonder if other people's feelings for us would change if we had nothing to offer them. *Would my husband still love me if I couldn't cook, clean, do laundry, and run errands? Would my wife stick by me if I lost my job or became physically unable to take care of the lawn or the car?*

People's feelings for us may fluctuate according to how well we're meeting their needs. They may even drop us when they no longer consider the relationship beneficial. But God's attitude toward us never changes. God didn't send Jesus to die for us because he needs us but simply because he loves us.

He isn't served by humans as if he needed anything.
Acts 17:25

Ask God **to help you show unconditional love to the people around you without looking for any benefits in return.**

MARCH

27

"What are you looking for?"

John 1:35–42

John the Baptist lost two of his disciples in one day. But that just meant he was doing his job—pointing people to the Messiah. As Jesus walked by, John said, "Look! This is the Lamb of God." The two men immediately started walking after Jesus. When Jesus saw them, he asked what they were looking for. Perhaps the men responded with the first thing that popped into their heads: "Where are you staying?"

After spending the rest of the day with Jesus, Andrew and the other man were convinced they had found the Messiah. Andrew rushed off to find his brother and share the news. When Jesus met Simon, he changed his name to "Cephas," or "Peter." From that point on, these men followed Jesus in a deeper sense, although they had no idea where the journey would lead them.

What would we say if Jesus confronted us with the question he asked John's disciples? "What are you looking for? Why are you following me?" If we take an honest look at our motives, we may find that we're looking ahead to the reward of heaven without thinking about what it means to be a Christ-follower here on earth. Or maybe we just "picked up" the Christian lifestyle because that's how we were raised, or because we think that's the way to have the best life.

As Jesus prepared his disciples for his approaching death, he compared discipleship with crucifixion. This implies a serious commitment with a high cost. It means we must die to our own desires and totally submit to his authority. Our primary motivation for following Jesus should never be what he might do for us but gratitude for what he's already done.

Then Jesus said to his disciples, "Those who want to come with me must say no to the things they want, pick up their crosses, and follow me."

Matthew 16:24

Ask yourself: **Am I following Jesus for the right reasons?**

"Can anything good come from Nazareth?"

John 1:43–46

When Sam and Dion's boss made them partners for a long-term project, they both had the same thought: *This can't be good.* Each one approached the assignment with feelings of distrust and suspicion, expecting the worst. After a shaky start, the two men discovered how much they had in common. Now their families enjoy spending time together, and Sam and Dion consider themselves brothers despite their differences in skin color.

Nathanael's initial reaction to Philip's news also sounded less than positive. Philip told his friend he had met the Messiah, a man called Jesus from the city of Nazareth. Nathanael answered with contempt: "Can anything good come from Nazareth?" Apparently, the town of Nazareth had a bad reputation. Perhaps the Jewish people despised the fact that a Roman army garrison had located there. Nathanael probably expected the Messiah to come from a prominent city.

We may not want to admit it, but we all carry around stereotypes, whether in our conscious or subconscious mind. These attitudes may have been ingrained in us since childhood. Our perceptions of people can be influenced by the media, by people around us, or by a personal experience from our past. Besides ethnicity, we often make assumptions about a person based on their accent, how they dress, and certain mannerisms.

These attitudes may seem harmless, but they displease the God who created us all. To avoid treating people like stereotypes, we must frequently examine our attitudes and be open to new relationships. If we shut people out for no reason, we may miss out on friendships that can enrich our life. If Philip had clung to his stereotype, he would have missed the discovery that someone wonderful did indeed come from Nazareth.

> *My brothers and sisters, practice your faith in our glorious Lord Jesus Christ by not favoring one person over another.*
>
> James 2:1

Ask yourself: **Am I allowing prejudices to keep me from enjoying relationships that God intends for me?**

MARCH
29

"How do you know anything about me?"

John 1:47–51

As she talked with the customer rep handling the credit card application, Cindy grew more bewildered. The department store just opened last week; she'd never shopped at this chain before. So how did this person already know so much about her—address, phone number, even her husband's name? As Cindy verified her place of employment, she had to ask. That's when she learned she was talking to her children's babysitter from ten years earlier.

Nathanael's situation didn't have such an obvious answer. He accepted Philip's invitation to meet Jesus in spite of his misgivings about the Messiah coming from a town like Nazareth. As Nathanael approached, Jesus declared, "Here is a true Israelite who is sincere." Jesus was saying that there was nothing false or deceitful in Nathanael, unlike the Jewish patriarch Jacob.

Nathanael appreciated the compliment, but it puzzled him. How could Jesus know anything about him? They had never met. Jesus responded that he had seen Nathanael under the fig tree even before his conversation with Philip. This revelation astounded Nathanael. "Rabbi, you are the Son of God! You are the king of Israel!"

As our Creator, there's nothing that God doesn't know about us. Jesus taught that God even knows the very number of hairs on our head, which continually changes. He knows our thoughts and our deep, unspoken needs and desires. He knows what we've done in the past and what we'll do in the future.

The thought of God's intimate knowledge of us can intimidate us if we're not secure in our relationship with him, or if we don't have a clear conscience. But once we begin to grasp the depth of our Father's love, it's comforting to understand that he knows all about us.

Every hair on your head has been counted.

Matthew 10:30

Ask yourself: **How do I feel about the fact that God knows me so intimately? Why do I feel that way?**

MARCH
30

"How can we know the way?"

John 14:1–7

As traffic whizzed past, I wished I'd taken my husband's advice. But why did I need to bring a boring atlas when I had a GPS plus step-by-step directions printed from MapQuest? Unfortunately, neither MapQuest nor the GPS knew that a portion of the interstate had been blocked off for repairs. My hotel lay just a few miles from the conference center, but in which direction? The detour signs only confused me more.

Jesus's disciples felt confused when he talked about going away. "You know the way to the place where I am going," he told them. Thomas voiced the question burning in all their minds: "Lord, we don't know where you're going. So how can we know the way?" Jesus's answer was simple and direct: "I am the way, the truth, and the life. No one goes to the Father except through me."

It may be popular to claim that many paths lead to God, but that contradicts what the Bible teaches. Jesus taught that access to God can only come through placing our faith in his sacrificial death and resurrection. The way is clear and open to everyone, blocked only by a person's unwillingness to believe. There is no alternate route. People who denounce the gospel as narrow-minded miss the wonder that God provided a way for us to come to him at all.

Jesus is more than the path to salvation and eternal life; he shows us the way to live a life of true meaning and purpose. Nurturing our relationship with him and following the directions in God's Word are the only way to travel. We may be tempted to let our life be guided by sources that seem more exciting, but we'll only end up feeling confused.

Jesus answered him, "I am the way, the truth, and the life. No one goes to the Father except through me."

John 14:6

Ask yourself: **Do I rely on the Bible to give me a sense of direction?**

MARCH

31

"Why are you men standing here looking at the sky?"

Acts 1:3–11

The men craned their necks toward the sky, trying to process what had just happened. The past forty days had been miraculous. After suffering such a horrible death, Jesus had come back to life. They hadn't just *seen* Jesus; they had touched him, eaten with him, and talked with him. When he'd gathered his apostles on the Mount of Olives, they expected something big. Surely this was the moment the Messiah would deliver and restore the nation of Israel.

But Jesus reminded them that historical events depended on God's timing. In the meantime, they had work to accomplish. Once again he promised the gift of the Holy Spirit and charged them to be his witnesses throughout the world. Then Jesus began to ascend upward. The apostles watched, awestruck, even after a cloud hid him from their sight. Suddenly, two angels appeared and addressed them: "Why are you men from Galilee standing here looking at the sky?"

The Bible tells us to live in anticipation of Jesus's return, but we're not to stand around looking toward the sky and waiting for it to happen. Like the apostles, we have plenty to keep us busy in the meantime. Once, while passing through Samaria with his disciples, Jesus told them to look and see the fields ready to be harvested.

We're surrounded by a world full of people ready to hear about Jesus. A part of the Christian life is finding the right balance between looking up and looking around. We can't let our focus on future events blind us to the spiritual needs around us. God does want us to be heavenly minded, but he also expects us to do a lot of earthly good.

[Jesus said] "I'm telling you to look and see that the fields are ready to be harvested."

John 4:35

Ask God **to open your eyes to the fields within your reach that are ready to be harvested.**

APRIL
1

"Is anything too hard for the Lord?"

Genesis 18:1–15

Jeannie replayed the conversation with her pastor's wife over and over. She wanted to believe what Ruth had said, but it just didn't seem possible. How many doctors had declared that Jeannie could never get pregnant? So many tests, so many years of praying. . . . Now Ruth claimed God had revealed to her that Jeannie and Mark would have children one day. Jeannie didn't know whether to laugh or cry. *Could it really be possible?*

Sarah had a hard time believing her ears when she overheard the Lord promising Abraham that she would bear a son within a year. Sarah laughed to herself. How many years had passed since she'd first heard of that promise? "Can I really have a child now that I'm old?" God knew Sarah's thoughts and confronted her doubts: "Is anything too hard for the Lord?"

We are thrilled by the biblical stories of God doing the impossible: parting the Red Sea, conquering powerful armies with a few men, healing the blind and lame, raising the dead. Why is it sometimes easier to believe those accounts than believe what God can do in our own life? *Can he really set me free from that lifelong addiction? Will I ever be healed from my childhood abuse? Isn't our marriage beyond repair?*

God is the same today as in Old Testament times. He often reveals his power by doing what's impossible in our eyes. Sarah had a son at the ripe old age of ninety. Today, Jeannie and Mark are busy with their four boys. While we live on earth, our faith will be imperfect. But whenever God asks us to believe something that seems impossible, we can remember that Jesus answered that question centuries ago.

But everything is possible for God.
Matthew 19:26

Ask yourself: **What impossible situation is God asking me to believe?**

APRIL

2

“Who do you think will love him the most?”

Luke 7:36–50

Simon looked at the woman with contempt. When he’d invited a rabbi to his dinner party, he’d expected extra people to stop by and listen to the conversation. That was perfectly acceptable. But this was too much—the way this woman cried over Jesus’s feet, and then unbound her hair to dry them off! *This proves Jesus is no prophet*, Simon told himself. *If he were, he’d know the woman’s reputation and wouldn’t let her touch him.*

Jesus answered Simon’s thoughts with a brief story about two men who owed money to a moneylender. One man owed five hundred silver coins and the other owed fifty. When they couldn’t repay their debts, the lender canceled them. “Now, who do you think will love him the most?” asked Jesus. “I suppose the one who had the largest debt canceled,” Simon replied.

Then Jesus pointed out that Simon had neglected to show him the basic common courtesies expected of a host. On the other hand, the woman had lavished affection and respect on Jesus, unconcerned about how she looked to the guests or how they might judge her. She had great love because of her awareness that she had been forgiven of many sins.

Sometimes it seems as though the people most fervently devoted to Christ are those who have been delivered from a background of blatant sin, such as drug abuse, sexual promiscuity, or criminal activity. The sense of how much they’ve been forgiven fuels a passionate love for the One who died to pay their sin debt. But even if our testimony is less dramatic, we all come to Christ from a background of shame and degradation. The more we understand the debt God paid for us, the deeper our love for him will be.

His Son paid the price to free us, which
means that our sins are forgiven.

Colossians 1:14

Ask God **to give you a deeper understanding of the debt that he paid on your behalf.**

APRIL
3

"Haven't you put a protective fence around him and everything he has?"

Job 1:6–12

I eased down the winding, wooded lane toward my friend's brand-new country home. Suddenly, a black metal gate blocked the road. Because of the trees, I hadn't even noticed the tall iron fence enclosing the property. Rolling down the car window, I pushed the button on the speaker. Inside the house, my friend called out a greeting and the heavy gate swung open.

Satan complained to God about the invisible fence around Job. When God praised Job's integrity and righteousness, Satan countered that Job only served God because of the way God had blessed him. "Haven't you put a protective fence around him, his home, and everything he has?" he asked. Satan issued a challenge: "But now stretch out your hand, and strike everything he has. I bet he'll curse you to your face."

Although "the whole world is under the control of the evil one" (1 John 5:19), Satan's power is limited by God. Satan couldn't test Job without God's permission. God allowed Job to be afflicted because he knew Job would stand firm and grow in his faith through the trials.

As believers, we have a protective fence surrounding us, our loved ones, and our possessions. Nothing can touch our life without God's permission. The removal of this protective barrier often reveals our true motives for worshiping God. Is it because we love him, or because we love his blessings?

Satan can't cross this boundary unless God allows it, and God always has a purpose. He may want to refine our faith and purify our heart. He may use our trials to draw someone else to himself as they watch our response. During times of testing, we can look forward to the day when God will completely strip Satan of any power, and we no longer need that protective fence.

The God of peace will quickly crush Satan under your feet.
Romans 16:20

Ask God **to strengthen your faith to endure times of testing.**

APRIL
4

"Are you still holding on to your principles?"

Job 2:1–9

A wave of disasters rolled over Job. Within a few minutes, he learned that his extensive herds of camels, donkeys, and oxen had been stolen, his flocks of sheep had been killed, and all his servants except four had been murdered. Then came the worst blow of all: a severe storm had knocked down his oldest son's house, killing all ten of Job's children.

Even in the midst of his grief, Job worshiped God. Then Satan challenged God that if Job had to suffer physically, he would deny God. When God gave Satan permission, Satan struck Job with a disease that covered his body with painful, festering sores, along with other symptoms. This once prominent citizen now sat outside the city, soothing his sores with ashes and scraping his itching skin with broken pottery.

Already devastated by the loss of her children, Job's wife watched him suffering. They both knew death would be a mercy compared to such unbearable pain. Seeing no reason to hope, she asked him, "Are you still holding on to your principles? Curse God and die!"

We all will face losses during our lifetime, whether we lose a job, our home, financial security, or people we love. In the midst of our suffering, will we despair and deny God or find something to cling to? When we don't understand what's happened, we can review what we *do* know: God is good, he loves us unconditionally, and he holds ultimate control over our life.

As we nurture our relationship with God day by day, we build up our faith for future times of testing. Then, when troubles hit us, we'll remember that God is trustworthy and that someday he will bring meaning to what now seems meaningless. And we'll learn how to hold on more tightly to the One who holds us.

I know whom I trust.

2 Timothy 1:12

Ask yourself: **How can I prepare myself now to hold on to my faith in future times of sorrow and loss?**

APRIL
5

"Shouldn't we also accept the bad?"

Job 2:7–10

"In sickness and in health, for richer, for poorer, for better, for worse, in sadness and in joy . . ." Young couples usually recite these traditional wedding vows with faces glowing and minds filled with visions of a fairytale life. They enter into the marriage covenant with no idea of what the future might bring. The test of their commitment comes later, when they have to decide whether they will accept the "for worse" times along with the "for better" times.

The ultimate test of Job's commitment to God came when he suddenly lost his ten children and all his possessions, and was struck with a painful skin disease. Despite his grief and misery, Job refused to deny God. "We accept the good that God gives us," he told his wife. "Shouldn't we also accept the bad?" God had given Job abundant riches, numerous servants, and a large family; now he had taken them away. Job enjoyed God's blessings during the good times; now he accepted the bad times that God allowed.

Many people become Christians with visions of a fairytale life filled with prosperity and blessings. Sooner or later, reality sets in. God permits good times and bad times to come into everyone's life; we never know which one lies just ahead. Both extremes test our commitment to him. During good times we may be tempted to forget God; during hard times Satan tries to make us doubt God's goodness—or even his existence.

Our response to change reveals a lot about our faith. When we enjoy good times, do we thank God and give him the glory? When bad times hit, do we allow troubles to draw us closer to him? Understanding God's sovereignty will help us handle all the "for better or worse" times of our life.

When times are good, be happy; but when times are bad, consider: God has made the one as well as the other.

Ecclesiastes 7:14 NIV

Ask yourself: **How do I handle sudden changes in my life?**

APRIL

6

"Aren't you one of this man's disciples too?"

John 18:15–18, 25–27

The couple drew curious stares as soon as they walked in. Their simple homemade clothing, with the woman's hair tucked under a white cap, straight pins instead of buttons on her dress, and the man's beard and straw hat, all set them apart from the other shoppers. It was obvious that the couple belonged to the Amish community down the road. There was no way they could blend in with this crowd, even if they'd wanted to.

On the night of Jesus's arrest, Peter tried to blend in with the crowd but didn't succeed. When he entered the chief priest's courtyard, the gatekeeper looked at him and asked, "Aren't you one of this man's disciples too?" Peter assured her that he was not. Later, as he stood warming himself by a fire, some men asked him the same question. "No, I'm not!" Peter repeated. But one of the high priest's servants insisted that he'd seen Peter with Jesus. For the third time, Peter denied being Jesus's disciple.

Can people around us tell that we're one of Jesus's followers? Do we openly talk about our faith? Does our behavior make it obvious that we try to live according to God's commands instead of the world's standards? Is the way we treat others an indication that God's love flows through us?

Or do we sometimes act like Peter and refuse to be identified with Jesus? Maybe we keep quiet during discussions about God in certain settings, or skip our usual mealtime prayer in public. God wants to give us the courage to live for him with a boldness that attracts attention. It might be easier and safer to blend in with the crowd, but a better goal would be to live in such a way that others can't help but notice that we've been with Jesus.

Never be ashamed to tell others about our Lord.

2 Timothy 1:8 NLT

Ask yourself: Do my words, actions, and lifestyle make it obvious that I'm one of his disciples too?

"If I've told the truth, why do you hit me?"

John 18:19–24

On the night of Jesus's arrest, he was taken to the high priest for questioning. Annas drilled Jesus about his teaching and his followers, hoping to get Jesus to say something that could be used against him. Jesus answered that he had always taught openly in public places. Why not ask those who heard him speak? Jesus's comment prompted one of the guards to slap him in the face.

Jesus could have angrily pointed out that it was illegal to strike a prisoner; instead, he responded with quiet dignity. "If I've said anything wrong, tell me what it was. But if I've told the truth, why do you hit me?" Jesus knew that Annas and the other Jewish leaders had no interest in learning the truth. They simply wanted to figure out a way to get rid of him.

Whenever we share the truth, we run the risk of someone lashing out at us. Jesus told his disciples that the world would respond to them the same way it had responded to him. In a letter to Timothy, Paul warned of a time when people would refuse to listen to the truth, preferring to believe myths instead. Such people would surround themselves with teachers who would say only what they wanted to hear.

The fact that someone doesn't want to hear the truth probably means they desperately need to hear it. Their hostility doesn't absolve us of our responsibility to share what God places on our heart. Today it's more important than ever to speak up with love and boldness. But we shouldn't be surprised if someone strikes out at us. When that happens, we can ask Jesus to help us follow his example and respond with quiet dignity.

People will refuse to listen to the truth and turn to myths.

2 Timothy 4:4

Ask yourself: **Do I let fear keep me from speaking up for God?**

APRIL
8

“Why are you looking among the dead for the living one?”

Luke 24:1–12

In May 2004, China loaned one of its most cherished relics to Hong Kong for ten days: a bone fragment. This fragment is purported to be a finger of Buddha, who died in 483 BC. Tens of thousands of people lined up to see the bone displayed in an elaborate case covered with bulletproof glass. Although officials herded the crowd past quickly, viewers expressed hope that their act of devotion would give them peace, protection, and good fortune.

When the women went to Jesus’s tomb to express their devotion, they expected to find his body. Instead, two angels shared some startling news. “Why are you looking among the dead for the living one?” they asked the women. “He’s not here. He has been brought back to life!” The heavenly messengers reminded the women that Jesus had told them exactly what would happen to him.

It’s hard to imagine the joy these women felt—after such incredible news finally sank in. They had gone to the tomb grieving, wanting to honor Jesus’s body by anointing it with spices. They left with the knowledge that death could not hold their Lord. This was not a time for mourning but for celebrating.

As Christians, our faith doesn’t focus on a prophet or leader who has died. We don’t express devotion to relics but to the One who left no physical remains on earth. Sometimes our worship and our daily life may look as though we worship a God who is dead. We forget the wonder that our Lord is sitting at God’s right hand, interceding for us. His Spirit lives within us to comfort, guide, and protect us. The question to ask ourselves is, “Can others see the joy of the Living One in us?”

You have turned my mourning into joyful dancing. You have taken away my clothes of mourning and clothed me with joy.

Psalm 30:11 NLT

Ask yourself: **Does my daily life show that I worship a living God?**

“Isn’t my word like a hammer that shatters a rock?”

Jeremiah 23:29–32

A blazing fire, a hammer breaking through solid rock, a sharp double-edged sword, rain and snow falling on the earth—God often uses vivid images to describe his Word and its power. When he sent Jeremiah to confront false prophets, he asked, “Isn’t my word like fire or like a hammer that shatters a rock?” The deceivers plagiarized each other’s prophecies and made up dreams that they’d had, calling them revelations. Their useless words did nothing to help the people, while God’s words were as powerful as fire or a hammer breaking a rock to pieces.

In Isaiah 55, God compared his words to rain and snow that fall from the sky. They water the earth, causing plants to sprout and grow, providing food for people. In the same way that rain and snow accomplish their purpose, the words that come from God’s mouth will achieve results. His words soak into a person’s life, causing faith to sprout and grow, and producing fruit in believers’ lives.

Today we have wonderful resources at our disposal to use for our spiritual growth and to help us share God’s truth with other people. Christian books, music, and movies can be a blessing, but they lack the power that God’s Word has to transform lives. His Word can burn away impurities, lies, and deception. It can cut straight through to the heart of a matter like a piercing sword, and water newly planted seeds of faith so they grow and bear fruit. God’s Word can break the hardest heart and change a hostile opponent of Christ into a tenderhearted believer. How can anyone else’s words ever compete with that?

[The Lord said] “My word, which comes from my mouth, is like the rain and snow. It will not come back to me without results. It will accomplish whatever I want and achieve whatever I send it to do.”

Isaiah 55:11

Ask yourself: **How has God’s powerful Word changed my life?**

APRIL
10

"What if ten are found there?"

Genesis 18:16–33

When God told Abraham that he planned to destroy Sodom and Gomorrah, Abraham immediately thought of his nephew Lot. Convinced of God's justice, Abraham asked, "Are you really going to sweep away the innocent with the guilty? What if there are fifty innocent people in the city?" God promised to spare the cities if fifty righteous people were there. Abraham continued to plead with God, until the hypothetical number had been reduced to ten.

At first glance, many people see God's destruction of Sodom and Gomorrah as an act of divine vengeance. But a closer look shows that his patience and mercy are woven throughout the story. Although the cities were guilty of terrible wickedness, God withheld punishment for a long time, giving the people a chance to repent. Eventually, his holiness required him to do something.

God did not respond in haste or anger. Although he had full knowledge of the situation, God acted only after carefully considering the evidence. "I must go down and see," he said. He would have spared the evil cities if ten righteous people had lived there. Lot's relationship with God left much to be desired, but God's angels rescued his family, even though they had to pull them out by their hands. When Lot begged for shelter in a small, nearby city, God spared Zoar because of him (see Gen. 19).

When we look at examples of God's judgment on sin purely from a human perspective, we can get a distorted view of his character. God would not be good if he didn't punish evil; he would not be holy if he ignored sin. When we look more closely at his dealings with people, the evidence of his mercy becomes clear. Then we see that he goes out of his way to show mercy, even to a single person.

But I show mercy to thousands of generations of those who love me and obey my commandments.

Exodus 20:6

Ask God **to open your eyes to see evidence of his mercy you may have overlooked.**

"Where did it fall?"

2 Kings 6:1–7

I rushed through the house searching for my car keys, which should have been in my purse. If I didn't leave right away, I'd be late for my appointment. *Why don't you ask God where the keys are?* I thought. But I pushed the persistent idea away. Prayer was for serious problems and spiritual issues, not little things like lost keys. Finally, however, I paused and asked God for help. After I obeyed a prompting to look inside the washing machine—an odd place, for sure—I found them. They had somehow slipped inside when I laid my purse on top.

As some of Elisha's disciples chopped wood to build new housing, an ax head flew off and sank in the river. The man who lost it was doubly distressed because he had borrowed the ax head and probably had no means to replace it. "Where did it fall?" asked Elisha. The prophet cut a stick, threw it into the water, and the heavy ax head floated to the surface.

At first glance, it might seem odd that God would include this incident in his Word. The story is sandwiched in 2 Kings between Namaan's healing from leprosy and God's supernatural defeat of the Aramean army. Apparently, God doesn't reserve miracles for "serious" problems and major issues only.

The story of the floating ax head assures us that God wants to be involved in every area of our life. His care and provision extends even to little details that we might consider too insignificant to address in prayer. God doesn't promise to give us everything we ask for; he does promise to always hear our requests and answer as he sees fit. We can feel free to talk with him about any concern, even if it's a lost ax head or a misplaced set of keys.

We know that he listens to our requests.

1 John 5:15

Ask yourself: **What "insignificant" concern or problem have I hesitated to bring before God?**

APRIL
12

"What do you say about yourself?"

John 1:1–26

Unlike many people, John the Baptist's favorite subject to talk about was not himself. As the crowds following John grew, the religious leaders in Jerusalem sent priests and Levites to investigate the man and his teaching. Apparently, they felt no need to be discreet. "Who are you?" they asked pointblank.

John immediately answered, "I am not the Messiah." Then he denied being Elijah or the prophet foretold by Moses. Exasperated, the priests finally asked, "What do you say about yourself?" John could have talked about his miraculous birth, described in Luke 1: how an angel predicted his conception to elderly parents and shared the name that God had chosen for him. Instead, John quoted his job description from the prophet Isaiah: to prepare the way for the Savior.

As Jesus's ministry gained attention, John's disciples complained that more people were following Jesus than John. Once again, John revealed an attitude of humility and fervent devotion to the Messiah. He compared Jesus to a bridegroom and himself to the best man. John felt joy that Jesus's influence was growing as his own diminished. He knew that his role was not to gain a permanent status or following for himself but to point people to the Savior.

It can be tempting to focus more on our accomplishments than on God's kingdom, especially if we have a highly visible role in the body of Christ. Our conversation reveals much about our attitude. When we talk about our service or ministry, do we draw attention to ourselves or do we point others to God and what he's done? Like John, we have a very important role: to become unimportant, as people see less of us and more of our Savior.

He must increase in importance, while
I must decrease in importance.

John 3:30

Ask yourself: **Does my conversation bring attention to me or does it point people to Jesus?**

APRIL
13

"Why are you sleeping, O Lord?"

Psalm 44:23–26

Psalm 44 was written as a cry for God to save his people. The nation had suffered a defeat in battle even though they had been obedient and faithful to God. Based on God's past deliverance and the people's clear conscience, they trusted God to rescue them. Even though it looked like God had abandoned them, the writer called out for God to "Wake up!" He wondered why God seemed to be sleeping at such a time.

When God the Son lived on the earth in a human body, his disciples wondered how he could sleep when they faced a sudden, violent storm that threatened to capsize the boat. As Jesus slept, exhausted from the day of ministry, his disciples woke him and cried out, "Don't you care that we're going to die?" Jesus stilled the wind and waves with a single command, but rebuked the men for their lack of faith.

The truth is, God the Father never sleeps but watches over us day and night (see Ps. 121:4). King David believed this promise with all his heart. Even as he fled from enemies, David was able to sleep soundly at night because he had learned to trust in God to keep him safe (see Ps. 3:5–6). Regardless of the dangers surrounding him, David placed his life in God's hands.

Not many of us could follow David's example. A variety of sleep disorders plague people in our society, and any number of things can keep us awake at night. But meditating on God's love and protection helps take our focus off the problems surrounding us. Whether we're struggling with insomnia or sleeping soundly like David, we can take comfort in the promise that God will be watching over us all through the night.

I fall asleep in peace the moment I lie down because
you alone, O LORD, enable me to live securely.

Psalm 4:8

Ask yourself: **Will God be sleeping tonight, or will he be standing guard over me?**

APRIL
14

"How long will my enemy triumph over me?"

Psalm 13

Warren turned on his computer and looked at the date. Two years, five months, and eighteen days. Nobody could say he hadn't done all the right things. He answered every relevant newspaper ad, checked online sites daily, attended job fairs, followed up on past business contacts. Most importantly, he prayed. Occasional freelance work helped supplement his wife's part-time job. But if he didn't land a job soon, they were headed for major debt. *How much longer will this drag on, Lord?*

David expressed the same feeling when he wrote Psalm 13. He may have been on the run from King Saul at the time, hiding out in caves and feeling cornered by his enemy. When David felt as though he couldn't bear his desperate situation any longer, he cried out to God. "How long will my enemy triumph over me?" David asked. By expressing his feelings to God, David found renewed hope, joy, and the strength to endure his troubles.

We can all identify with that feeling of desperation, when it looks like our troubles will go on indefinitely. Although our human nature screams for a way out, the first chapter of James urges us to see the value of trials that test our stamina. By clinging to God during such times, we develop perseverance and learn to be steadfast in our faith. God wants us to have a positive outlook, knowing that the process is necessary for our spiritual maturity.

Desperate times call for desperate prayers, as David modeled. The book of Psalms shows that there's no reason to be afraid to express our true feelings to God. When there seems to be no end in sight and we feel like crying out, "How long?" God understands. He wants us to endure the trial through his power and come out stronger on the other side.

> *Endure until your testing is over. Then you will be mature and complete, and you won't need anything.*
>
> James 1:4

Ask yourself: **What desperate situation do I need to talk over with God?**

"What will you pay me if I hand him over to you?"

Matthew 26:1–5, 14–16

The chief priests could hardly believe their ears. Surely this had come from the hand of God. They had all agreed on the necessity of getting rid of Jesus for the good of the nation, but they had to be careful about it. If they waited until the Passover celebration ended, there would be less chance of a riot breaking out when they arrested him.

But now, one of Jesus's own disciples had come to them with an unexpected offer. "What will you pay me if I hand him over to you?" Judas Iscariot asked. After a short consultation, the priests offered thirty silver coins. Judas agreed to the amount, and from that point on he searched for an opportunity to betray Jesus when there would be no crowds around.

Many people have speculated on Judas's motivation for betraying Jesus. The Bible does tell us that he was a thief, even though he was in control of the disciples' money (see John 12:6). We also know that Satan entered Judas just before he visited the priests (see Luke 22:3) and again at the Last Supper (see John 13:27). Jesus chose Judas to be one of the Twelve, knowing that he would not believe in him (see John 6:64).

We shudder at Judas's evil decision to betray Jesus for thirty silver coins, yet we sometimes betray him for much less. Do we put our Christian beliefs on the back burner in order to get ahead in our career? Would we hide our faith in order to be accepted or popular? Have we stood by and listened as someone verbally abused Jesus? Instead of letting go of our faith when it proves inconvenient, we need to hold on even more tightly.

We need to hold on to our declaration of faith.

Hebrews 4:14

Ask yourself: **In what ways am I tempted to betray Jesus?**

APRIL
16

"What do we care?"

Matthew 27:1–5

She looked at the strip of plastic in her hand and waited. Thinking back, she could see how she'd let her friends pressure her to give in to her boyfriend's demands for sex. It only took a few weeks to reveal how unhealthy the relationship was, and for her to regret the decision she'd made to go against what she'd been taught about right and wrong. How she wished she could undo her rash actions! But now, a plus sign on the test strip indicated consequences beyond anything she'd expected.

It didn't take long for Judas to regret his betrayal of Jesus. Maybe he had thought his action would force Jesus to free Israel from Roman oppression, as the Messiah was expected to do. Perhaps he had become disillusioned with Jesus's ministry, or was simply greedy for money. Whatever his motivation, Judas hadn't expected this outcome.

The next morning he tried to return the money to the chief priests, admitting that he had betrayed an innocent man. "What do we care?" they responded coldly. "That's your problem." The leaders had no interest in his apparent change of heart. Overwhelmed by guilt, Judas threw the money into the temple and then hanged himself.

We can't always stop something we've set in motion, no matter how much we regret our decision. Any time we go against God's will, our behavior carries the risk of permanent consequences for ourselves and for others. Even after we repent and receive forgiveness, we may have to live with the sin's negative effects on our health, our relationships, and our lifestyle. It's always best to carefully consider the far-reaching implications of our actions instead of doing something that we later wish we could undo.

After desire has conceived, it gives birth to sin; and sin, when it is full-grown, gives birth to death.

James 1:15 NIV

Ask yourself: **Do I need to look ahead and consider the potential consequences of any behavior that I'm engaging in?**

APRIL
17

"Will you give your life for me?"

John 13:33–38

Kayden's face grew hotter by the minute. *I can't let her down now.* Darla had been so happy when he'd promised to stay with her throughout the delivery. *I can do this.* They'd taken the classes; they knew what to expect. *She can't get through this without me.* But Kayden hadn't been prepared for the screams, the panic, the grip that almost broke his hand. *I'm not about to wimp out. . . .* Then the baby's head crowned, and Kayden almost knocked down a nurse in his rush to get out.

Peter also had good intentions but misplaced confidence during his last Passover meal with Jesus. When Jesus told the disciples he would be going away to a place where they would join him later, Peter protested. "Lord, why can't I follow you now? I'll give my life for you," he vowed. "Will you give your life for me?" Jesus challenged. "I can guarantee this truth: No rooster will crow until you say three times that you don't know me."

These words must have shocked all of the disciples. Matthew and Mark both recorded that Peter and the others answered, "Even if I have to die with you, I will never say that I don't know you." But within hours, what sounded unbelievable would become a sad reality.

Being overconfident in our abilities can be a dangerous thing, especially in spiritual matters. Even mature Christians can fall into sin at any moment. We're especially vulnerable during those times when we feel most safe and secure, because we're less likely to be on our guard against temptation. God is the only One who can help us stand against sin. We can't afford to lose our sense of dependence on him. If we start to trust ourselves too much, we may have to face a sad reality check.

People who think they are standing firmly
should be careful that they don't fall.
1 Corinthians 10:12

Ask yourself: **Am I in danger because of overconfidence in my ability to resist certain temptations?**

APRIL
18

"Couldn't you stay awake with me?"

Matthew 26:36–46

Myra looked at her sleeping husband and wanted to scream. She understood that Anthony felt worn out from working overtime. But after caring for two preschoolers all day, she wasn't full of energy either, especially after this midnight run to the hospital. For the next five hours, Myra struggled through intense labor pains alone. The nurses stayed out of the room because, after all, her husband was with her.

Jesus wasn't alone in the Garden of Gethsemane, but sleepiness kept his disciples from offering any support. Before Jesus walked off to pray, he shared his great anguish with Peter, James, and John and asked them to stay awake with him. Knowing the horrors that awaited, Jesus's sweat became like drops of blood falling to the ground (see Luke 22:44).

When he returned to the disciples, Jesus found them asleep. "Couldn't you stay awake with me for one hour?" he asked Peter. Jesus left them again to pray, and once again the men fell asleep. This time Jesus didn't wake them. Soon, their opportunity to be of service during Jesus's time of great need had passed.

The Bible warns us to guard against spiritual lethargy or sluggishness. We have good reason to stay spiritually alert. Each day that passes brings us that much closer to the end of our time on earth, either through death or Christ's return. Soon our opportunity to participate in God's work will have passed.

With our salvation secured and our future life with God guaranteed, we may be tempted at times to slack off and do some spiritual napping. But we don't want to miss a single opportunity to impact someone for Christ. With God's help we can keep our mind vigilant and alert so that Jesus won't ever find us sleeping on the job.

You know the times in which we are living.
It's time for you to wake up.

Romans 13:11

Ask yourself: **How can I make sure that I stay spiritually alert?**

APRIL
19

"Should we use our swords to fight?"

Luke 22:47–54

As the disciples tried to shake off their exhaustion, a crowd armed with clubs and swords stepped out of the darkness. The fact that Judas Iscariot led the way added to the confusion. Suddenly the reality of the situation hit the disciples. "Lord," they cried, "should we use our swords to fight?" Without waiting for an answer, Peter struck at one of the men, cutting off his right ear. Jesus intervened. "Stop! That's enough of this," he told them. Then Jesus touched the man's ear and healed him.

Just minutes earlier, Jesus had warned his disciples of a change coming in the world's treatment of them. "The person who doesn't have a sword should sell his coat and buy one," he'd said. Jesus's followers would need to protect themselves in coming days, but this was not the right moment to fight back. The events of this night would follow God's plan, ordained so long ago.

Ephesians 6 talks about a different kind of sword that God wants us to use every day. God has provided spiritual armor to protect us from Satan's attacks. Our offensive weapon is the sword of God's Word. Jesus used this sword when Satan tempted him three times in the wilderness (see Matt. 4:1–11). Several verses of Revelation picture him as having a two-edged sword coming out of his mouth (see Rev. 1:16).

God's Word is sharper than any double-edged sword and cuts deep, exposing thoughts and intentions (see Heb. 4:12). We need this weapon to subdue our sinful urges, to ward off Satan's deceptions, and to provide discernment for daily decisions. Spiritually speaking, it's always the right time to use our sword to fight.

Also take salvation as your helmet and the word of God as the sword that the Spirit supplies.

Ephesians 6:17

Ask yourself: **Do I use the sword of God's Word every day?**

APRIL
20

"How, then, are the Scriptures to be fulfilled that say this must happen?"

Matthew 26:47–56

The events on the night of Jesus's arrest and trials seemed chaotic to his disciples, but Jesus knew exactly what to expect. When Peter tried to resist the armed mob with a sword, Jesus stopped him. "Don't you think that I could call on my Father to send more than twelve legions of angels to help me now?" Jesus asked. "How, then, are the Scriptures to be fulfilled that say this must happen?"

Jesus had all the angels of heaven at his disposal, but he knew that the events unfolding were the fulfillment of ancient prophecies concerning him. Many passages, including Psalm 22 and Isaiah 53, describe how the Messiah would suffer and die for the sins of the world. Rather than use his power to escape a horrible fate, Jesus gave his life up in accordance with God's plan to redeem the human race.

It can be frightening when we seem to be surrounded by chaos. The daily news makes it look as though world events are spiraling out of control. But we can rest assured that nothing takes God by surprise. He has foreseen every little detail, and he's already decided how he will use each one. Everything that happens will line up somehow with God's ultimate plan for the world, laid down in Revelation and other prophetic passages.

We can also be confident that all of the Scriptures about believers will be fulfilled. Our troubles and suffering will make us more like Christ. If we are obedient, we will be blessed with a fruitful life. God's power will enable us to accomplish more than we can imagine. He will use everything in our life for our good and his glory. Even when life seems chaotic, we can trust these Scriptures to be fulfilled.

All of this has happened so that what the prophets have written would come true.

Matthew 26:56

Ask yourself: **Do I have trouble believing that God's written promises concerning me will come true?**

"Should I say, 'Father, save me from this time of suffering'?"

John 12:23–30

In her memoir, *Trading Fathers*, my friend Karen Rabbitt remembers the phone call that alerted her to her electrician husband's accident.[4] Racing across town to the emergency room, Karen's prayers and tears gushed out. "Jesus, Jesus, is he alive? The guy didn't say. . . . Sweet Jesus, our lives are in your hands!" Karen's next thought surprised her in the middle of such turmoil: "If twenty years is all I get with him, so be it."

Jesus's mind was in turmoil as the time for his death drew near. "I am too deeply troubled now to know how to express my feelings," he told his disciples. "Should I say, 'Father, save me from this time of suffering'?" His mind recoiled in horror at the agony that faced him, and his human nature cried out to be delivered from it. But Jesus knew that he had been born for this very hour, and he submitted to the Father's will. "Father, give glory to your name," he prayed.

We will never comprehend the depth of Jesus's suffering as he took on the sins of the human race and paid for them all. We'll never know what that brief separation from the Father meant to him. But God does want us to understand that our suffering here on earth is temporary, and it always has a purpose.

Suffering keeps us from becoming prideful and helps make us more like Christ. It gives God a chance to demonstrate his power through our life. Trials and pain keep us from loving this world, and they shift our focus to our heavenly home. It's hard to submit to God's will in the middle of a crisis when our only desire is to be delivered, but it helps to remember that our pain will never compare to what Jesus endured.

Our suffering is light and temporary and is producing for us an eternal glory that is greater than anything we can imagine.

2 Corinthians 4:17

Ask yourself: **How does my attitude toward God change when I experience suffering?**

4. Karen Rabbitt, *Trading Fathers* (Enumclaw, WA: Winepress Publishing, 2009), 270.

APRIL
22

"So you're really the Messiah, are you?"

Luke 23:33–43

Bob wondered how two people could see the same thing and respond in such drastically different ways. He and his sister had been teens when their mom became a Christian. They'd both listened to her "Jesus talks" and they'd watched the changes in her life. But it wasn't until their mom faced terminal cancer with such grace and peace that Bob understood. While he finally embraced the gospel message, his sister reacted with even more hostility than before.

The two criminals who were crucified with Jesus may not have seen how he lived, but they saw how he died. Matthew and Mark recorded that in the beginning of the six-hour ordeal, both thieves ridiculed and insulted Jesus. At one point, one of them mocked him by saying, "So you're really the Messiah, are you? Well, save yourself and us!"

However, a change had taken place in the other thief's heart. He rebuked the first thief and reminded him that they deserved their punishment. Then he acknowledged Jesus's innocence and asked Jesus to remember him when he entered his kingdom. Jesus promised the second thief that he would join him in paradise that very day.

People respond to the gospel message in drastically different ways. If we worry too much about how people might react, we can become intimidated and hesitant to share our faith. We are only accountable to share God's truth as he leads us—to warn others about punishment for sin and tell about his offer of forgiveness and eternal life. The other person bears the responsibility for how they choose to respond. Even if their initial reaction is hostility or ridicule, it's possible that their heart can change, like the criminal who followed Jesus from a cross to paradise.

Listen to what I say, and warn them for me.

Ezekiel 3:17

Ask yourself: **Do I use God-given opportunities to share the gospel without being overly concerned about how people will respond?**

APRIL
23

"My God, my God, why have you abandoned me?"

Matthew 27:45–54

The soldiers nailed Jesus to the cross around nine in the morning. He'd been beaten so badly that he hardly looked like a human being (see Isa. 52:14). The crowds passing by hurled insults at him; the religious leaders mocked him. His pain grew more unbearable as the hours passed. At noon, Jesus faced the part of his ordeal that he dreaded the most.

The sun disappeared under a darkness that blanketed the whole land. For the next few hours, Jesus experienced a separation from God the Father that he had never known. As Jesus became the sin offering for the world, he was temporarily cut off from fellowship with God. He expressed his anguish by crying out in a loud voice the opening line of Psalm 22: "My God, my God, why have you abandoned me?"

Several minutes later, Jesus gave up his spirit into God's hands. He had accomplished what he came to earth to do. In order to free us from the curse of sin, Jesus had become a curse himself (see Gal. 3:13). The sinless Son became an object of God's wrath in order to pay the penalty for our sins.

We'll never comprehend the horror that Jesus felt as he took the sins of the human race upon himself. And he suffered all of it for our benefit. Jesus endured a temporary separation from God so that we would never have to be separated from him. He felt abandoned by his Father so that we could live with the assurance that God would never abandon us. As believers, our sins can erect a barrier in our relationship with God until we acknowledge them and repent, but because of what Jesus willingly faced, we never need to cry out, "My God, why have you abandoned me?"

The Lord will never desert his people or
abandon those who belong to him.

Psalm 94:14

Ask God **to help you be mindful every day of what Jesus's temporary separation from God accomplished for you.**

APRIL
24

"Who will roll away the stone for us?"

Mark 16:1–7

The women walked with heavy hearts in the dawn's light. They had purchased spices the previous evening after the Sabbath ended at sundown. Now they planned to sprinkle these on the body of Jesus. It was the least they could do for their beloved rabbi who had done so much for them. But they worried about how they would get inside the tomb.

Two of the women had watched Joseph of Arimathea lay Jesus's body in the tomb and roll a large stone in front of the opening. "Who will roll away the stone for us from the entrance to the tomb?" they wondered aloud. However, when they arrived at the burial place, the women found the stone already pushed aside. Before they had time to wonder at this surprise, an angelic messenger informed them that Jesus of Nazareth had risen from the dead.

Even though the women had no idea how they would get past the huge stone that blocked Jesus's tomb, that didn't stop them from going. Their love and devotion to Jesus drove them forward even when it seemed that the trip might turn out to be wasted. If they had let practical concerns keep them from going that early morning, they would have missed the amazing privilege of being the first to hear the news of Jesus's resurrection.

Sometimes we let obstacles keep us from boldly serving God. When the odds seem stacked against us, it's tempting to do the "sensible" thing and hold back. Our concerns may be valid, but whenever we act out of love and devotion to God, our efforts are never wasted. When we serve God with a sincere heart, we can count on him to roll away any obstacles too big for us to handle.

When they looked up, they saw that the stone had been rolled away.

Mark 16:4

Ask yourself: **What obstacles do I allow to block my service and devotion to God?**

APRIL
25

"Are you the one, or should we look for someone else?"

Luke 7:18–23

One of the best-known writings of St. John of the Cross, a sixteenth-century monk, is a treatise called *Dark Night of the Soul*. Down through the ages, many people have used that phrase to describe a period of time in their life when they struggled with doubts about God and their faith.

John the Baptist experienced his own "dark night of the soul" as he languished in a dungeon, facing possible execution. He had fulfilled his role in pointing people toward Jesus as the Messiah, but now confusion set in. Although his disciples reported Jesus's miracles and powerful teachings, perhaps John wondered why Jesus had not set up God's kingdom. Wouldn't the Messiah have freed Israel from Roman rule by now?

John sent two disciples to Jesus with a question that cut to the chase: "Are you the one who is coming, or should we look for someone else?" Jesus instructed the men to report back to John what they had observed: sick people healed, dead people brought back to life, and the spreading of the Good News. The Messiah had ushered in a different kind of kingdom from the one people expected.

After the messengers left, Jesus made an astonishing remark about John: "I can guarantee that of all the people ever born, no one is greater than John" (Luke 7:28). This should certainly put to rest any worries we might have about admitting our doubts to God. He's not offended by honest questions and doesn't think less of us for voicing them.

As long as we live on earth, our faith will be imperfect. We may struggle with periods of doubt about God or our relationship with him. God understands, and wants to help us work through those times. When we honestly face our doubts, they can become stepping-stones to a stronger faith.

I believe! Help my lack of faith.

Mark 9:24

Ask yourself: **Am I honest with God when I experience doubts?**

APRIL
26

"Why don't you sleep with my slave?"

Genesis 16:1–6

"It seemed like a good idea at the time." How many of us have said those words as we looked back at actions that turned out to be terrible decisions? Sarai's suggestion for Abram to sleep with her maid seemed logical to her, and represented a perfectly acceptable custom at the time. If Hagar got pregnant by Abram, her child would be considered as belonging to her mistress, removing the stigma of barrenness from Sarai. If the child was male, Abram could choose to adopt him as his legal heir.

Although God had promised that Abram would have numerous descendants, his wife had long passed childbearing age. Abram agreed to Sarai's suggestion and slept with Hagar. Their action may have seemed reasonable, but it was not part of God's plan. They had no idea of the far-reaching consequences of their "Plan B." Besides conflict in their relationship, the hostility between Ishmael's descendants (Arabs) and Isaac's descendants (Jews) still affect the nation of Israel today.

Our culture condones many things that are unacceptable to God, like premarital sex, infidelity, homosexuality, and abortion. Society encourages materialism, greed, and self-love. Other issues may not be spelled out in the Scriptures but are still inappropriate for a child of God. We can't base our decisions on the approval of those around us, or even on what seems a reasonable course of action to us.

Our main criteria should always be whether or not an action is in line with God's will. We need prayer, Bible study, and his Holy Spirit's guidance to keep us from getting off track. Our "Plan B" might seem like a good idea at first, but it could lead to consequences that we regret for a long time.

Someone may say, "I'm allowed to do anything," but not everything is helpful.

1 Corinthians 6:12

Ask yourself: **Do I tend to base my decisions on God's Word and guidance, or on what seems reasonable to me?**

APRIL
27

"Where have you come from, and where are you going?"

Genesis 16:7–16

As Susan's car neared her exit, her whole body tensed up. When was the last time she looked forward to coming home from work? Her two teenagers grew more arrogant and rebellious by the day, and her husband had no inclination to get involved. Some days she wanted to just keep driving instead of going home.

Running away from our problems sometimes seems easier than dealing with them, especially if messy relationships are involved. Hagar tried to run away from her problems, but God intercepted her. When Hagar became pregnant by her owner's husband, she grew arrogant and treated Sarai with contempt. Sarai responded by mistreating Hagar so badly that Hagar tried to go back to her native Egypt.

The Lord confronted her in the desert: "Hagar, Sarai's slave, where have you come from, and where are you going?" Then he told her to return to Sarai and submit to her authority. After God gave her assurances about the son she would bear, Hagar called him "The God Who Watches Over Me." Then Hagar returned to Sarai and Abram with a new attitude and a new relationship with God.

All of us have probably felt like running away at some point in our life. Our situation may have been triggered by our own improper attitude or behavior, or we may have endured unfair treatment we didn't deserve. Either way, we simply felt unable to face the situation any longer.

There *are* times when we need to remove ourselves from relationships or situations—when we're endangered, or when blatant sin is involved. But trying to avoid difficulties doesn't help solve them. God wants to help us face our problems and work through them. We can trust the One who knows exactly where we've come from and where we're going.

Hagar named the LORD, who had been speaking to her, "You Are the God Who Watches Over Me."

Genesis 16:13

Ask God **to help you face any situation you feel like running away from.**

APRIL
28

"Why are you crying like this and breaking my heart?"

Acts 21:7–14

Joyce listened to her excited daughter and son-in-law. From the first time Curt and Leanne had shared their heart for missions work, Joyce had tried to dissuade them. She pointed out the financial risk of leaving their careers, the hardship of raising two toddlers on the mission field, and the potential danger of working in a hostile nation. Now everything had lined up and they had a departure date. *Don't spoil their joy by blubbering again*, Joyce reminded herself.

The believers at Caesarea worried about Paul's safety as he journeyed to Jerusalem. When Paul stopped to visit there, a prophet came down from Judea. Using Paul's belt, Agabus tied up his hands and feet and warned that Paul would be bound and handed over to the Romans. The local believers, along with Paul's traveling companion Luke, immediately tried to talk him out of going to Jerusalem.

The message from Agabus came as no surprise to Paul. He knew that he would face suffering and imprisonment in order to carry the gospel to Rome. He also knew that his friends wanted to protect him. But he had resolved to obey God's will at all costs. "Why are you crying like this and breaking my heart?" he asked. Paul declared that he was ready not only to be tied up in Jerusalem but also to die there for Jesus's sake.

We're naturally concerned when family or friends plan to do something that could prove dangerous, even if God is directing them. But if we give in to our emotions, we can become a hindrance to their obedience rather than an encouragement. It's hard to see loved ones walk into a situation that may include suffering, but if they're following God's will, that's the best place for them to be.

May the Lord's will be done.

Acts 21:14

Ask yourself: **Am I willing to commit my loved ones to God's will, even if it means danger and hardship?**

"Who will hear us?"

Psalm 59

The opening session ended with thunderous applause. The speaker had impressed everyone with his sensitivity and compassion for people, and his humble attitude despite his star status. During the intermission, however, the audience got a different view of him. He spat orders at his assistant, complained about the venue, and even made a derogatory remark about the sponsoring organization—which everyone heard. He had forgotten to take off his lapel microphone.

In Psalm 59, David prayed for God to protect him from his enemies. He described the words that came from their mouths as sharp swords, and asked God to bring them down "because of the sins from their mouths and the words on their lips." David thought a fitting end for such people would be for their own words to trap them and expose their arrogance in thinking that no one would hear them.

The Bible makes it clear that God hears every word we say, and he holds us accountable for what comes out of our mouth. Many Scriptures advise us to keep our speech free from lies, gossip, slander, seductive talk, obscene jokes, and pointless arguing. Unless we live in isolation, we're probably exposed to these negative elements nearly every day, making it easy for them to infiltrate our conversation.

Some Christians talk one way at church and a different way at work or around neighbors. Whether we do it to "fit in" or because we think it's okay to let down our guard sometimes, we can't afford to be careless about our speech. What comes out of our mouth can influence those around us—for good or bad. If our words don't line up with God's standards, our witness for Christ will be damaged. And even when our microphone is turned off, God still hears every word.

Everything you say should be kind and well thought out.

Colossians 4:6

Ask yourself: **How would my conversation be different if I remembered that God hears every word?**

APRIL
30

"Can we find anyone like this?"

Genesis 41:15–43

Lee sat down in the break room, surprised to find that the topic of conversation seemed to be ancient religions. "What do you believe?" someone asked him. "Well, I'm a Christian," he answered. "That explains a lot," his coworker next to him said with a smile. "I knew there was something different about you."

The king of Egypt could see something different about Joseph. When Pharaoh's wise men couldn't interpret his troubling dream, someone recommended Joseph. After acknowledging God as the source of his wisdom, Joseph explained that the dream warned of seven years of severe famine that would follow seven years of plenty. Then Joseph advised Pharaoh to appoint an intelligent man who would implement a plan to set aside a reserve supply of food for the country.

Pharaoh knew he didn't have to look far to find someone to fit the bill. "Can we find anyone like this—a man who has God's Spirit in him?" he asked. A few moments earlier, Joseph had been locked up in prison; now the worldly, sophisticated Egyptians gazed at him in awe of his understanding and wisdom. Pharaoh put the young Hebrew in charge of Egypt, second in command only to himself.

Godly people stand out from the crowd. If we're living according to God's standards, the world can't help but notice a difference. Our lifestyle serves as a testimony to people who would never set foot in a church or crack open a Bible. In a world darkened by sin, God calls us to shine like stars. When people look at us, they should see a reflection of God's love, mercy, and righteousness. With God's Spirit living in us, our life can shine like a bright light in a dark sky.

You will shine like stars among them in the world
as you hold firmly to the word of life.

Philippians 2:15–16

Ask yourself: **Does my lifestyle make me stand out from the crowd?**

MAY
1

"Where can we buy bread for these people to eat?"

John 6:1–14

Did Jesus ask Philip a trick question? Since Philip came from Bethsaida, a few miles away, he would have been the disciple most familiar with the resources of the surrounding villages. But the crowd that had gathered to hear Jesus numbered between fifteen and twenty thousand people. Philip did the math. Even if they could find that much bread so late in the day—which they couldn't—how would they pay for it?

John tells us that Jesus asked the question to test Philip's faith, already knowing how he would handle the situation. Jesus wanted to reinforce the truth that the problem had no human solution. Even with Andrew's discovery of a boy willing to share a few small loaves of bread and fish, the situation seemed impossible. But in Jesus's hands, the little bit of food gave the crowd plenty to eat, with twelve baskets of leftovers.

God often tests our faith by allowing us to face a need that can't be met through our normal resources. We might lack the money to pay a bill or meet some other physical need such as a car repair, a new appliance, or different housing. Or we may stand in need of strength, courage, or wisdom as we work our way through a difficult problem. The situation looks hopeless from a human standpoint.

Our first step is to make sure that we have a genuine need and not simply a desire. We need to examine our life to make sure we're living in obedience and being generous in our giving to God. Once we admit we can do nothing on our own, we can freely ask for help from the One who promises to meet all our needs, the same God who showed compassion for a hungry crowd so long ago.

My God will richly fill your every need in a glorious way through Christ Jesus.

Philippians 4:19

Ask yourself: **What need am I currently facing that has no human solution?**

MAY
2

"Couldn't I wash in them and be clean?"

2 Kings 5:1–14

The Aramean army commander rode away in a rage. Why had he ever listened to his Israelite slave girl's advice to seek healing from Elisha? What a wasted trip! Instead of showing the proper respect, Elisha had sent out a messenger—with an insulting message. Naaman had expected some type of dignified cleansing ceremony, but Elisha simply told him to dip himself in the Jordan River seven times. How could bathing in such a muddy little river do any good? His hometown had two rivers far superior to any in Israel. "Couldn't I wash in them and be clean?" he asked.

His devoted servants urged him to reconsider. After all, they reasoned, if Elisha had asked him to do something difficult or complicated, wouldn't he have done it? Why shouldn't he try this simple thing? Naaman swallowed his pride and obeyed the prophet's instructions. God not only healed his disease but restored his skin to a youthful condition.

Many people discount the gospel message because of its simplicity, preferring to explore what seem like more sophisticated ways to "find God." Salvation requires us to put aside our pride and admit we can't do anything to save ourselves: God has done it all. Even after becoming a Christian, pride can still wreak havoc in our relationship with God and with other people.

The desire to do things our own way instead of God's way can lead us into disobedience and sin. And, like Naaman, we may become incensed when someone doesn't give us the respect we feel is due us. God promises to honor those who replace their self-will with an attitude of humility. If we don't deal with our pride, we'll miss out on God's blessings, just as Naaman almost missed out on his healing.

A person's pride will humiliate him, but
a humble spirit gains honor.

Proverbs 29:23

Ask yourself: **How does my pride interfere with my daily walk with God?**

“How could you accept silver or clothes?”

2 Kings 5:15–27

My husband and I had decided to stop and see what the inside of a casino looked like; now I couldn’t wait to get out. It wasn’t quite like what the billboards with the smiling models had portrayed. The background music combined with the rhythmic noises of the slot machines to create a hypnotic beat. Countless rows of people sat holding their change on their laps, staring at the machines as if hypnotized, all hoping to strike it rich.

Gehazi saw a chance to strike it rich when his master refused to accept a gift from Naaman. After Elisha left, Gehazi pretended that Elisha had changed his mind and asked for seventy-five pounds of silver and two sets of clothes. Naaman, filled with gratitude for being healed of a serious skin disease, insisted on giving twice as much silver.

As soon as Gehazi hid the plunder, Elisha questioned him. “I didn’t go anywhere,” Gehazi lied. But Elisha exposed Gehazi’s deception and greed. “How could you accept silver, clothes, olive orchards, vineyards, sheep, cattle, or slaves? Naaman’s skin disease will cling to you and your descendants permanently!”

The Bible warns us to fight against the temptation to try to get something for nothing and the desire to want what we don’t have. Greed is included in a list of sins to avoid in Romans 1:29 and many other passages. Since our culture constantly bombards us with the pressure to buy, we must always be on our guard. Always wanting more keeps us from enjoying what we already have. God wants us to learn to be content with what he provides for us. Once we adopt that attitude, we’ll understand that we’ve already struck it rich.

He told the people, “Be careful to guard yourselves from every kind of greed.”

Luke 12:15

Ask yourself: **Does my attitude reflect greed or contentment with what God provides?**

MAY
4

"Do you understand what I've done for you?"

John 13:3–17

The young businessman rolled up his sleeves and thought about the unpleasant chore that awaited—cleaning his muddy shoes. He didn't regret his decision to accompany his pastor on this trip. The response to the revival meetings had been rewarding, and he enjoyed the people. But how could they stand to live in such poverty? This morning's visit took them down a muddy lane and had left his shoes caked in filth. Pulling a bucket of water from the well, he stepped on the back porch to see his shoes freshly cleaned, and his pastor walking away.

Even while facing the approaching agony of his crucifixion, Jesus took the time to model humility and selfless giving. Wrapping a towel around his waist, Jesus washed and dried his disciples' feet. They sat stunned as they watched their leader perform a menial chore that was reserved for non-Jewish slaves whenever possible. After he finished, Jesus asked them a question: "Do you understand what I've done for you?" Since he, as their Lord and teacher, had washed their feet, the disciples were to do the same for each other.

Jesus gave the ultimate object lesson in humility when he laid aside his glory to take on human form for a period of time. He demonstrated the ultimate selfless love when he went to the cross. Now he asks us to give our lives for each other, even though our human nature fights against it. Do we serve others without a thought of getting something back? Or do we consider some acts of service beneath us? The more we understand what Jesus did for us, the more we'll want to serve others, even to the point of washing dirty shoes—or feet.

We understand what love is when we realize that Christ gave his life for us. That means we must give our lives for other believers.

1 John 3:16

Ask yourself: **How does my attitude toward serving others measure up against Jesus's model?**

"What does grain have to do with straw?"

Jeremiah 23:16–28

One Sunday morning when I was too sick to go to church, I flipped through television stations looking for a church service. The first church I "visited" had a pastor whose hair had more substance than his message, which was about thinking positive and feeling good. Then I turned to another station and watched a pastor deliver a biblically based sermon, focusing on a passage of Scripture and how to apply it to daily life. Both men had great speaking skills and seemed equally sincere and passionate, but their messages were as different as night and day.

In Jeremiah's day, God contrasted the difference between true messages from him and false prophecies by asking, "What does grain have to do with straw?" Instead of showing the people of Judah their need to repent, the false prophets spread messages of peace and security. Rather than warn of God's judgment, they told the people, "Everything will go well for you." True prophets, on the other hand, would have helped turn Judah from evil by sharing God's real message.

Many popular speakers and authors today offer messages that are more like straw than grain. Sermons often sound like motivational speeches or positive thinking seminars. Some churches ignore Bible passages that talk about the suffering and sacrifice expected of a follower of Christ. They avoid using words like "sin" and "repentance" because those concepts don't fit in with their feel-good approach.

Teaching based directly on God's Word can transform our thinking and help us live a godly lifestyle. The heart of that teaching will be the message of Jesus's death on our behalf and will encourage us to develop the habits of a committed disciple, such as prayer, obedience, and service. That kind of teaching won't always make us feel good, but it will never blow away in the wind like straw.

Every Scripture passage is inspired by God. All of them are useful for teaching, pointing out errors, correcting people, and training them for a life that has God's approval.

2 Timothy 3:16

Ask yourself: **Does my church offer biblically based teaching?**

MAY

6

"Did you sell the land for that price?"

Acts 5:1–11

Ananias and Sapphira reviewed their plan: they would sell that piece of property and donate the money to the church, as so many other believers had done. Only they'd keep part of the money for their own personal use. It was *their* property after all, and no one needed to know how much they got for it. When Peter confronted Ananias and accused him of trying to deceive the Holy Spirit, Ananias dropped dead.

A few hours later, Sapphira arrived, oblivious to what had happened. "Tell me," Peter questioned, "did you sell the land for that price?" Sapphira answered, "Yes, that was the price." When Peter asked how she and her husband could agree to test God's Spirit, Sapphira also dropped dead and was buried alongside her husband.

God judged this incident harshly to purge deception and hypocrisy from the developing church. Today, lying has almost become an art form. It no longer seems unusual to read of a "memoir" that turns out to be more fiction than fact, or a newspaper reporter who broke big stories by fabricating interviews and sources. Sometimes we even learn about incidents of people staging fake harassment or physical attacks in order to bring attention to a cause.

God despises dishonesty in any form. Even if we're careful not to tell an outright lie, we may deceive others by withholding information or by presenting the truth in a way that influences their perception. We can also lie with our behavior by acting in ways that deliberately give a false impression of us. God wants our conversation, our actions, and our lifestyle to reflect total honesty, so he can take delight in us.

Lips that lie are disgusting to the Lord,
but honest people are his delight.

Proverbs 12:22

Ask yourself: **Do I make every effort to keep my speech and my behavior free from dishonesty and deception?**

MAY
7

"Who wins the victory over the world?"

1 John 5:1–12

In the 1930s, an undersized, knobby-kneed colt turned out to be an unlikely champion. Considered lazy, Seabiscuit was given limited training and used only in minor races. Then a new owner and a new trainer saw his potential. By the time he retired, Seabiscuit was horse racing's all-time leading money winner.

The book of 1 John talks about another surprising win. In the world's eyes, Christians may look like losers, but our faith in Christ makes us conquerors. "Who wins the victory over the world?" John wrote. "Isn't it the person who believes that Jesus is the Son of God?" Once we place our faith in Christ, we receive the power to follow God's commands and live a victorious life.

Our culture values winning in sports, military conflicts, political campaigns, and at the Academy Awards. But Christians win a different type of victory. Our faith enables us to resist the pressure to conform to the world's way of thinking. It helps us withstand the hostility the world directs at us. We can endure life's disappointments, trials, and sorrows because we live with the certainty that Christ has the final victory over the world.

Jesus has already conquered sin and death; someday he will rule the earth in righteousness. Since our faith makes us one with him, we share in his victory. But that doesn't mean we always live like a winner. If we forget who we are in Christ, Satan can get the upper hand. When we stop depending on God's strength to help us live an obedient lifestyle, the world can beat us down. Each day we have a choice: Will we let the spirit of the world rule us, or will we live in the victory that Christ died to make possible?

The one who loves us gives us an overwhelming victory in all these difficulties.

Romans 8:37

Ask yourself: **In what area of my life am I failing to live as a victor?**

MAY
8

"Can a woman forget her nursing child?"

Isaiah 49:14–18

Christina sat at her desk, wondering why she couldn't concentrate. She'd looked forward to coming back to work after her maternity leave; now it seemed that her heart had stayed at home. Moment by moment, her thoughts centered on her five-week-old son. Was he sleeping well today? Would the sitter remember to use that special cream on his rash? Hadn't his forehead felt a little warm this morning? And just when Christina finally got interested in her current project, the milk started flowing and she had to reach for the breast pump.

God compared a mother's love and attention to his care for Israel. During the Babylonian captivity, the people wondered if God had forgotten about them. He assured them that he had not. "Can a woman forget her nursing child?" God asked them. "Will she have no compassion on the child from her womb?" God said that although it *is* possible for mothers to forget their children, he could never forget his people. God had even engraved their names on his hands, so that his thoughts were continually focused on them.

What a comforting thought to know that God is thinking about us all through the day and night. How incredible to think that the Creator of the universe has us at the center of his thoughts. No matter what's happening in our life, God tenderly watches over us like a mother caring for her baby. And like a mother, he always wants what's best for us.

When we face troubles that seem to have no end, we can start to feel like God has forgotten all about us. During those times it helps to read Scriptures that remind us of his love and care. We may forget about God sometimes, but thankfully, we are never out of his thoughts.

Although mothers may forget, I will not forget you.

Isaiah 49:15

Ask yourself: **What types of situations tempt me to feel like God has forgotten me?**

"What do you want with us, Jesus from Nazareth?"

Mark 1:21–28

Heads turned as the man's cries pierced the subdued atmosphere in the synagogue. One look and the worshipers knew that this tortured soul suffered from demon possession. "Oh, no! What do you want with us, Jesus from Nazareth?" the demon shouted. "Have you come to destroy us? I know who you are—the Holy One of God!"

Many of the people had witnessed or heard of exorcisms involving incantations, strange rituals, or props. Jesus spoke only a few simple words: "Keep quiet, and come out of him!" The evil spirit threw the man down on the floor in convulsions and left his body with a shriek. A few minutes earlier, Jesus had amazed the people in the synagogue with the way he taught with such authority; now they were stunned by his power over evil spirits.

During his time on earth, Jesus spoke and taught about God with wisdom and authority. He demonstrated power over the weather, evil spirits, diseases and infirmities of all kinds, and even death. Yet most people refused to do what every demon Jesus encountered did—acknowledge him as the Holy One, the Son of God. Today, many Christians call Jesus "Lord," but refuse to submit to his authority in their daily lives.

Before Jesus ascended into heaven, he commissioned his followers to make disciples on the basis of the authority given him by God the Father. As we obey that command, our life becomes infused with his authority as we tell others about God, teach from the Scriptures, confront evil in the world, and bring healing to wounded people. If we fully submit to Jesus's lordship *over* us, then people will see his authority *through* us as well.

Jesus . . . said, "All authority in heaven and on earth has been given to me."

Matthew 28:18

Ask yourself: **Does my life reflect Jesus's authority over me and through me?**

MAY
10

"Who is David? Who is Jesse's son?"

1 Samuel 25:2–13

So this is what kissing up to the CEO gets you, Sean thought as he looked around the spacious office. His supervisor cleared his throat. "Sean, we have a problem here." Sean laughed. "Yeah, we have a lot of problems—and they're all sitting out there in cubicles." His supervisor started again. "You know that we decided to divide up into teams to tackle this current project. It seems that nobody wants to work with you." Sean snorted. "Afraid I'll make them pull their weight?" "Actually," his supervisor said, with a frown, "no one wants to put up with your constant stream of sarcasm."

The man in today's passage let sarcasm put more than his job as stake. David had a right to request food for his men from Nabal; after all, they had protected Nabal's workers and helped him prosper. Nabal was rich enough to spare the provisions, and his culture's traditions required that hospitality be shown when requested.

But Nabal responded to David's message with rudeness. "Who is David? Who is Jesse's son? So many servants nowadays are leaving their masters." Nabal wanted to know why he should give his bread, water, and meat to "men coming from who knows where." When David heard Nabal's answer, his anger flared. Four hundred men strapped on swords and rode off with David to pay Nabal back.

Our culture seems to value sarcasm. Television sitcoms filled with zingers and put-downs are popular, as are columnists and commentators who rely on biting, edgy, sarcastic wit. No wonder it slips into the everyday conversation of so many people. While sarcasm may not endanger our life, it holds the power to kill the spirit of a child or fatally damage a relationship with a spouse, friend, or coworker. When it comes to sarcasm, it's best to remember just how dangerous it can be.

The tongue has the power of life and death.

Proverbs 18:21

Ask yourself: **Do I ever let sarcasm slip into my conversation?**

MAY
11

"What is truth?"

John 18:28–40

This was one case the Roman governor of Judea would have preferred to avoid. Pilate knew that although Jesus was popular with the people, the Jewish leaders wanted him executed. After a personal conversation with his prisoner, Pilate seemed to believe that Jesus was innocent of any crime and did not represent a threat to the civil government. Wanting to guard his own political career, Pilate looked for a compromise.

Pilate asked Jesus several questions, until Jesus declared he had come into the world to testify to the truth, and that anyone who belonged to the truth would listen to him. At that point, Pilate stopped listening. "What is truth?" he asked. Without waiting for a response from Jesus, Pilate walked out to the Jews to try once again to get himself off the hook.

We can't be sure what Pilate had in mind when he asked his question. His words could have expressed a sincere wish for enlightenment, a philosophical comment on the difficulty of ascertaining genuine truth, or a sarcastic jab at Jesus's statement. But we do know that he didn't wait for Jesus to respond. Pilate had no idea that he was walking away from the One who called himself the Truth (see John 14:6), the One who had prayed for his followers earlier that evening, saying, "Use the truth to make them holy. Your words are truth" (John 17:17).

It's often not easy to recognize the truth today. We can't always trust newspapers and television programs; internet hoaxes and tabloids fool many. Some people latch on to any bestselling book claiming to disclose some secret truth. Just as Pilate walked away from Jesus, many people ignore God's Word and search for truth elsewhere. The human race still has the same question, and the answer is still the same.

Your words are truth.
John 17:17

Ask yourself: **Have I been looking for truth in the wrong places?**

MAY
12

“Do you have only one blessing, Father?”

Genesis 27:30–40

Isaac’s frail body trembled all over as he realized what had just happened. *So, my suspicions were right*, he thought. His younger son Jacob had deceived him, pretending to be Esau. Isaac had officially handed over the birthright of the firstborn son to Jacob, along with blessings of prosperity, domination over his brothers and other nations, and curses on anyone who cursed him. Now his real firstborn son stood before him, demanding to be blessed.

“Haven’t you saved a blessing for me?” Esau cried. Isaac explained that he had nothing left to give Esau; Jacob had gotten the best of everything that an heir could receive. As a formal oath, the father’s blessing was irrevocable. “Do you have only one blessing, Father?” Esau pleaded. “Bless me too, Father!” The words that Isaac pronounced over Esau’s future contrasted sharply with what the son had hoped to hear.

We never have to worry about God running out of blessings to pass on to his children. There’s no need to feel jealous or threatened when we see him pour blessings into someone else’s life. God has more than enough to go around. We don’t need to trick him into blessing us; it’s one of his favorite things to do. God’s unlimited love, grace, and mercy are the source of an unending supply of blessings.

God doesn’t show favoritism among his children; he wants to shower blessings on us all. We can practice habits, attitudes, and behaviors that position us to receive more of his bounty. When we obey God’s commands, and stay close to him through prayer and Bible study, we’ll enjoy the blessings that come only to someone walking closely with him. There’s no limit to God’s blessings, and they are freely given to us all.

God does not play favorites.

Romans 2:11

Ask yourself: **What changes can I make in my life so that I enjoy more of God’s blessings?**

MAY
13

"Why should I lose both of you in one day?"

Genesis 27:41–46

Jan prides herself on being a "free spirit" and a "free thinker." She boasts about living life on her own terms with no compromises. For her funeral, Jan says the perfect song would be one of her favorites—Frank Sinatra's "I Did It My Way." Her friends wonder if she's joking, but they have to admit that it would be an appropriate selection.

That song would also be fitting for Rebekah after she helped Jacob deceive his father. At the twins' birth, God had predicted that the younger son would be the leader of the family. But Rebekah devised her own plan to make sure her favorite son got the blessing that normally went to the firstborn. And things had worked out beautifully—or so she thought.

Esau, livid with rage, comforted himself by planning to kill Jacob after their elderly father died. When Rebekah found out, she had to devise another plan—this time to save Jacob's life. Rebekah urged him to run away. "Why should I lose both of you in one day?" she asked. He could stay with her uncle in Haran for a short while, just until Esau's anger cooled. Then Rebekah would send for him and everything would be fine—or so she thought.

Rebekah never saw Jacob again. By the time he returned, twenty years later, she was dead. Rebekah may have "won" by doing things her way, but she lost far more than she gained. Our human nature fights for the right to live life on our own terms instead of God's. Sometimes we even convince ourselves that we're helping carry out his plans. But any time we devise a scheme that goes against God's will or interferes with his timing, we lose. The only way to have a winning life is to do things his way.

Blessed are all who fear the LORD and live his way.

Psalm 128:1

Ask yourself: **Are my plans usually based on doing things my way or God's way?**

MAY
14

"Why did you cheat me?"

Genesis 29:15–27

As Jacob fled from home in the face of his brother's anger, he had an encounter with God at Bethel that changed him forever. But God still had some refining to do. Arriving in Haran, Jacob found a warm welcome from his uncle Laban. The two men struck a deal: Jacob would work for Laban seven years in return for the hand of Laban's beautiful younger daughter Rachel.

The years passed quickly for Jacob, and finally Laban threw a wedding feast. That night, however, he substituted his older daughter Leah. An angry Jacob confronted his uncle the next morning. "What have you done to me?" he demanded. "Didn't I work for you in return for Rachel? Why did you cheat me?"

Jacob had gotten a taste of his own medicine, and he found it hard to swallow. He had deceived his father by pretending to be the firstborn son; now Laban deceived him by pretending that his firstborn daughter was the younger one. Although Jacob also married Rachel a week later, he had to commit himself to another seven years of work.

Many times what we call "irony" or "poetic justice" is actually God's discipline. He may want to point out some flaw in our character or behavior that needs to be corrected. Sometimes he gives us a taste of what we've dished out so we can learn how our actions make others feel. We can avoid the need for such divine retribution if we follow Jesus's command to treat others the way we would like to be treated. Living by this principle can only be done with God's help and it's not easy. But at least it ensures that when we get a taste of our own medicine, it's not so bitter.

[Jesus said] "Whatever you want men to do to you, do also to them, for this is the Law and the Prophets."

Matthew 7:12 NKJV

Ask yourself: **Do I remember a time when God let me have a taste of my own medicine?**

"Can these bones live?"

Ezekiel 37:1–14

Ezekiel gazed at the sun-bleached bones filling the valley and pondered God's bizarre question. "Son of Man, can these bones live?" The prophet answered, "Only you know, Almighty Lord." Then God instructed Ezekiel to prophesy to the bones, to tell them that God would bring them to life and they would know him.

Ezekiel obeyed and began to preach to the bones on the ground. Suddenly he heard a rattling noise. As Ezekiel watched in amazement, the bones lined up and attached to each other. First ligaments formed, then muscles, and finally, skin covered the bones. Following God's next command, Ezekiel called for breath to enter the bodies. A sound of wind rushed through the valley, and the bodies stood on their feet.

God explained to Ezekiel that the bones represented the Jewish people in their spiritually dead condition. Scattered and living in exile, most of them had given up. "Our bones are dry, and our hope has vanished," they said. "We are completely destroyed." But God promised to bring them back to their homeland like bringing bodies back from the grave, infused with new life. Someday, God would put his Spirit in them and everyone in Israel would acknowledge what the Lord had done for them.

Who else besides God could turn a heap of dry bones into living people? Who else but God can put his Spirit in someone so they can walk in new life, or restore a believer who has fallen away from following him? Who else can breathe life into a dead marriage, or renew old dreams that died long ago? No person or situation is beyond his reach. The same God who breathed life into the first man, and later turned dry bones into living bodies, can surely bring life to our dead hopes.

I will put my Spirit in you, and you will live.

Ezekiel 37:14

Ask yourself: **What situation or person in my life needs God's life-giving breath?**

MAY

16

"With whom was God angry for forty years?"

Hebrews 3:7–19

Jason sank down against a tree and pulled off his hat. This trail had turned out to be a lot more challenging than he'd expected, with markers almost impossible to find. He wondered where those teens were now—the ones who'd tried to steer him in a different direction a while back. *Why should I take the advice of some young—wait a minute, that rock formation over there sure looks familiar.* After taking a better look around, Jason had to admit that he'd just spent a couple of hours wandering in a circle.

The Israelites spent a lot of time wandering around after God delivered them from slavery in Egypt. The writer of Hebrews used their example to warn against the consequences of stubbornness and disobedience. "Who heard God and rebelled?" he asked. "With whom was God angry for 40 years?"

Although Israel had witnessed many miracles, they refused to believe that God would help them conquer the Promised Land. So God let them wander in the wilderness until that generation died, with the exception of Joshua and Caleb.

We risk losing something precious whenever we let a lack of trust keep us from following where God wants to lead us. He may decide to let us wander around in a wilderness for a while until we learn to rely on his guidance. We can face serious consequences when we stray from the path of his commands.

The choice is ours: Will we wander aimlessly through life, depending on our own sense of direction, or will we live a life of blessing and purpose by following God's instructions? If we feel like we've been going in circles, that's a sign that we need his help in getting back on the right path again.

I follow the straight paths of your guiding principles.

Psalm 119:128

Ask God **to show you how you're doing at staying on the path of his principles for living.**

"What should we do?"

Acts 2:32–41

Ray shifted uncomfortably in his chair as the pastor ended his sermon about the responsibilities of a father. The list of negative effects on children with uninvolved parents sounded frightening. *He could have had me in mind when he wrote that!* Ray told himself during the closing prayer. Ray's troubling thoughts nagged him all afternoon, until he picked up the TV remote. By the end of the first quarter, his conviction had evaporated—and he hardly remembered the morning message.

Peter preached a message that convicted thousands of people and changed their lives. With boldness and passion, he used Old Testament prophecies to prove that Jesus was the Messiah. He reminded them of Jesus's crucifixion and resurrection, and confronted them with their own guilt in Jesus's death. His words pierced deep into the people's hearts. They had crucified their Messiah! "Brothers, what should we do?" they cried out in desperation. Peter told the crowd that they must turn to God and, on the basis of their repentance, be baptized.

Repentance means more than just feeling sorry for our actions, as even Judas did. It means that we turn away from sin and toward Christ for forgiveness. We reverse the direction our life is going to follow God's commands instead of our own way. After we become a Christian, God's Spirit convicts us of sin. If we choose to ignore that nagging feeling, it eventually fades away. We miss the opportunity to receive forgiveness, restore our relationship with God, and make any needed restitution or correction in our behavior. When we sense that uncomfortable feeling of conviction, the best response is to ask, "Father, what should I do?"

To be distressed in a godly way causes people
to change the way they think and act and leads
them to be saved. No one can regret that.

2 Corinthians 7:10

Ask yourself: **How do I respond when God's Spirit convicts me of wrongdoing?**

MAY
18

"Has anyone condemned you?"

John 8:1–11

Every eye in the temple courtyard stared at Jesus. *Let's see him get out of this one*, the Pharisees and scribes thought smugly. The law demanded that anyone guilty of adultery be killed. If Jesus advocated letting the woman go free, he would be contradicting Moses's law. If he agreed to the woman's stoning he could get into trouble, since Rome didn't permit Jewish executions. Either outcome would affect his popularity.

The accused woman stood in the middle of the crowd, head bowed in shame. It had all happened so fast, but a feeling began to grow that she'd been set up. Now her fate seemed to hang on the man who was stooped down, writing in the dust.

Jesus knew the religious leaders weren't interested in upholding the law; otherwise they would have brought the guilty man too. He understood their desire to discredit him. "The person who is sinless should be the first to throw a stone at her," he said. One by one the men slipped away.

Finally, Jesus faced the woman. "Where did they go? Has anyone condemned you?" he asked. "No one, sir," the woman answered. Then Jesus replied, "I don't condemn you either. Go! From now on don't sin."

Every human being stands convicted of sin that separates us from God. But Jesus's death made it possible for us to receive a full pardon. Since we still sin after we become a Christian, God promises to forgive us when we repent and turn away from wrongdoing. God's Spirit convicts us of any unconfessed sins in our life, prompting us to take appropriate action. But sometimes we have false condemnation heaped on us by Satan, other people, or our own confused thinking. For the answer to the question, "Has anyone condemned you?" we need only go to the eighth chapter of Romans.

So those who are believers in Christ Jesus
can no longer be condemned.

Romans 8:1

Ask yourself: **Do I struggle with feelings of condemnation even after confessing sins?**

MAY
19

"Who are you to judge your neighbor?"

James 4:11–12

I wondered how the woman could keep on dancing her heart out like that. One of the *America's Got Talent* judges apparently didn't like what he was seeing, so he pushed his button. The huge red "X" by his name above the stage lit up and an irritating buzzer sounded. Seconds later, a second judge followed suit. But the woman wasn't through yet; the viewers across the country would make their own judgment about her performance, and their vote would decide her fate.

If people carried around buzzers like these judges use, the world would be a noisy place. James used strong language to address the tendency of people to judge and criticize each other. He wrote that when we slander or judge another person, we're actually passing judgment on God's law itself. Since God is the author of the law and the only rightful judge, we display a haughty attitude when we put ourselves in his place. "So who are you to judge your neighbor?" James asked.

Many people look at others' behavior and lifestyle with the mindset of "guilty until proven innocent." We rush to pass judgment, even though we have no way of fully knowing the person's motives or situation. First Corinthians 4:5 urges us to refrain from judging anything before the appointed time when the Lord returns. He will bring hidden secrets to light and expose the motives of people's hearts before dispensing justice.

Only God knows the details of a situation, and only he has the right to judge. How can we be in such a hurry to condemn another person's motives, conduct, or lifestyle, when we're accountable to the same judge as they are? When we remember that our own hidden secrets and motives will be revealed one day, we won't be so hasty to whip out our "buzzer."

God alone is the judge.

Psalm 75:7

Ask yourself: **Do I tend to look at people with a judgmental attitude?**

MAY
20

"What were you thinking when you did this?"

Genesis 20:1–13

"Year graduated from high school." Brad stared at the application. *Well, I almost went four years*, he reasoned. *Easier to just put down a year than explain how I dropped out to work and help my family. After all, a GED is just as good as a diploma—and I really need this job.* Several weeks later, Brad was fired for giving false information on his application.

Sometimes Abraham took the easy way out too. After he moved to Gerar, Abraham feared that someone would kill him for his beautiful wife. So he told everyone that Sarah was his sister. After all, Sarah really was his half sister, and this seemed to be the only way he could protect himself from the godless people living in this land.

When King Abimelech took Sarah into his harem, God warned him in a dream that she was a married woman. Abimelech proclaimed his innocence and returned Sarah to her husband. "What have you done to us?" he rebuked Abraham. "What were you thinking when you did this?" By relying on deception instead of trusting God, Abraham put Abimelech and Sarah at risk of adultery, and endangered the marriage through which God had promised him descendants.

What looks like the most reasonable course of action is not always the right thing to do. We may convince ourselves we're being smart and heading off potential problems, when in reality we're simply taking the easy way out. The right path is often difficult and scary. It's tempting to choose the way that doesn't require much effort or courage on our part. But what looks to be in our best interests can lead us away from God's will. When we take the easy way out, we may find ourselves later wondering, *What was I thinking?*

There is a way that seems right to a person,
but eventually it ends in death.

Proverbs 14:12

Ask yourself: **When I'm faced with a difficult decision, do I sometimes take the easy way out?**

MAY
21

"Do you really want to go back there?"

John 11:1–16

The disciples could hardly believe their ears. Had Jesus forgotten how the Jews in Jerusalem had recently tried to kill him? Why would he want to put his life in danger by going back to Judea? But Jesus had just announced his intention to go to Bethany in response to a message that his friend Lazarus was sick. "Rabbi, not long ago the Jews wanted to stone you to death," they reminded him. "Do you really want to go back there?"

Jesus answered with a metaphor contrasting walking in the light versus walking in darkness. People who walk during the "day" don't have to worry about stumbling because they have God's light to guide them, but those who walk in the darkness of their own will can fall. Jesus knew that as long as he submitted to God's plan for his life, he could not be harmed until the appointed time of his crucifixion.

God has given each one of us a purpose and specific work to do. As long as we're following his plan for our life, nothing and no one can interfere with his purposes. But it's dangerous to leave the light of God's truth and walk down a path of disobedience. It's foolish to let ourselves be guided by the world or by our own understanding.

Any time we stray from God's will, we make ourselves vulnerable to temptations, Satan's traps, and unwise choices that bring serious consequences. The only safe place to be is in the center of God's will. As long as we follow where he leads, we'll be protected. We may have to walk through some dark valleys, but even in the shadow of death, we have the security of knowing that we're not walking alone.

Yea, though I walk through the valley of the shadow of death, I will fear no evil; For You are *with me.*

Psalm 23:4 NKJV

Ask yourself: **Am I walking in the safety of God's will for my life?**

MAY

22

"Have you met a person who is quick to answer?"

Proverbs 18:13; 29:20

Cynthia drove home from the PTA meeting with a burning face. She'd stood up and given those board members what-for concerning the policy changes in the sports program. But then the principal had shared the reasons for the changes. Cynthia hated to admit it, but this wasn't the first time she'd spouted off before hearing the whole story. When would she learn not to blurt out the first thing that popped into her mind? *Well*, she thought, *I could try taping my mouth shut—if I could keep my foot out of it long enough!*

Proverbs has something to say about this universal problem and the trouble it causes. "Have you met a person who is quick to answer?" the writer asked. "There is more hope for a fool than for him." He also warned that giving an answer without listening is shameful and foolish (see 18:13). In contrast with a wicked person who gushes out evil words, godly people carefully consider their words and the effect they will have before they speak.

Most of us have been on the giving *and* the receiving end of a thoughtless, insensitive remark blurted out. Sometimes we answer a person without really hearing what they said, or we express an opinion without getting all the facts first. Speaking without thinking usually makes us look foolish; sometimes it leads to hurt feelings. Inappropriate words can also ignite serious misunderstandings or damage relationships. With God's help we can learn to slow down and evaluate our words before they leave our mouth. We can set aside the tape—once our words change from "careless" to "carefully considered."

The heart of a righteous person carefully considers
how to answer, but the mouths of wicked
people pour out a flood of evil things.

Proverbs 15:28

Ask yourself: **Do I sometimes blurt out remarks that I wish I could take back?**

Ask God **to help you remember to consider your words before speaking.**

"If the Lord is with us, why has all this happened to us?"

Judges 6:11–24

"The LORD is with you, brave man." The angel's words could hardly have seemed more out of place in such a setting. For seven years, the Midianites and their allies had swooped across Israel during harvest times and stripped the crops. These seasonal invasions forced the Israelites to hide in caves and mountain strongholds. Unable to thresh his grain out in the open on a threshing floor as usual, Gideon hid in a winepress to beat out his small wheat harvest.

Gideon ignored the angel's personal greeting and questioned God's presence with his people in light of their present circumstances: "But if the Lord is with us, why has all this happened to us?" Why had God performed miracles on Israel's behalf in the past only to hand them over to their enemies now? Gideon accused God of abandoning the nation, even though prophets had warned about the consequences of disobedience.

Many of us have asked similar questions of God during times of trouble or suffering. "If you're really with me, then why has this happened?" Sometimes our troubles result from sin or disobedience, so a good first response is to examine our life for unconfessed sins or behaviors that may have caused the problem. But often the hard things in life simply come from living in a world under the curse of sin.

We'll all face tough times while we live on this earth. We'll struggle with financial stresses and health issues. We'll deal with disappointments and dysfunctional relationships. If we live long enough, we'll eventually experience the loss of loved ones. It may be tempting at times to feel like God has abandoned us. But no matter how badly we hurt, we can find comfort in his promise to never leave us. God's presence will give us the strength to face whatever happens.

I will never neglect you or abandon you.

Joshua 1:5

Ask God **to help you sense his presence in your life during difficult times.**

MAY
24

"Where is the lamb for the burnt offering?"

Genesis 22:1–14

"Sacrifice him there as a burnt offering on one of the mountains that I will show you." God's command was clear—and also confusing, unreasonable, and terrifying. Isaac's birth had been miraculous, born when Sarah was ninety and Abraham a hundred years old. God had promised Abraham that he would have numerous descendants through Isaac. How would God fulfill his promises if Abraham sacrificed his beloved son?

Although Abraham didn't understand what God had in mind, he had learned the importance of obedience over the years. Abraham didn't question God, but as he climbed up Mount Moriah with his son, Isaac had a question: "Father? We have the burning coals and the wood, but where is the lamb for the burnt offering?" Abraham answered, "God will provide a lamb for the burnt offering, son."

Later, as Abraham raised the knife over his bound son, God stopped him. Turning around, Abraham saw a ram caught in a bush. Because of Abraham's trust, God first gave Abraham the strength to carry out such a heartbreaking command, then he provided a substitute for the sacrifice.

We usually think of God as providing for our needs in the physical sense, but his provision goes far beyond that. God provided a ram for Abraham's sacrifice; centuries later he offered his Son as the Lamb of God to be sacrificed for the world's sins. In our personal life, God has promised to provide us with everything we need for our Christian walk. He will give us the wisdom and courage to live a godly life. He will supply the strength to obey his commands, even when they seem impossible or unreasonable. Whenever we take a step in obedience, God will provide what we need to see the journey through.

God's divine power has given us everything
we need for life and for godliness.

2 Peter 1:3

Ask yourself: **Do I trust God to provide what I need to obey his commands that are tough or hard to understand?**

“What is your advice?”

1 Kings 12:1–13

Solomon’s son received some good advice and some bad advice, and he chose to follow the latter. During Rehoboam’s coronation, the people requested the new king to lighten the heavy labor and tax burden that Solomon’s extensive building programs had demanded. Rehoboam promised to give an answer two days later. First, he sought guidance from the older men who had served as his father’s counselors. They recommended a favorable answer to gain the people’s loyalty. Rehoboam rejected this advice.

Then Rehoboam brought the same question to the young men who had grown up with him: “What is your advice?” His peers urged the opposite approach. “This is what you should tell them: ‘My little finger is heavier than my father’s whole body. If my father put a heavy burden on you, I will add to it.’” Rehoboam’s decision to follow the young men’s counsel triggered the rebellion of the northern tribes and the splitting of the kingdom.

We have many sources for advice these days: newspaper columns, self-help books and seminars, professional counselors, and the emerging trend of “life coaches.” While Proverbs 15:22 urges the wisdom of forming plans with many advisers, it’s best to carefully and prayerfully evaluate any advice we receive. Is it biblically sound? Is it wise? What could the long-term effects be if I follow this counsel? Following the wrong advice can bring disastrous results.

Advice from trusted friends or professionals can be helpful and sometimes necessary, but believers have an ongoing appointment with the ultimate Counselor. When faced with a decision, a good first step is to lay out the situation before God, open his Word, and prayerfully ask, “What is your advice?” We’ll never go wrong if we follow what he recommends.

God has wisdom and strength. Advice and insight are his.

Job 12:13

Ask yourself: **What sources do I depend on when I need advice?**

MAY

26

"Don't you know that what goes into a person can't make him unclean?"

Mark 7:14–23

Years ago, I heard a story on the radio about a daughter who wanted to see a movie that her mother deemed inappropriate. One evening, after another heated discussion, the girl came into the kitchen as her mom prepared a salad. On top of the lettuce sat dirty carrot peelings, the tops of tomatoes and radishes—the parts of veggies that are usually discarded. "You can't expect me to eat that garbage!" the girl gasped. The mother responded, "That wouldn't be as bad as putting garbage in your mind."

Jesus made a similar point when the Pharisees criticized his disciples for not performing the Jewish ceremonial washing before meals. The Pharisees diligently followed all the purifying rituals and dietary restrictions, priding themselves on their avoidance of anything that might defile them. "Don't you know that whatever goes into a person from the outside can't make him unclean?" Jesus asked.

Jesus taught that what really makes a person morally unclean is what resides in their heart and mind. Evil thoughts produce evil actions: "sexual sins, stealing, murder, adultery, greed, wickedness, cheating, shameless lust, envy, cursing, arrogance, and foolishness." No amount of ceremonial washing can cleanse us from those.

Sin begins in the mind with an impure thought, fantasy, or attitude. These eventually come out in our behavior. Everything we read, see, and hear affects our thought life. It doesn't make sense to monitor the cleanliness and nutritional value of what we eat but fail to guard what enters our mind through television, books, interactions with other people, and the internet. If we don't like what's coming out of us, it might be time to evaluate what we're letting in.

Keep your thoughts on whatever is right or
deserves praise: things that are true, honorable,
fair, pure, acceptable, or commendable.

Philippians 4:8

Ask yourself: **How can I be more careful about what I put into my mind?**

"Who can notice every mistake?"

Psalm 19:7–14

Steven came home from work and went straight to the kitchen. One look at his wife told him what he wanted to know. Still no eye contact. When he'd tried to kiss her good-bye that morning, she'd turned her face away. *I sure wish I knew what I did wrong this time*, he thought. All he'd been able to get out of her was her standard: "If you don't know, I'm sure not going to tell you." Too bad she wouldn't accept his standard apology: "I'm sorry—I didn't mean to do whatever it was."

David expressed concern about unintentional sins in Psalm 19. As he meditated on the benefits of living by God's holy laws, he wanted to be completely cleansed of sin and live an upright life. David asked to be forgiven not just for the sins that he confessed but also the ones he might forget about or overlook. "Who can notice every mistake?" he prayed. "Forgive my hidden faults."

Self-examination is helpful and recommended in Scripture, but it's possible to take it too far. God doesn't want us to be consumed with worry, wondering if we have sins in our life that we don't notice. We shouldn't be plagued with anxiety that we've done something with impure motives, or neglected to do something we should have done. Excessive or false guilt can paralyze our spiritual growth and make us miserable.

Once we recognize sin in our life, we're responsible to deal with it through prayerful confession, repentance, and restitution when necessary. Then we can invite God to look closely into our heart and mind to reveal any unknown or unintentional sins. Rather than wonder if we've left anything out or obsess over possible wrongdoing, we can trust him to tell us what we need to know.

Examine me, O Lord, and test me. Look closely into my heart and mind.

Psalm 26:2

Ask God **to examine your heart and reveal any unconfessed sin you've overlooked.**

MAY
28

"What about him?"

John 21:18–23

Justin laid the papers down and looked at the sullen teenager sitting on the other side of his desk. He always felt relieved when a first-time offender received supervised probation and community service instead of a jail sentence. But he didn't get the usual response from this kid. Justin had outlined the requirements for the next eighteen months, emphasizing what could have happened with a harsher judge. "Any questions?" he asked. "Yeah," the boy said. "What about the other two guys?"

When Jesus told Peter something of what his future held, Peter was curious about what would happen to another disciple. Jesus predicted that Peter would be crucified as an old man. Then Jesus told Peter, "Follow me!" When Peter turned around and saw John behind them, he asked Jesus, "Lord, what about him?" Jesus rebuked Peter for the question: "If I want him to live until I come again, how does that concern you?" Then he repeated, "Follow me!"

Many people seem to have excessive curiosity about the details of other people's lives, as evidenced by the success of tabloids and so-called reality television shows. For some, this might be an entertaining escape, but for others it can become an obsession that lets them avoid focusing on their own lives. It becomes easier to watch someone else's struggles than to deal with their personal problems.

Christians can fall into the trap of comparing their lives with those of other believers. Our focus can shift from our own spiritual growth to curiosity about God's dealings with others. *Why did he choose to bless her so much? Is he going to let him get away with that?* We all have different abilities, different ministries, and different paths to travel. Our main concern needs to be the responsibilities God has given us, and how well *we* obey Jesus's call of "Follow me!"

Assume your own responsibility.
Galatians 6:5

Ask yourself: **Does curiosity about other people's lives distract me from my own walk with Christ?**

"Should I get one of the Hebrew women to nurse the baby for you?"

Exodus 2:1–9

Missy looked at the headline and felt sick. The "Cash for Clunkers" rebate program had ended, and she hadn't taken advantage of it. Missy had certainly qualified—she had the clunker, and she sure could use the cash. Plus, Missy planned to buy a new, gas-saving car anyway. *How could I have let such a golden opportunity slip through my fingers?* Missy asked herself.

Miriam was a young slave girl, but she seized a golden opportunity when she saw it. Pharaoh had ordered that all Hebrew newborn boys be thrown into the Nile. After hiding baby Moses for three months, his mother crafted a boat from a basket and placed it in the shelter of the dense reeds along the river. Then Miriam kept watch from a distance to see what would happen to her brother.

When Pharaoh's daughter came to bathe, she spotted the basket. Miriam heard the compassion in her voice when she recognized that the baby was Hebrew. In a flash, Miriam appeared with a suggestion: "Should I go and get one of the Hebrew women to nurse the baby for you?" Because Miriam grabbed this God-given opportunity, Moses's life was saved and his mother was paid to care for him during his first few years.

God wants us to be alert for opportunities that he sends our way. We want to make the most of openings to share the gospel and chances to encourage someone, do a good turn, or take a stand against evil. It's important to use our limited time on earth to the fullest instead of letting valuable opportunities slip through our fingers. God provides us with unexpected opportunities every day; it's up to us to recognize them and seize them.

Make the most of your opportunities
because these are evil days.

Ephesians 5:16

Ask yourself: **Do I actively look for ways to make the most of my God-given opportunities?**

MAY
30

"What do these stones mean to you?"

Joshua 4:1–9

In her large family Bible, my mother keeps a newspaper clipping from May 1969. Below a photo of a crumpled car driven by my brother are these words:

> Thomas E. Neal, 20, a sophomore at UTM, suffered only a minor nose cut and his passenger escaped uninjured at 7:25 Sunday when the 1968 Plymouth collided with a car in an adjacent lane, ran down a small ditch, struck a concrete fence, flipped over, and crushed its top on the pavement of a Loeb's Tasty Bar-B-Q near Reelfoot and Miles in Union City. Police said his car was estimated a total loss.

God knows how visual reminders can strengthen our faith. As the Israelites entered the Promised Land, God held back the spring floodwaters of the Jordan River while two million people crossed on dry ground. To help the Israelites remember this miracle, God had them take twelve stones from the middle of the Jordan and erect a memorial on the riverbank. In the future, when their children asked, "What do these stones mean to you?" they would be prompted to share what God had done that day.

When God works in our life in a powerful way, we feel as though we'll remember the details forever. But day-to-day living and the passing of time can dim even our most cherished memories. We can nurture our spiritual growth by following the Old Testament examples of having memorials to mark important events. Modern "memorials" might include a journal, a bulletin from a baptism or church service, photos, or decorative objects with Scriptures that hold special meaning for us. Anything that reminds us of how God has worked in our life will strengthen our faith and serve as a witness when someone asks, "What does this stone, or newspaper clipping, mean to you?"

I will remember the deeds of the L*ORD*.

Psalm 77:11

Ask yourself: **What events in my life call for a visual reminder of God's goodness?**

"Do I bring a mother to the moment of birth and not let her deliver?"

Isaiah 66:5–11

Ron opened his desk planner and almost sprayed coffee through his nose. "It can't be the thirtieth already!" he moaned. He'd promised his boss to finish those blueprints by the end of the month, but the rolled-up plans lay on his desk at home, untouched for weeks. *Why do I always do this?* Ron wondered. He'd always admitted being a procrastinator, but *this* unfinished project jeopardized his job.

God sometimes reminded Israel that he always finishes what he starts. Through the prophet Isaiah, God pronounced coming judgment on Israel for substituting external rituals for true worship while practicing idolatry. Even as he predicted their Babylonian captivity, God encouraged them to look forward to the day when Israel will be fully restored during the millennium.

Throughout Israel's history, people were tempted to believe that God had given up on the nation. God used a powerful image to drive home his point: "Do I bring a mother to the moment of birth and not let her deliver?" he asked. Just as the birth of a baby can't be stopped when the time comes, God will deliver on his promise to restore Israel when the due date arrives.

We can also trust God to finish what he started in us the moment we became a Christian. God's goal is to transform us into Christ's image, an ongoing process that will last throughout our lifetime. Some days we may feel we take two steps backward for every one step forward in our spiritual maturity. But God promises that someday we will be completed. In God's hands, we don't have to worry about ending up as an unfinished project.

I'm convinced that God, who began this good work in you,
will carry it through to completion on the day of Christ Jesus.

Philippians 1:6

Ask God **to help you trust him to finish transforming you into Christ's image, even when you don't see any progress.**

JUNE

1

"Why did you make me like this?"

Romans 9:14–21

Most people have something they would like to change about their appearance. If our hair is straight, we try to curl it; if we have naturally curly hair, we straighten it. Plastic surgeons rake in billions from people wanting to change the contours of their body, the shape of their nose, or the look of their skin. Even though Christians know that God created us, we can struggle with dissatisfaction. We may unconsciously ask God, "Why did you make me like this?"

In Romans 9, Paul used this question in a discussion about God's sovereignty. Paul had already addressed God's right to work out his purposes through people he created. Knowing that Jacob had a heart of faith and Esau did not, God chose the younger brother to form the nation of Israel. Later God used Pharaoh's rebellious heart to reveal himself to the world and demonstrate his power.

Then Paul used an analogy of a potter making things out of clay. How ludicrous to think of a clay object demanding to know why the potter shaped it in such a way. This illustration shows how silly it is for us to question the way God shaped us, or why he assigned us to a specific work or ministry. Since God is our Creator, he alone has the right to decide our life's purpose.

There's nothing wrong with wanting to improve our appearance—within reasonable boundaries. But we dishonor God when we continually compare ourselves with others and question how he made us. *Why didn't you give me that talent? Why couldn't I have had her opportunities? Why is his ministry growing more than mine?* After we learn to be content with how the Potter shaped us and where he put us, our question will be, "How can I bring you glory?"

I've learned to be content in whatever situation I'm in.

Philippians 4:11

Ask God **to help you learn to be content with the way he created you.**

JUNE
2

"How long will you gullible people love being so gullible?"

Proverbs 1:20–23

Lucky me! I laughed as I opened my email. Once again I had the incredible opportunity to make a ton of money by helping a Christian widow in Nigeria get her late husband's fortune from the bank. All I had to do was advance her a sum of money so the funds could be transferred. I couldn't hit the delete button soon enough.

Variations of the Nigerian Scam (also called Advance Fee Fraud or 4–1–9 Scam) have circulated for years and financially ruined countless people; some cases have even led to beatings or murder. There's never been a shortage of people who'd rather work hard at scamming somebody than do honest work; there's never been a shortage of people naïve enough to fall victim to them.

The book of Proverbs lists one of its purposes as "to give insight to gullible [also translated as 'simple' or 'naïve'] people." It pictures wisdom as a woman crying out in the streets, "How long will you gullible people love being so gullible?" Lady Wisdom then offers to pour out her spirit on gullible and foolish people, ending with a warning that trouble and calamity lie ahead if they refuse to listen.

Being susceptible to fake emails that are after our money can be costly; we also can't afford to be gullible about spiritual matters. Many Christians without a thorough knowledge of the Bible are taken in by bestselling books or popular movies claiming to share spiritual truth. They evaluate what they see and hear on the basis of their emotions or what sounds right. Paul praised the believers at Berea for examining the Scriptures to check out everything he taught (see Acts 17:11). Every day we have a choice: Will we be like the Bereans or the gullible people mentioned in Proverbs?

Your word is a doorway that lets in light, and
it helps gullible people understand.

Psalm 119:130

Ask yourself: **Do I rely on the Bible to check out spiritual teachings before I accept them as truth?**

JUNE
3

"Can you drink the cup that I'm going to drink?"

Matthew 20:20–23

Jonathan rubbed his neck and looked at the stack of files. How could he still have so much work to do after such a long day? He'd expected more responsibilities with the new position, but he hadn't been prepared to deal with this heavy load, plus handling all the customer complaints. Was the modest salary boost and private office worth it? His wife hated the work he brought home and the evening phone calls, even though she'd urged him to apply for the promotion in the first place.

The mother of James and John wanted a promotion for her sons. As a favor, she asked Jesus to seat her sons on his right and left, the positions of highest honor, in his future kingdom. "You don't realize what you're asking," Jesus replied. "Can you drink the cup that I'm going to drink?" Even though James and John had no idea what lay ahead, they answered without hesitating, "We can." Jesus affirmed that they would drink from the same cup, but he could not grant their request. God had already determined who would occupy positions of honor in his kingdom.

God has assigned each one of us a cup—our unique destiny as determined by him. Jesus knew his future included the bitter cup of crucifixion that he had to endure to reach the glory of the resurrection. Our destiny includes sharing in Christ's suffering to reach the day when we'll share his glory. We may face discrimination, ridicule, or even persecution. God may call us to give up things that we hold dear in order to serve others. Parts of our cup will be bitter, and parts will be sweet—but it's all a mixture prepared by God.

If we share in Christ's suffering in order to share his glory, we are heirs together with him.

Romans 8:17

Ask yourself: **Am I prepared to suffer as part of the cup assigned to me by God?**

"Who will rescue me from my dying body?"

Romans 7:14–25

A friend once told me about her son getting his arm stuck between the spindles of a kitchen chair when he was four years old. She didn't know it had happened until she went to see why he was so quiet. As she walked down the hall, she heard a whimpering voice saying, "Isn't somebody going to rescue the boy?"

Paul cried out to be rescued from a more common situation, one that we all face. In Romans 7 he describes the ongoing struggle between his old corrupt nature that pulled him toward sin and his new spiritual nature that desired to obey God. He loved God's standards in his mind, but the power of sin still waged war to take him captive. "What a miserable person I am!" he wrote. "Who will rescue me from my dying body?"

Christians are still vulnerable to temptation. Every day we have to live with the conflict between our old sinful nature and our new desire to obey God and live by his Spirit. Like Paul, we find ourselves doing the things we don't want to do, and failing to do the good that we intend. And like him, our failures can make us feel like a "miserable person."

We can't get our sinful nature under control through our own willpower or sheer determination not to sin. Following a set of rules won't work. We find freedom by calling on the only One who can rescue us. Through his death, Jesus liberated us once and for all from the penalty for sin. He also stands ready to free us day by day from sin's power as we ask for help and do our best to obey God's standards. One day Christ will deliver us forever from the presence of sin. Until then, he's always ready for a rescue mission when we feel stuck.

I thank God that our Lord Jesus Christ rescues me!

Romans 7:25

Ask yourself: **Do I remember to call on God to rescue me in my daily battles with my old sinful nature?**

JUNE

5

"Why did you despise my word by doing what I considered evil?"

2 Samuel 12:1–10

King David sat enthralled, listening to Nathan explain a legal case that needed judgment. A wealthy man with plenty of livestock had stolen a poor neighbor's only pet lamb to provide a meal for a guest. David erupted in anger, declaring that the rich man deserved to die for his actions. Then the prophet revealed the true purpose of the story.

"You are the man!" he declared. God had sent Nathan to confront David for his sin of sleeping with Bathsheba and then arranging to have her husband killed. "Why did you despise my word by doing what I considered evil?" the Lord demanded. As much as a year may have passed since the incident, and David had become so desensitized that he didn't recognize himself in the story until Nathan identified him as the villain.

God called David "a man after my own heart" (Acts 13:22). In the psalms David wrote, he often expressed love for God's laws and the importance of following them. Yet even David sometimes failed to honor God's Word by obeying it. The book of James reminds us to be doers of the Word, not just hearers of it. A person who reads Scripture without doing what it says is as foolish as someone who examines their reflection in a mirror and immediately forgets what they look like.

It's possible to be committed to Bible study without ever applying the Scripture to our life. God wants his Word to transform our attitudes, behavior, and lifestyle. We treat his Word with contempt when our Bible study turns into a mere intellectual exercise or an ingrained ritual that doesn't impact our thinking. We can read, study, meditate, and memorize but it won't do us any good unless we "do" too.

Do what God's word says. Don't merely
listen to it, or you will fool yourselves.

James 1:22

Ask yourself: **Do I sometimes despise God's Word by failing to apply what I read to my life?**

"Can I bring him back?"

2 Samuel 12:13–23

The young mother cradled the newly delivered baby in her arms and studied the tiny face, every feature perfect. Her husband gently stroked the dark hair and soft cheeks. They'd waited nine long months for a look at their baby; now they could hardly tear their eyes away—especially since this would be their last look for a long while. Their son's life had ended before he drew his first breath.

David and Bathsheba knew the pain of losing a baby. When their infant son became ill, David began to fast and pray. The child died after seven days, but the servants and palace officials dreaded telling David the news. They feared that he might do himself harm; instead, he bathed, worshiped in the Lord's house, and asked for food.

This shocked the people around him, who expected fasting and mourning *after* a death. "But why should I fast now that he's dead? Can I bring him back?" David asked them. "Someday I'll go to him, but he won't come back to me." David's words have brought comfort to countless families down through the ages who have lost infants or young children through illness, accidents, miscarriage, or abortion.

It would be hard to find someone who hasn't been impacted by the death of a baby or young child, either by personal experience or through a relative or friend. God recorded David's words to remind us that the souls of babies or young children go to be with God. Regardless of how their lives began or how they ended, he now holds them safe in his hands. David looked forward to being reunited with his lost son. We may not understand the details, but if we know Christ, then we can also look forward to a special family reunion someday.

[David said] "Someday I'll go to him,
but he won't come back to me."

2 Samuel 12:23

Ask yourself: **Whom do I look forward to being reunited with in heaven?**

JUNE
7

"Will you catch only a fleeting glimpse of wealth?"

Proverbs 23:4–5

Years ago, I watched a television program that followed up on several people who had won huge amounts of money in a lottery. In many of the cases, the winners lost their money due to foolish choices. Some of them were no better off than before. But even when people make wise investments and follow sound financial principles, they can wake up and find their money gone. Banks can fail, companies sometimes cut off retirement funds, and the stock market can nosedive.

The writer of Proverbs reminded his readers about the temporary nature of earthly wealth. For this reason, he advised them not to wear themselves out trying to get rich. "Will you catch only a fleeting glimpse of wealth before it is gone?" he asked. "It makes wings for itself like an eagle flying into the sky." Instead of spending our lives as workaholics, always pursuing more wealth, he recommended we become smart enough to know when we have enough.

Paul warned believers to watch their attitudes toward wealth (see 1 Tim. 6:17–19). God wants us to be careful not to let earthly riches pull us away from relying on him. Instead of hoarding our money, we are to be generous about sharing with others and investing in God's work. Growing rich in good deeds is the best way to build a solid foundation for our future.

How foolish to spend our life chasing temporary riches and neglect to build up heavenly treasures. Even if we spent our entire life on earth as a billionaire, that still represents a mere fleeting glimpse of wealth compared with eternity. What really matters is the riches that we'll have waiting for us in heaven. Those we get to enjoy forever.

Store up treasures for yourselves in heaven, where moths and rust don't destroy and thieves don't break in and steal.

Matthew 6:20

Ask yourself: **How am I storing up treasures in heaven?**

"Is there someone left to whom I can show God's kindness?"

2 Samuel 9:1–7

Brent groaned as he recognized the driver pulling up behind his stalled car. *Once I get out of my car, he won't be so willing to lend a hand*, he thought. It was no secret around the factory that Darren, the other driver, had been in line for the next opening in management. It also wasn't a secret that Brent had pulled some strings to secure the position for a relative. An hour later, Brent watched Darren drive away after making a trip to the auto store, getting Brent's car started, and following him home just in case.

Mephibosheth was also stunned when someone who should have been his enemy showered him with kindness. Saul had pursued David and tried to kill him numerous times, but David didn't follow the usual policy of a new king and wipe out his predecessor's family. "Is there someone left in Saul's family to whom I can show God's kindness?" he asked. Jonathan's disabled son came before the new king, trembling with fear. But David gave Mephibosheth Saul's property, a royal pension, and arranged for him to eat at the king's table.

Romans 12 explains that God expects us to resist the temptation to pay back evil for evil. Instead, we're to do good to our enemies, meeting their needs when we get the chance. Unexpected acts of kindness may soften the heart of someone who's done us wrong and make them penitent. Our obedience helps open the way for God's power to overcome evil with good.

David's treatment of Mephibosheth largely sprang from the covenant he had made with Jonathan to show kindness to his descendants. Our treatment of others should be based on our covenant with Christ. Since we've received such undeserved kindness from God, why wouldn't we want to pass that on?

Don't let evil conquer you, but conquer evil with good.

Romans 12:21

Ask yourself: **Do I give in to the desire to pay back evil for evil?**

JUNE
9

"Why was this man born blind?"

John 9:1–9

Bitterness consumed Marilyn for several years after the accident left her in a wheelchair. *What did I do to deserve this?* she cried out to God over and over. After her sister coaxed her into attending a Bible study, Marilyn gave her life to Christ. At first, she prayed for healing, but as time passed Marilyn's prayers changed. Now she grabs every opportunity to share her powerful testimony of how God used her disability to open doors for the gospel.

Seeing the blind man begging by the roadside reminded the disciples of a question they had wrestled with before. At the time, Jewish people believed that all suffering and tragedy resulted from sin. When a person was born with a disability, they wondered, did that person sin while in the womb, or did the disability represent payment for some sin of the parents?

"Rabbi," the disciples asked, "why was this man born blind? Did he or his parents sin?" Jesus answered that the man's blindness had not been caused by anyone's sin. God had permitted this disability in order to display his power and mercy. Then Jesus made mud, applied it to the man's eyes, and told him to wash it off in the pool of Siloam. The blind man received the gift of sight from the One who had earlier proclaimed himself "the Light of the world" (John 8:12).

Our natural human response when confronted with a disability is to wonder why it happened and to ask God to remove it. Sometimes God heals, but often he displays his mercy in other ways. Afflictions force us to rely more heavily on God. When he fills us with his power, we become stronger than we could ever be on our own. Our weakness and limitations are the perfect stage to display God's strength and power.

[The Lord said] "My power works best in your weakness."

2 Corinthians 12:9 NLT

Ask God **how he wants to be glorified through your limitations and weaknesses.**

JUNE
10

"How did he give you sight?"

John 9:10–26

I slipped into my seat as the opening scene began. Looking up at the screen, I was surprised how blurry and fuzzy the movie looked. Then I put on my 3D glasses and noticed a dramatic change. The image on the screen looked crystal clear, with rich color and depth. Water seemed to splash toward me and a butterfly tempted me to reach out my hand to touch it. I wondered how a cheap pair of plastic glasses could achieve such amazing effects.

Everyone wanted to know how the blind man in John 9 had received his sight. First his neighbors asked him. When some people took him to the Pharisees, they questioned him. Dissatisfied with his explanation, the Pharisees summoned his parents. They confirmed that their son had indeed been born blind, but were afraid to say more to the Jewish leaders.

Once again the Pharisees resumed their questioning of the man, hoping to find a flaw in his testimony or force him to recant. "What did he do to you?" they persisted. "How did he give you sight?" By now the ex-blind man had tired of repeating his story to people who obviously were determined not to believe him. He reminded them that since time began, no one had heard of a man born blind receiving sight (see John 9:32).

When we become a believer and God puts his Spirit in us, we have a new way of looking at things. God gives us discernment to understand spiritual concepts that didn't make sense before. Bible verses and familiar hymns take on new meaning. We see the world in a different way, from God's perspective. When we look through God's eyes, our spiritual vision switches from fuzzy to crystal clear—and the effects are amazing.

I am your servant; give me discernment that
I may understand your statutes.

Psalm 119:125 NIV

Ask God **to increase your discernment and understanding of his truth.**

JUNE
11

"Do you think we're blind?"

John 9:27–41

The formerly blind man saw something that the religious leaders couldn't see. As the Pharisees persisted in their questioning, the man pointed out that since time began no one had ever heard of a man born blind receiving sight. Didn't this prove that his healer had come from God? His words infuriated the self-righteous Pharisees, who accused him of being full of sin at birth and threw him out of the synagogue.

Soon the man saw his healer for the first time. When Jesus revealed his identity as the Son of Man, the ex-blind man bowed in worship. Then Jesus made a startling statement: "I have come into this world to judge: Blind people will be given sight, and those who can see will become blind." Jesus had come to reveal the true spiritual condition of people and to open the spiritual eyes of those who admitted their need.

Some Pharisees who heard the conversation knew that Jesus referred to spiritual blindness. "Do you think we're blind?" they asked. Jesus responded that the Pharisees were not blind in the sense of having no knowledge of God or his laws. But while they claimed to have spiritual insight, they rejected the Messiah and his message. They couldn't claim ignorance, yet they refused to see the truth before their very eyes.

Satan blinds the minds of unbelievers to keep them from seeing the light of the gospel. They don't understand who Christ is or why they need him. Spiritual principles make no sense to people until God's Spirit breaks through and brings light to their spiritual eyes. When we share God's truth with someone, it helps to remember that we see something they can't see yet, and only God can heal their spiritual blindness.

The god of this world has blinded the
minds of those who don't believe.

2 Corinthians 4:4

Ask God **to open the spiritual eyes of those who need to see the truth of the gospel.**

JUNE
12

"Who will go to heaven to get this command for us?"

Deuteronomy 30:6–14

Marcus hung up the phone and got ready to tell his wife the frustrating news. They'd waited for his new assignment for weeks, only to discover it had been sent to the wrong office. His sergeant couldn't help; things had to move through the proper chain of command. Now Marcus's marching orders sat on a clerk's desk, but he couldn't get his hands on them until the holiday weekend was over.

As the Israelites prepared to enter the Promised Land, Moses reminded them that God's commands were not inaccessible. God didn't keep his law in heaven, so that they needed to ask, "Who will go to heaven to get this command for us so that we can hear it and obey it?" It wasn't so distant that they should wonder, "Who will cross the sea to get it for us so that we can hear it and obey it?"

God had engraved the Ten Commandments in stone with his own finger. He had given Israel detailed instructions regarding worship, relationships, and civil law. "These words are very near you," Moses told them. "They're in your mouth and in your heart so that you will obey them." The people couldn't plead ignorance, and God had promised to enable them to obey his commands if they allowed him to change their hearts.

The Israelites had no excuse for not knowing and obeying God's will, and neither do we. Today we have access to his Word in written form, and his Spirit living inside us to help interpret the Scriptures and to guide us in making godly choices. We may sometimes wish God would write his will concerning a specific situation on a sticky note for us and post it where we can't miss it, but if we keep his Word close, we already have our marching orders.

Take these words of mine to heart and keep them in mind.

Deuteronomy 11:18

Ask yourself: **Do I study and meditate on God's Word to help me discern his will?**

JUNE

13

"Should people humble themselves for only a day?"

Isaiah 58:1–5

Mandy stepped back from the doorway. *I can't believe what I'm hearing!* she thought. She'd never expected her boss to be perfect, but she did think that working for a Christian would be different. But right now, there he stood in the copy room, blasting away at a secretary in language she never heard anyone using in church. Could this be the same man who'd helped serve communion last Sunday?

God sent a message through the prophet Isaiah to confront the hypocrisy of people who attended religious services but didn't obey God in their everyday lives. The people went to the temple regularly, offered sacrifices, and boasted about how often they fasted. They complained that although they'd done their part, God still didn't bless them. God let them know that outward rituals were no substitute for a real relationship with him.

While these people sometimes acted pious, the rest of the time they quarreled, mistreated their workers, and ignored the needy. When they fasted, they made sure everyone knew it. "Should people humble themselves for only a day?" God asked. "Is fasting just bowing your head like a cattail and making your bed from sackcloth and ashes? Is this an acceptable day to the Lord?"

God doesn't think much of our church attendance if we curse someone, lie, cheat, or flirt with a coworker during the week. It's easy to look like a devout Christian on Sunday, but the true test of our relationship with God starts on Monday. How do we reflect our faith when we're out in the real world facing difficult situations and tough choices? That's when our faith is on display for everyone to see. And that's why every day—not just Sunday—is a good day to humble ourselves before God.

This is the day the LORD has made.

Psalm 118:24

Ask yourself: **Does my life reflect my faith seven days a week, or only on Sundays?**

JUNE
14

"How long must I see the battle flag?"

Jeremiah 4:19–21

A political demonstration erupts into violence and bloodshed. Neighboring countries on the brink of war exchange threats. Innocent bystanders are killed by suicide bombers. A dictator continues his program of mass genocide. Rumors surface of nuclear weapons poised to strike. Sometimes I wonder, how can a person stay informed about world events without getting overwhelmed?

Jeremiah felt overwhelmed when he glimpsed his nation's future—judgment for their sin and rebellion. God described how the Babylonian army would invade from the north like a hot wind sweeping through and destroy the cities. Overcome with anguish at the impending disaster, Jeremiah cried out, "My heart is beating wildly! My heart is pounding! How long must I see the battle flag and hear the sound of rams' horns?"

We live in a time when extensive media coverage brings war right in front of our faces. Images and footage are played and replayed around the clock on televisions in homes and in public places. Even though we may not suffer the agony of those struggling to survive in war-torn countries, we identify with Jeremiah's question. *How long*, we wonder, *will we have to live in a world ripped apart by conflict and war?*

Jesus told his disciples that there would be wars until the end of time (see Mark 13:7). Although wars are consequences of human sin, God always works out his own purposes through them. Even though we're surrounded by violence and terrorism, we can know the peace that comes from trusting God's control over world events. The more we focus on his sovereignty, the more we'll be overwhelmed by his peace instead of what's going on around us.

Then God's peace, which goes beyond anything
we can imagine, will guard your thoughts
and emotions through Christ Jesus.

Philippians 4:7

Ask yourself: **How can I experience the peace of God more fully while living in a world filled with conflict and violence?**

JUNE
15

"Why are you so angry with your people?"

Exodus 32:1–14

The Israelites had grown restless. Apparently something had happened to their leader. They hadn't seen Moses since he climbed Mount Sinai forty days ago. Since Moses had left Aaron in charge, the people asked him to make gods who would go before them. They wanted the comfort of something tangible to see and worship. Aaron melted the Israelites' gold earrings and fashioned a statue of a calf, similar to the Egyptian and Canaanite gods. The next day, the people celebrated a festival, supposedly to honor the Lord. After making offerings to the statue, their feasting dissolved into an orgy.

Up on the mountain, God threatened to destroy the Israelites for their idolatry. "Lord," Moses pleaded, "why are you so angry with your people whom you brought out of Egypt using your great power and mighty hand?" Moses appealed to God's mercy on the basis of his promises to Israel's ancestors and on how the nation's destruction would look to the Egyptians.

God had recently commanded Israel to have no other gods, warning that he would not tolerate rivals (see Exod. 20:3–5). The people had promised to obey, but then they tried to add the calf statue to their worship of God. We look back on the Israelites' weird mix as ludicrous—without seeing that we often do the same thing. Any time we elevate someone or something next to God, or above him, we engage in idolatry. Our ministry, our family, or a gift from him can become an object of worship. Even an element of our worship, such as music or Bible study classes, can take God's rightful place. God still doesn't tolerate any rivals for our affection, and it still makes him angry.

Never worship any other god, because the LORD
is a God who does not tolerate rivals.

Exodus 34:14

Ask yourself: **Have I allowed anything or anyone to become God's rival in my heart?**

"What did these people do to you that you encouraged them to sin?"

Exodus 32:15–28

Moses walked down the mountain carrying a hard copy of the commandments that God had already given in verbal form to the Israelites. When he saw the people in the process of breaking at least three of the Ten Commandments, he smashed the stone tablets inscribed by God's hand. After Moses destroyed the calf statue, he demanded an explanation from Aaron: "What did these people do to you that you encouraged them to commit such a serious sin?"

Aaron had proved to be a poor substitute leader; now he showed that he was also a poor liar. First, he called the Israelites "evil" and emphasized that the problem stemmed from the people's feelings that Moses had deserted them. Then Aaron claimed he had merely thrown gold into the fire, and "out came this calf!" His absurd excuses did nothing to lessen the seriousness of what had happened. Three thousand people died that day as punishment.

Aaron had been given the special privilege of serving as Moses's spokesman before Pharaoh. He had witnessed God's miraculous powers time after time. Moses had entrusted him with leadership of the Israelites while he spent time with God on Mount Sinai. But when faced with pressure from the people, Aaron caved. Then he tried to deny any personal responsibility for the mess that resulted.

We're all susceptible to pressure from other people in some form. It may be subtle encouragement to change the way we think on an issue. Sometimes it's outright pressure to commit some immoral behavior. When faced with such pressure, it helps to look ahead to the potential long-term effects—and to remember that we can't lie our way out of personal responsibility. It can be hard to stand firm, but God will give us the strength to keep from caving.

But honorable people act honorably and
stand firm for what is honorable.

Isaiah 32:8

Ask yourself: **Do I have a hard time standing firm against pressure from others to compromise my beliefs?**

JUNE

17

"Didn't you realize that I had to be in my Father's house?"

Luke 2:41–50

According to a 2008 report by the Barna Group, one in four American adults had not attended a conventional church or any faith community gathering within the past year.[5] Yet 59 percent of this group considered themselves Christians.

Even at age twelve, Jesus felt irresistibly drawn to places of worship. When the Passover festival ended, Mary and Joseph started home with their caravan as usual. After a day's traveling, they discovered that Jesus had been left behind. The frantic parents returned to Jerusalem to search for their son, and finally found Jesus in the temple courtyard, deep in discussion with the teachers and rabbis. "Son, why have you done this to us?" Mary asked. Jesus seemed surprised that his parents would look anywhere besides the temple. "Why were you looking for me?" he responded. "Didn't you realize that I had to be in my Father's house?"

It was only natural that the Son of God would be found in his Father's house; as children of God, church is a natural place for us to be found. God created us to be part of a community, growing and sharing together. Members of a church family can comfort the hurting, strengthen the weak, and help with practical needs. We can study the Word together, pray for each other, join together in worship, and be a witness of God's love to the world around us.

When the letter to the Hebrews was written, some believers had abandoned the habit of gathering with other Christians. The writer urged them to continue meeting. With our busy lives, we may be tempted to skip Bible studies or church services. But there's no better place to be than in our Father's house.

We should not stop gathering together with other believers, as some of you are doing.

Hebrews 10:25

Ask yourself: **Do I place a high priority on worship and fellowship with other believers?**

5. "New Statistics on Church Attendance and Avoidance," March 3, 2008. www.barna.org.

"Why do you eat with tax collectors and sinners?"

Luke 5:27–32

I don't think I can do this, Cameron thought as he climbed out of the church van. It seemed like such a noble idea when they discussed it in church. But now he wished he hadn't joined the team that witnessed to the inner-city homeless. The ragged man sitting in the alley lifted up a dirt-smudged face as they approached. *Do I really want to spend time here?* Cameron asked himself.

Jesus never hesitated to spend time with anyone who needed or wanted to hear about God. When Levi (also called Matthew) responded to Jesus's call of "Follow me," he left his profession but brought his bad reputation with him. Tax collectors were hated for supporting the Roman government, and often for cheating people by overcharging them and then pocketing more than their fair share.

Levi wanted others to meet Jesus, so he hosted a large reception in his home for his friends and former associates. The Pharisees reacted in disgust when they saw Jesus having a meal with such people. "Why do you eat and drink with tax collectors and sinners?" they asked. Jesus responded that he came to call those ready to repent, not waste time on self-righteous people who refused to recognize their own sin.

The Pharisees prided themselves on distinguishing between the "righteous" and the "sinners." They guarded their reputation by avoiding people who might make them unclean by association. While we don't use the word "unclean" today, we're still familiar with the principle.

Many of us have groups that we avoid associating with, whether it is the poor, the mentally challenged, the physically handicapped, certain ethnic groups, or the over-pierced and tattooed. However, sometimes the people we avoid are the very ones who need our attention. Why would we associate with such people? Simply because God loves them.

There is no difference between people. Because all people have sinned, they have fallen short of God's glory.

Romans 3:22–23

Ask yourself: **Have I been avoiding someone who needs to hear about God's love and forgiveness?**

JUNE
19

"Whose daughter are you? Whose son are you?"

Genesis 24:23; 1 Samuel 17:58

In biblical times, a person's identity was rooted in their parentage. The Bible often introduces people as "son of" or "daughter of" someone. When Abraham sent his servant to find a wife for Isaac, God directed him to a beautiful young woman. The servant didn't ask her name; he asked, "Whose daughter are you?" Rebekah answered, "I'm the daughter of Bethuel, son of Milcah and Nahor."

When King Saul watched a teenage boy striding out to take on the giant who terrified the Israelite army, he told his army commander to find out whose son he was. As David stood before Saul with Goliath's head in his hand, Saul asked, "Whose son are you, young man?" David replied, "The son of your servant Jesse of Bethlehem."

As Christians, our identity is rooted in our heavenly Father. It may be popular to say that "we're all God's children," but that's not true. God only gives that right to those who believe in Jesus Christ (see John 1:12). The Bible labels those who don't believe in him as "children of the devil" (1 John 3:10). When God adopts us, he puts his Spirit in us to let us know that we belong to him. As we learn to be led by that Spirit, it becomes obvious to the world whose son or daughter we are.

Human fathers are imperfect and prone to mistakes. Some seem distant; others appear to be nonexistent. But our heavenly Father is perfect and loves us unconditionally. He provides for us and guards our future inheritance. And he encourages us to call out to him as our "Abba," an intimate term used by young children to address their father. Regardless of who our earthly father is, we have a heavenly Father who will never let us down.

He loves us so much that we are actually called God's dear children. And that's what we are.

1 John 3:1

Ask yourself: **Can other people tell who my Father is?**

"What has happened that you are going to reveal yourself to us and not to the world?"

John 14:22–31

As I glanced out the window, the huge harvest moon caught my eye. *Hard to believe that glowing ball is just reflecting light from another source*, I mused. From my vantage point on earth, I hadn't been able to see the sun for a few hours. But the moon clearly revealed the sun's presence by reflecting its light in the dark sky.

Just before his death, Jesus told his disciples that in a little while the world would no longer be able to see him, but *they* would. He promised he would show himself to those who loved him. "Lord," one of them asked, "what has happened that you are going to reveal yourself to us and not to the world?"

In his response, Jesus said that he and the Father will make their home with those who love him and obey his teachings. When the disciples received the promised gift of the Holy Spirit after Jesus returned to heaven, they began to understand what Jesus had tried to teach them. It became clear that just as Jesus had revealed God the Father to people, his followers had the responsibility to reveal Jesus the Son to the world.

God designed us to be reflections of his glory. People who don't know him have a veil covering their mind that keeps them from understanding the truth. As believers with the Spirit living in us, we can see God's glory. As we grow more like Christ, we reflect his image to those around us. It's amazing how bright the moon can be as it reflects the sun's light. And it's amazing how beautiful our life can be when we reflect the light of the Son.

As all of us reflect the Lord's glory with faces that are not covered with veils, we are being changed into his image with ever-increasing glory.

2 Corinthians 3:18

Ask yourself: **How brightly does my life shine with a reflection of God's glory?**

JUNE
21

"What do we gain if we pray to him?"

Job 21:7–15

Job's friends claimed that wicked people never prosper because God judges them during their lifetime, but Job knew this wasn't always the case. He argued that the evil often lead happy lives with thriving families, even while they mock the idea that they need God. "Who is the Almighty that we should serve him?" Job imagines them asking. "What do we gain if we pray to him?"

We might not want to admit it, but most of us have felt that way at some time. Maybe we got discouraged after covering a situation in prayer but not noticing any change. Or maybe we grew tired of praying for the same person every day for years without seeing an answer. We might have felt overwhelmed when we looked at a situation that seemed completely hopeless and asked, "What good would my prayers do?"

In spite of what we're feeling at the moment, a good reason to pray is that God commands it. He instructs us to pray continually. In addition to our regular time of extended prayer, God wants us to hold on to a prayerful attitude at all times. As we go through the day with an awareness of his presence and our dependence on him, we'll automatically react to any situation with short, spontaneous prayers.

God knows how much we need prayer for our own benefit. Even when our prayers don't visibly change our circumstances, they change us. We begin to see things from his viewpoint instead of from our narrow, self-centered perspective. Our faith grows as we learn to trust his control over our life. Prayer doesn't guarantee that we'll always get the answers we want, but any time we engage in heartfelt conversation with God, we gain something.

Never stop praying.

1 Thessalonians 5:17

Ask yourself: **Do I ever feel that my prayers are useless?**

Ask God **to renew your passion for prayer and give you a deeper understanding of its power.**

"What do I have left?"

Judges 18:11–26

The couple stared at the pile of debris that bore their address. As the shock gradually subsided, the memories flooded back. Years of saving for their dream home had been followed by several years of building, as they did much of the work with their own hands. Then came the decision to celebrate its completion with a vacation in Hawaii. Now, all those years of planning and hard work had been wiped out within moments. Even the cars in the garage had been totaled. The tornado had made sure they had nothing left.

The man in today's passage felt as though he had nothing left. As a band of warriors from Dan passed by Micah's house, they stopped to steal his collection of idols. When the Levite hired by Micah to be his household priest questioned them, the men persuaded him to come away and serve the tribe of Dan instead of Micah's family.

Micah soon discovered his loss and confronted the rear guard of the Danites. "You've taken away the gods I made as well as my priest," he complained. "What do I have left?" Since Micah had traded true worship of God for manmade idols and a hired priest, the removal of those things left him feeling empty.

Manmade things can be stripped away from our life at any moment. The work of our hands can be lost without warning. If that happens, will our relationship with God be enough to see us through? Earthly losses can devastate us and make us feel empty—for a while. But we can trust God to fill our life with what we truly need. Losing material possessions we value is painful, but God can use the experience to help our faith grow as we learn to depend on what really counts—and what can never be taken away.

These things that I once considered valuable,
I now consider worthless for Christ.

Philippians 3:7

Ask yourself: **If I lost everything except my relationship with Christ, would that be enough for me?**

JUNE
23

"Are you as loyal to me as I am to you?"

2 Kings 10:12–17

God had determined to wipe out King Ahab's evil dynasty, and Jehu became the instrument of his judgment. But in his zeal and desire for personal power, Jehu went too far and slaughtered innocent people, an act for which God would later condemn Jehu's dynasty. After killing a group of Ahab's relatives that he met on the road to Samaria, Jehu met Jehonadab coming to meet him.

Jehonadab and his family faithfully followed God and obeyed the Mosaic law. Jehu knew that he and Jehonadab agreed on the need to rid Israel of Baal worship and restore worship of Yahweh. But his burning question was whether Jehonadab would align himself with Jehu's policy of ridding the nation of Ahab's family line. "Are you as loyal to me as I am to you?" Jehu asked. When Jehonadab answered in the affirmative, Jehu asked for his hand. Jehonadab's ride in the chariot with Jehu signified agreement and commitment.

None of us could answer in the affirmative if God asked us the question that Jehu asked. Even though we want to have faith that never wavers, most of us will have temporary lapses. We may act like we don't know him in certain surroundings. We may let other pursuits temporarily turn our heart away from him. There may even be times when we've endured so much disappointment and suffering that we wonder if we have any faith left.

Thankfully, God's faithfulness doesn't depend on ours. He will never turn his back on his children even when our loyalty is questionable. It would go against his character and his Word. Since God has pledged such faithfulness to us, how can we do less than try to keep our heart loyal to him?

If we are unfaithful, he remains faithful
because he cannot be untrue to himself.

2 Timothy 2:13

Ask yourself: **How can my life demonstrate more loyalty to Christ?**

"How can I be certain that I will take possession of it?"

Genesis 15

God had made some incredible promises to Abram: to make him into a great nation, to bless the entire world through him, to give him the land of Canaan, and to make his descendants as numerous as the dust of the earth. Now Abram was old and still childless. It appeared that his servant Eliezer would be his heir.

God declared that a son from Abram's own body would be his heir, and he compared Abram's future descendants to the stars in the sky. Abram had believed and followed God, but now he needed assurance that God would fulfill these promises that seemed impossible from a human standpoint. "Almighty LORD, how can I be certain that I will take possession of it?"

God responded to Abram's question by enacting a formal covenant with him and giving more specific details about the future of Abram's descendants. The ancient customs associated with making a covenant seem strange to us today, but Abram knew the transaction meant a binding agreement. God had given him the assurance he asked for—and more.

God has made incredible promises to anyone who has become his child through believing in Jesus: forgiveness and freedom from the penalty of sin, his daily presence to fill our earthly life with meaning and purpose, and a glorious eternity with him after our body dies.

When we struggle with our sinful nature, we may need assurance that these promises will come to pass. God has already given us the confirmation we seek. As part of the new covenant, we are sealed with God's Spirit. The Holy Spirit serves as a deposit on a binding agreement, guaranteeing what is to come. If we're God's child, then our inheritance is a sure thing.

This Holy Spirit is the guarantee that
we will receive our inheritance.

Ephesians 1:14

Ask yourself: **Do I ever doubt God's promises concerning my future?**

JUNE
25

"What causes fights and quarrels among you?"

James 4:1–3

When Pete and Lorraine moved to a new town, they quickly found a church that felt like home. But soon, the couple decided to keep looking. The congregation seemed more like a group of cliques competing with each other than a church family coming together to worship God. Committee meetings resembled debates, and tempers flared at business meetings as members argued about details of the new building program.

Dissension within the church has been a problem since its earliest days. "What causes fights and quarrels among you?" James asked his readers. The strong language he used indicates the seriousness of the problem. The Greek word translated as "fights" literally refers to "a state of war." James answered his own question with another question for his readers to ponder: "Aren't they caused by the selfish desires that fight to control you?"

James pointed out that conflicts within the church usually stem from our self-centered desires. Many times we convince ourselves that we're courageously taking a stand when we're really just trying to get our own way. Just before his crucifixion, Jesus prayed for unity among believers (see John 17:21). He wanted us to be united on the basis of our relationship with him rather than divided by our differences.

A church family united in love and obedience to God's will presents a powerful witness to the world. But too often outsiders look at a church and see a group of people letting personal opinions turn into petty disagreements, which sometimes escalate into serious conflicts. How can we maintain unity among a diverse group of people? We can avoid gossip and useless arguing, respect our leaders, and accept each other's individual differences in matters not related to core doctrine. And we can pray that what we hold in common will hold us together when divisive issues crop up.

Through the peace that ties you together, do your best to maintain the unity that the Spirit gives.

Ephesians 4:3

Ask yourself: In what ways do I contribute to the unity of my church family?

"What is life?"

James 4:13–16

The family climbed down the steps, disappointed that they hadn't found what they expected. The sign on the lookout tower had promised breathtaking views of the nearby mountains, but the early morning fog and mists rising from the valley had blocked the view. However, when the family returned a few hours later they found that the fog had cleared, and busily snapped photos of the beautiful scenery.

The Bible uses the image of a mist or vapor to remind us how brief our earthly life is in the overall scheme of things. James warned against taking our future plans for granted without considering God's will. "What is life?" he wrote. "You are a mist that is seen for a moment and then disappears." In the middle of setting goals and mapping out our future, we can easily forget how uncertain life really is.

Many people spend their lives pursuing pleasure, accumulating material possessions, and making lofty plans while leaving God out of the picture. How would we live differently if we remembered to weigh the brevity of earthly life against eternity? Would our activities change if we evaluated them on the basis of how much lasting value they have? Would some worries and concerns fall away as we concentrated on using what time we have to live for Christ?

No matter how many years God grants us, life is short and can fade away at any moment. This thought can be frightening if we don't know what lies ahead. Believers know that when this fleeting time on earth ends, then our real life begins—an eternity spent with God in a place completely free from the influence of sin. The mist of our earthly life will disappear—and boy, will we see some breathtaking views then.

Teach me about the number of days I have left so that I may know how temporary my life is.

Psalm 39:4

Ask yourself: **Does my daily life reflect awareness that my time on earth is temporary?**

JUNE
27

"Isn't there medicine in Gilead?"

Jeremiah 8:18–22

Jenny unlocked her sister's apartment and headed straight for the bathroom. One look in the medicine cabinet told her what she needed to know. *Why does she always do this?* Jenny wondered. Ever since her sister had been diagnosed with schizophrenia, the family had struggled to convince her to stay on her medication. But after she felt better for a while, she often stopped taking it—and ended up hospitalized. Jenny slumped against the shower door and thought about how much misery could be avoided if her sister would just take her pills.

Jeremiah felt deeply about the misery his people had brought on themselves because they refused to stay faithful to God. Even as they worshiped idols, the people complained that the Lord had deserted them. God countered that their punishment had been caused by their own sin. Sharing God's words, Jeremiah cried out, "Isn't there medicine in Gilead? Aren't there doctors there? Then why hasn't the health of my dear people been restored?"

Gilead was renowned for the healing ointments and medicines available there—for people who chose to use them. God had made his healing Word available to Israel, but they had rejected it. They preferred to seek advice from false prophets rather than the Great Physician. Even now, God held the cure for their self-inflicted wounds—but they refused to take it.

God's Word offers the cure for all sorts of spiritual ailments, whether we suffer from the effects of sin, pain from past hurts, a distorted self-image, or false guilt. Sometimes we reject his advice and look to another source, then ask why we haven't been healed. God writes the prescription, but we choose whether or not to take the medicine we need.

> *I said, "O LORD, have pity on me! Heal my soul because I have sinned against you."*
>
> Psalm 41:4

Ask yourself: **How do I need to apply God's healing Word in my life right now?**

"Death, where is your sting?"

1 Corinthians 15:42–57

As I left the memorial service, I couldn't help contrasting it with other funerals I'd attended. Family and friends browsed through photos from the past and looked at examples showing the young mom's love of crafts. As people shared favorite memories, their words painted the picture of a life spent loving God and others. Her husband and children missed her, but they embraced the knowledge that she had gone home, freed at last from pain and suffering. This truly was a celebration of life and hope.

Paul reminded the Christians at Corinth that death is necessary, since we can't go into God's presence in our earthly body that's corrupted by sin. We have to be changed, either by death or by instant transformation when Jesus returns to earth. Death means that we trade in our weak, imperfect physical body for one that is eternal, perfect, and not limited by the laws of nature.

Adam's sin allowed death to enter the world; Jesus's death and resurrection broke sin and death's power over the human race. We still inhabit a decaying physical body for a while, but when it dies our life will go on forever. "Death, where is your victory?" Scripture asks. "Death, where is your sting?"

The hope of the resurrection lies at the center of our faith. It strengthens us to face the hardships of this life because we can look forward to eternal life with God. It reminds us that any pains, disabilities, or physical ailments are only temporary. And it gives us the comfort of knowing that we will someday be reunited with our loved ones who had faith in Christ. We'll still grieve and feel hurt when someone dies, but we can rejoice that death no longer has the power to destroy.

Those who believe in me will live even if they die.

John 11:25

Ask yourself: **How does the hope of the resurrection affect my attitude toward death?**

JUNE
29

"Whom will I send?"

Isaiah 6:1–8

Isaiah had the privilege of glimpsing God's splendor and holiness, and the vision changed him forever. The prophet saw God lifted up on a throne, with the bottom of his robe filling the whole temple. Angelic beings flew around the throne proclaiming God's glory. As they cried out, the doorposts shook and the temple filled with smoke. In the same instant that Isaiah saw God's purity, his eyes were opened to his own sinfulness.

One of the angels touched Isaiah's lips with a burning coal from the altar, symbolizing that Isaiah's guilt had been removed. Now that Isaiah had been cleansed, God offered an opportunity for service. "Whom will I send? Who will go for us?" he asked. Knowing that his people needed to be cleansed, too, Isaiah answered at once: "Here I am. Send me!"

God still reigns on his throne today, and he still looks for people to send out. We may feel as inadequate as Isaiah did initially, but each one of us is called to be God's spokesperson. The more we understand God's holiness, the more we become aware of our sinfulness. After God cleanses us and removes our guilt, why wouldn't we be ready to take every opportunity to share with others who also need to hear about his forgiveness?

God probably won't put a hot coal on our lips, but he may place a burning desire in our heart. He gives some people a burden to go into full-time ministry to a specific country or group of people. Other times, he prompts people to support missionaries with financial support or prayer. Sometimes he leads people to get involved in short-term missions projects. And he often lays a specific person with needs on someone's heart. Whatever the destination, God wants us ready to go whenever he calls.

Here I am. Send me!

Isaiah 6:8

Ask yourself: **Am I ready and willing to go wherever God wants to send me?**

JUNE
30

"Didn't I tell you that if you believe, you would see God's glory?"

John 11:38–44

In his popular meditation *My Heart, Christ's Home*, Robert Boyd Munger illustrates Christian discipleship with a vivid metaphor of a person inviting Jesus to come and live in his home.[6] Each room represents a different aspect of the person's life. After a while, Jesus confronts the owner about a locked closet giving off a foul stench. The owner argues and debates but reluctantly gives Jesus the key. He later marvels at the difference in his home that resulted from letting Jesus clean out that closet.

When Jesus wanted to unseal Lazarus's tomb, Martha protested that the stench would be too great. Her brother had been dead for four days and his body would already be decaying. Jesus gently rebuked Martha for not trusting him. "Didn't I tell you that if you believe, you would see God's glory?" he reminded her. Martha relented. A few moments later she witnessed God's glory in a way she never expected as her beloved brother returned to life.

Most of us have aspects of our life that we try to seal off from God. In our head, we know we can't hide anything from an all-knowing God. But whether consciously or subconsciously, we avoid dealing with a certain problem area and hope he won't notice. If God truly knew what was stuffed in that smelly closet, wouldn't he be offended? Would it change his feelings for us?

God does not force his help on us if we're not willing to accept it. But he wants to clean up every area of our life. Once we trust God enough to turn complete control of our life over to him, we'll see amazing changes. As we let him clean out all the garbage from our life—even that closet we've tried to seal away—we'll see his glory in ways we never expected.

Jesus said, "Take the stone away."

John 11:39

Ask yourself: **Is God asking permission to uncover a sealed area of my life?**

6. Robert Boyd Munger, *My Heart, Christ's Home*, expanded ed. (Downers Grove, IL: InterVarsity, 1986).

JULY

1

"Who wants to listen to him anymore?"

John 6:48–60

The Jewish people loved to hear the story of how God gave their ancestors manna, the bread from heaven, during their forty years of wandering in the wilderness. They probably felt a little uncomfortable when Jesus referred to himself as the bread of life that came from heaven. Their confusion increased when he said that his flesh was the bread that gave everlasting life.

Then Jesus made comments that really shocked them. He stated that only those who ate his flesh and drank his blood would receive eternal life. His words sounded absurd to them. "What he says is hard to accept," they complained. "Who wants to listen to him anymore?"

Jesus used the eating and drinking illustration to show that discipleship calls for an intimate relationship with him. How his listeners responded revealed their true motivation for following him. Watching Jesus heal sick people, drive out evil spirits, multiply food, and perform other miracles had proved exciting. Listening to his messages of God's lavish love and mercy was rewarding. But many found either the wording or the meaning of this new teaching unacceptable.

Jesus has many followers today who react in similar ways. Some people come to church for the pretty music, potlucks, and holiday programs. They're willing to sit through a message as long as it's positive and affirming. But they draw the line at a message that calls for self-denial and sacrifice. Even committed Christians may display a similar attitude, avoiding Scripture passages that seem difficult to obey or comprehend. But being a disciple means trusting in God even when we find his commandments disagreeable or hard to understand. It means that we *always* want to listen to him.

Trust the LORD with all your heart, and do
not rely on your own understanding.

Proverbs 3:5

Ask God **to help you trust him even when what he says is difficult to understand.**

“To what person could we go?”

John 6:61–69

Jesus’s words about eating his flesh and drinking his blood offended many of his followers. “Did what I say make you lose faith?” he asked. “The words that I have spoken to you are spiritual. They are life. But some of you don’t believe.” At that point, the religious leaders and many who had professed to be his disciples deserted him, proving that their initial faith was not genuine.

Turning to the twelve disciples, Jesus asked, “Do you want to leave me too?” Peter answered for the group, “Lord, to what person could we go? Your words give eternal life. Besides, we believe and know that you are the Holy One of God.” There was still much about Jesus and his mission the disciples didn’t understand, but they recognized him as the Messiah. Although the deserters had called Jesus’s words “hard to accept,” the apostles knew that his words represented the only source of life.

As Christians, we know that salvation can be found only through faith in Jesus. But many believers get into the habit of following too closely after someone else. Maybe we live for the latest Bible study or television broadcast of a charismatic leader or teacher. Or maybe we eagerly await the latest release of our favorite author. Or maybe we run to our pastor whenever we need spiritual guidance.

There’s nothing wrong with drawing on any of these resources as long as the teaching is based on the solid foundation of God’s Word. But we sometimes forget that we have the privilege of going directly to Jesus with our needs. With the help of his Spirit, prayer, and the Bible, we can find guidance, comfort, and instruction. Sometimes we don’t need to go to another person.

No one else can save us. Indeed, we can be saved only by the power of the one named Jesus and not by any other person.

Acts 4:12

Ask yourself: **Am I following after a person or leader when I should be going directly to Jesus?**

JULY
3

“What example can I give you?”

Lamentations 2:13–14

When Jeremiah began his ministry, Jerusalem faced impending judgment even as false prophets delivered messages of peace and safety. The people chose to listen to these lies instead of admitting their sins. As Jeremiah warned the people of their need to repent, he asked, “What example can I give you? What parallel can I show you, people of Jerusalem?”

God has given us his Word filled with examples to comfort, warn, instruct, and encourage us. Israel’s history illustrates how rebellion against God leads to slavery to sin, but also reminds us that he stands ready to restore if we repent. The book of Judges demonstrates how low people can sink when God’s absolute standards of right and wrong are rejected and people do what seems right to them.

Noah shows that faith can keep us afloat in the storms of life. Ruth’s life demonstrates that God may have a wonderful surprise waiting when he calls us to leave our comfort zone. Jonah shows that it doesn’t pay to run away from God; the prodigal son proves that you *can* go home again. Martha’s life warns that enthusiasm for serving can distract us from what really matters. Abraham’s and Sarah’s lives illustrate that God always keeps his promises but it’s best to wait for his timing.

Every story, character sketch, conversation, letter, and poem in the Bible contains an important lesson for us. Each one offers a chance to deepen our understanding of God and nurture our spiritual growth. We can often avoid failure and pain by heeding the lessons from biblical characters and events that parallel our current circumstances. But by far, the most important example to study is Jesus, the ultimate pattern of a life pleasing to God.

Everything written long ago was written to teach us so that we would have confidence through the endurance and encouragement which the Scriptures give us.

Romans 15:4

Ask God to lead you to the biblical example that relates to your life right now. What does he want you to learn?

JULY
4

"How can you say that we will be set free?"

John 8:30–36

Parades, picnics, fireworks, and sales at the mall—we have a lot to choose from on this national holiday. But our observance doesn't always honor the meaning of our nation's birthday. The United States was born when the Continental Congress formally adopted the Declaration of Independence in 1776, signaling our intention to become an independent nation and break ties with Great Britain. It's easy to get wrapped up in the festivities of the holiday and miss the chance to celebrate the hard-won freedom we enjoy.

Many of the Jews who listened to Jesus were so wrapped up in their pride and self-righteousness that they missed the true freedom he offered. When Jesus said the truth would set them free, they protested: "We are Abraham's descendants, and we've never been anyone's slaves. So how can you say that we will be set free?"

Jesus accused them of being slaves to sin. Even though they were physical descendants of Abraham, they were not his spiritual children because they refused to believe in God's Son. These men had no sense of their bondage to sin, so they didn't see how desperately they needed the freedom that the Son offered.

Jesus suffered and died to set us free from sin's control and Satan's grip. Once that bondage is broken, we have the freedom to follow God and to be the person he created us to be. But pride, rebellion, legalism, and compromising with sin can keep us from fully living out our freedom in Christ. Through his sacrificial death, Jesus offers us the ultimate Independence Day. But here's the paradox: in order to experience that wonderful freedom, we have to submit and be dependent on him.

If the Son sets you free, you will be absolutely free.

John 8:36

Ask yourself: **Do I live in the freedom from sin's bondage that Jesus died to secure for me?**

JULY
5

"Where's your big mouth now?"

Judges 9:26–41

In 2002, talk show host Linda Goldfarb launched her radio program. "I knew God did not want a show that condoned bobble-head Christianity, where we nod in agreement but don't put feet to our faith," she explained. As a result, her program *Not Just Talkin' the Talk* is based on James 1:22: "Do what God's word says. Don't merely listen to it." Each week Linda invites expert guests in different fields "to share their stories and equip our listeners to walk-the-walk spiritually, physically, and relationally in their everyday lives."

Talk is cheap and always has been. After the people of Shechem turned against Abimelech, Gaal moved into the area and won their trust. At a festival celebration, Gaal ridiculed both Abimelech and Zebul, his officer. He boasted about what he would do if *he* were in charge, how he would challenge Abimelech to get himself a big army and come out to fight.

Zebul reported Gaal's words to Abimelech, who set up an ambush. When Gaal saw the troops coming, Zebul challenged him. "Where's your big mouth now?" Zebul reminded Gaal of his boastful claims and urged him to fight. Gaal led a force against Abimelech, but ended up running away and being thrown out of Shechem.

God could ask that same question to a lot of believers. Some of us talk a lot about what we believe but fail to live it out. It's easy to talk about obedience and then ignore difficult commands, or claim we serve him but run away from anything that challenges our faith.

The Christian life isn't about knowing the right words to say; it's about living a life transformed by our trust in God and a desire to do his will. What we say means nothing if there's no evidence of God's power working through us. God doesn't want our empty words; he wants us to put our faith into action and "walk the walk."

God's kingdom is not just talk, it is power.

1 Corinthians 4:20

Ask yourself: **Is my Christianity more about saying the right things, or living a righteous lifestyle?**

"Do you know that the Lord is going to take your master from you today?"

2 Kings 2:1–6

That will be Dad calling to reschedule our fishing trip, Troy thought, as the phone rang. His relationship with his father had been strained—to put it mildly—since Troy's rebellious teen years. But lately the two men had actually been learning how to get along with each other. Still, Troy hadn't been able to pass up canceling their plans last Saturday in order to hang with the guys and watch the game at the sports bar. *I'll do something with him this weekend*, Troy told himself as he picked up the phone. A few minutes later, he sat in shock after hearing the news of his dad's fatal heart attack.

We never know when we'll see someone for the last time on earth, but Elisha had a heads-up concerning his mentor. As he traveled with Elijah, two different groups of prophets asked him, "Do you know that the Lord is going to take your master from you today?" Each time, Elisha answered, "Yes, I know. Be quiet." Three times Elijah urged him to remain behind, but Elisha refused. He had determined to be with his spiritual father until the last possible moment.

Our family members and friends can be taken away from us at a moment's notice. It's vital that we make the most of the time we have with each other. Today might be our last chance to apologize and ask for forgiveness, to say "I love you," or to just sit and listen to a loved one. This day may be the last opportunity to learn from a mentor, encourage a brother or sister in Christ, or share the gospel with an acquaintance before they leave this earth. Since we don't know when we'll see someone for the last time, we can spare ourselves future regrets by not leaving things unsaid.

Encourage each other every day while
you have the opportunity.

Hebrews 3:13

Ask yourself: **Is there someone I need to spend time with today?**

JULY
7

"What should I do for you before I'm taken from you?"

2 Kings 2:7–15

As Elijah spent his last hours on earth, he thought of his son in the faith who would be staying behind. As they walked and talked together, Elijah asked, "What should I do for you before I'm taken from you?" Elisha answered, "Let me inherit a double share of your spirit." Although Elijah didn't hold the power to grant such a request, he offered a sign that would confirm God's decision. If Elisha saw his master taken away, then he could expect to receive what he asked for.

Later, the two men's conversation halted when a fiery chariot and horses separated them and Elijah was swept up to heaven in a whirlwind. Elisha cried out in grief and then picked up Elijah's coat. When he used it to strike the Jordan River as Elijah had done earlier, the waters parted. This repeat of the miracle further confirmed that God had appointed Elisha to carry on Elijah's work.

Since we don't know when our last day on this earth will be, it's important that we stay mindful of those we'll leave behind. What should we do for our loved ones before we're taken away? If we do our best to live a godly life and honestly share about our faith journey with others, we'll leave a legacy that will have a lasting impact long after we're gone.

God expects each of us to pass on truths we've learned to fellow believers, who will in turn pass them on to others. That way, the inheritance of God's riches gets handed down through successive generations. A trust fund is nice, but when it comes to legacies, a life lived for Christ is the ultimate gift to leave behind.

Now teach these truths to other trustworthy people
who will be able to pass them on to others.

2 Timothy 2:2 NLT

Ask yourself: **What kind of legacy am I preparing to leave behind?**

"Who can oppose the descendants of Anak?"

Deuteronomy 9:1–6

The odds didn't look good. As the Israelites got ready to cross the Jordan River into their Promised Land, Moses sized up the situation. They would face enemies with superior strength and numbers who lived in walled cities that seemed invincible. The Canaanites included a race of people who stood seven to nine feet tall and had a frightening reputation. "You've also heard it said, 'Who can oppose the descendants of Anak?'" Moses admitted.

Forty years earlier, the Israelites had been on the verge of entering Canaan. But the spies' report about the people and cities there terrified them. Because of their disbelief, they ended up wandering in the wilderness until the older generation had died. Moses wanted this new generation to be prepared for what difficulties lay ahead. But he also reminded them of the good news: God himself would go ahead of them and crush their enemies. Their victory was already assured, because they had God on their side.

All of us can identify with that feeling of facing enemies who seem too powerful to take on. Maybe God has called us to a task that looks overwhelming. Maybe we struggle with a relationship that seems hopeless, or a habit or sin that threatens to overpower us. Or maybe we're the target of attacks and hostility because of our faith.

When our problems look so much bigger than we are, we have a choice to make. Will we let fear keep us from everything that God has promised us, or will we remember who is on our side? Even when the odds are stacked against us from a human standpoint, our victory is assured. By obeying God's will and trusting him, we can take on any giants that we encounter.

You, dear children, are from God and have overcome them, because the one who is in you is greater than the one who is in the world.

1 John 4:4 NIV

Ask yourself: **What giant am I facing in my life right now?**

JULY

9

"How can a Jewish man like you ask a Samaritan woman like me for a drink of water?"

John 4:1–9

"Give me a drink of water." Those few words from Jesus astonished the Samaritan woman. She'd felt curious when she saw a Jewish man sitting by the well. Since the Jewish people despised the mixed-race Samaritans, many of them went out of their way to avoid passing through Samaria. It was also shocking for a man to talk to a woman, especially a stranger, in public. But a Jewish man speaking to a Samaritan woman? That was unheard of. "How can a Jewish man like you ask a Samaritan woman like me for a drink of water?" she asked.

The Samaritan woman had no way of knowing that Jesus deliberately took the direct route through her town because he had an appointment—with her. He could see her emptiness and disappointment with life, so he set up a meeting to offer her a new one. God has also set up divine appointments for us throughout each day. It may be a conversation with someone who needs to hear about God's offer of a new life, or a believer who needs words of encouragement to strengthen them. Every encounter has been arranged for a purpose.

The most important divine appointment in our day is the one that we most often miss—time spent in prayer and communion with God. It's tempting to skip our quiet time when faced with a busy schedule. But taking a few moments to focus on God and discuss our plans and concerns with him makes a huge difference in our attitude and in how we handle our daily pressures. If we begin our morning with a conversation with Jesus, we'll be less likely to miss the other appointments God has scheduled for us.

My heart has heard you say, "Come and talk with me." And my heart responds, "Lord, I am coming."

Psalm 27:8 NLT

Ask yourself: **How can I be more alert to the divine appointments that God has scheduled into my day?**

"Where are you going to get this living water?"

John 4:10–15

The Samaritan woman came to the well to draw water; instead, Jesus drew her into a conversation with statements that stimulated her curiosity. After she expressed shock at his request for a drink, Jesus told her that if she knew his identity, *she* would have asked *him* for a drink. And he would have given her living water. The woman pointed out that Jesus hadn't brought anything with which to draw water from the deep well, as she had. "So where are you going to get this living water?" she asked.

Jesus explained that people who drank the water he gave never became thirsty again. In fact, his water became a spring within them "that gushes up to eternal life." Missing the spiritual implication, the Samaritan woman thought only of how much easier her life would be if she no longer had to traipse to the well to draw water every day. "Sir, give me this water!" she said.

When we drink the water that Jesus offers, it satisfies our soul's deepest longing forever. We find the joy of entering into a personal relationship with God, knowing him and being intimately known and cherished by him. He forgives our sins and gives us the gift of eternal life. Never again will we be spiritually thirsty.

God never intended for us to slake our thirst and then keep this water all to ourselves. Jesus explained that the Holy Spirit would flow from deep within a believer, like streams of running water. We can be a source of blessing to others by sharing the life-giving message of God's love and forgiveness. We can also refresh other believers with God's truth. It's important to keep our faith from growing stagnant, because a thirsty world is dying for a drink of living water.

[Jesus said] "Streams of living water will flow from deep within the person who believes in me."
John 7:38

Ask yourself: **How does the Holy Spirit bubble over in my life and touch others?**

JULY
11

"Could he be the Messiah?"

John 4:16–30

The woman at the well had another shock in store as she continued her conversation with Jesus. When Jesus asked to speak with her husband, the woman responded that she didn't have one. Jesus then outlined the sordid details of her love life: she had been married five times and currently lived in a sinful relationship with a man. The woman was astonished at his supernatural knowledge, but uncomfortable with having her guilt exposed. She immediately steered the conversation to an old debate between the Jews and Samaritans about the proper place to worship God.

Jesus explained that since God is a spirit, a worshiper's attitude is what matters, not location. When the woman longed for the days when Messiah would come and explain everything, Jesus identified himself. "I am he," Jesus proclaimed, "and I am speaking to you now." The woman left her water jar and ran into the city to share her discovery. "Come with me, and meet a man who told me everything I've ever done. Could he be the Messiah?"

Like the woman at the well, we have burdens that we lug around—burdens that are much heavier than a clay water jar. Like her, we have met the One who knows every sordid detail of our life—past, present, and future. The Samaritan woman's response reminds us of the amazing fact that instead of condemnation, Jesus offers forgiveness and unconditional love.

God doesn't want us carrying around heavy burdens that weigh us down. He wants us to trust him enough to let him take care of them. When we talk with Jesus and then leave our burdens at his feet, we'll feel freer to run out and tell others about the Messiah, like the Samaritan woman did.

Turn your burdens over to the LORD,
and he will take care of you.

Psalm 55:22

Ask yourself: **What burdens do I need to lay down at the Messiah's feet?**

"Did someone bring him something to eat?"

John 4:31–41

The disciples felt confused. They had left Jesus sitting by the well tired and thirsty. When they returned from buying food in the village, he showed no interest in eating. Jesus responded to their urging with a mysterious answer: "I have food to eat that you don't know about." The men looked at each other. "Did someone bring him something to eat?" they wondered aloud.

John doesn't record that Jesus ever received the drink of water he requested from the Samaritan woman. But he didn't need it or the disciples' food to feel satisfied. "My food is to do what the one who sent me wants me to do and to finish the work he has given me," Jesus told the disciples. He was filled with the joy of having done his Father's work. Another soul had been set free from Satan's kingdom of darkness and brought into the light of God's truth. And at that very moment, many more Samaritans were on their way to see for themselves if the Messiah had truly come.

During Jesus's forty day fast at the beginning of his ministry, Satan urged him to turn stones into bread. Jesus reminded Satan that people don't live solely on physical food; we also need the sustenance of God's Word. We need food to nourish our body, to provide fuel and energy, and to help every part function. We also need a well-rounded spiritual diet that contains study of God's Word, obedience to his commands, prayer, worship, and fellowship with other believers. If we skimp on any of these, we can't grow or function as God intended. Spiritual malnourishment is far more serious than physical hunger. A good steak dinner is nice, but it's more important to satisfy our soul than our stomach.

Jesus answered, "Scripture says, 'A person cannot live on bread alone but on every word that God speaks.'"

Matthew 4:4

Ask yourself: **What improvements do I need to make in my spiritual diet?**

JULY
13

"If I am a father, where is my honor?"

Malachi 1:6

It's hard to find a television show these days that portrays a family where the parents are respected. As a matter of fact, respect and honor are missing ingredients in most relationships portrayed in the media—and often in real life too. One of the Ten Commandments instructs people to honor their parents. In Leviticus 19:32 God commanded the Israelites to honor the elderly as a way to "show respect for your God." The New Testament calls for honor and respect in marital relationships and for those under our authority, as well as those who hold authority over us.

God accused Israel of failing to give him the honor and respect they themselves insisted on in their earthly relationships. "So if I am a father, where is my honor?" he asked. "If I am a master, where is my respect?" God was a father to the nation of Israel; the people were his servants. Instead of having the proper attitude toward him, they had become disrespectful, disobedient, and callous to the point of feigning innocence when God confronted them.

Showing honor to other people can transform our relationships. And what a powerful witness it is of our faith when we treat everyone with respect simply because they are created by God and someone whom Jesus died for. But God deserves our highest honor and respect—more than we could ever express to him.

If we let ourselves be influenced by our culture, a casual attitude can creep into our relationship with God. We can lose a sense of his majesty and power. It's important to meditate on Scriptures about who God is and what he has done. God shouldn't have to ask us, "Where is my honor?" It should come through in our thoughts, our words, and our actions.

O Lord, you are my God. I will highly honor you; I will praise your name.

Isaiah 25:1

Ask yourself: **Do I sometimes let a casual attitude toward God rob him of the honor and respect due him?**

JULY
14

"When you bring such offerings, should I accept them from you?"

Malachi 1:6–14

Jackie looked at the wrapped gift her husband had left on the kitchen table. Several years ago, she'd told him that she preferred a birthday present chosen by him, not his secretary. Now each year she had to remind herself that "it's the thought that counts." The trouble was, she wondered if he gave it any thought at all. Last year she got an orange sweater, even though she'd always hated orange. The year before it was a scarf, even though she'd mentioned that scarves irritated her neck. Slowly, she opened the box and pulled out . . . an orange scarf.

God complained about the Israelites' attitude toward giving to him. The priests failed to enforce the guidelines for proper offerings and sacrifices, allowing people to bring obviously defective animals. God accused the priests and people of showing contempt for him by begrudging the sacrifices and seeing them as a nuisance. Instead of bringing God their best, they brought in stolen, lame, and sick animals. "When you bring such offerings," God asked, "should I accept them from you?"

When Jesus introduced the new covenant, a new system of giving replaced the compulsory sacrifices and offerings of the old law. But God still examines our attitude toward giving. As we prayerfully decide what to give back to him, God wants us to do it freely and joyfully, not because we feel forced to give. God doesn't want our leftovers; he wants our best, whether it's our time, money, or energy. Our love for God and gratitude for what he's done will motivate us more than strict laws ever could. When it comes to giving, God counts the attitude more than the amount.

Each of you should give whatever you have decided.
You shouldn't be sorry that you gave or feel forced
to give, since God loves a cheerful giver.

2 Corinthians 9:7

Ask yourself: **What is my attitude toward giving time, money, or service to God?**

JULY
15

"Who hopes for what can be seen?"

Romans 8:18–25

As summer neared its end, Corey's hopes got higher and higher. *This could be the day*, he thought each morning as he woke up. Corey's parents had promised to give him a car before he started classes at the community college. He didn't know what kind of car it would be, or exactly when they'd spring it on him, but it was as good as in the garage. His parents wouldn't promise him something and then not follow through—and besides, didn't they give him a pair of fuzzy dice on his birthday last month?

Paul wrote about the hope that believers have as we wait for the day when God will redeem our body from the presence of sin and its effects. We can already see evidence of our salvation in our changed desires, transformed life, and God's hand in our circumstances. But we're looking forward to so much more that God has promised. He asks us to live in expectation of things that can't be seen with our eyes. "If we hope for something we already see, it's not really hope," Paul wrote. "Who hopes for what can be seen?"

We don't base our lives on wishful thinking but on the unshakeable foundation of God's character and his Word. The essence of faith is having a firm confidence that God will do all that he's said he will do; it's living in anticipation of things that we hope for but have no visible evidence of right now. We don't know when all of God's promises will come to pass or exactly how they will happen. But if God said it, it's as good as done. God would never promise something and then not follow through—and besides, didn't he give us his Holy Spirit when we were born again?

Now faith is the assurance of things hoped for, the conviction of things not seen.

Hebrews 11:1 NASB

Ask yourself: **How does my life reflect hope in things not yet seen?**

“Why didn’t you answer me today?”

1 Samuel 14:24–41

As the Israelite army fought the Philistines, King Saul made a foolish oath: he cursed any person who ate anything before the battle’s end. His soldiers obeyed, even though they were exhausted during the fighting. Afterwards their hunger caused them to slaughter and eat animals without first draining the blood as God had commanded. Saul put a stop to this sinful action, but he didn’t know about another problem that his rash words had caused.

Before Jonathan heard about his father’s oath, he ate a little bit of the honey that was so plentiful in the woods. Later that day, when Saul decided to keep pursuing the Philistines, the priest urged him to first consult God. This time no answer came. Saul assumed someone had committed a sin, and he called on the priest to use the Urim and Thummim to identify the guilty person. “O God of Israel, why didn’t you answer me today?” Saul prayed.

Sometimes when it seems as though God isn’t listening to our prayers, it’s because he isn’t. According to Proverbs 28:9, if we refuse to listen to God and obey him, then he finds our prayers detestable. Isaiah warned the people that their sins had separated them from God; as a result, he chose not to listen to their prayers (see Isa. 59:2).

Any unconfessed sin in our life creates a barrier between us and God. And if we confess a specific sin without intending to give it up, God sees our hypocrisy. His promises about answered prayer are for those who share his opinion about sin. It’s important that we continually examine our heart to search for any unrepentant attitudes toward sin. If we want God to listen to our prayers and answer them, then we need to hear and obey him.

If I had thought about doing anything sinful,
the Lord would not have listened to me.

Psalm 66:18

Ask yourself: **Does God have any reason not to listen to my prayers today?**

JULY

17

"And for that I am to die?"

1 Samuel 14:42–45

Saul had no idea of the trouble his words would cause when he made his troops swear to fast until they'd won the battle. His hasty, self-centered order weakened the soldiers during the fighting and prompted them to sin by disobeying God's dietary laws when the fasting ended. The oath also nearly caused the death of his son.

When Saul requested divine guidance and God didn't answer, Saul suspected someone had broken the fast. He rashly uttered another oath, swearing the guilty person would die—even if it was his own son. The priest drew lots, and Jonathan admitted tasting a little honey on the end of his staff. Then he asked, "And for that I am to die?"

Saul could have admitted he had acted foolishly, but he was more concerned about how he looked in front of his men. He swore Jonathan would die. The soldiers declared it would be unthinkable for Jonathan to die after leading them to victory in battle. They swore an oath of their own: not a hair of Jonathan's head would be harmed.

While most of us don't go around swearing a lot of oaths, we can identify with the tendency to blurt out rash words before thinking through the possible implications. Whether making promises we're not prepared to keep, throwing out false accusations, or giving advice when we're not qualified—our words can come back to bite us. And they often hurt other people too.

When something we've said causes trouble, our concern shouldn't be to save face or to cover up our mistake. We can honestly admit our error and try to correct the situation. And we can ask God to help us be more guarded with the words that come out of our mouth.

A fool starts out by talking foolishness and ends up saying crazy things that are dangerous.

Ecclesiastes 10:13

Ask yourself: **Do I have a tendency to blurt out foolish things that I later regret?**

“What is this sound of sheep and cows that I hear?”

1 Samuel 15:10–26

We all stopped talking when my three-year-old granddaughter sauntered into the family room after just a moment’s absence. “Lacey Grace,” her daddy asked, “have you been in Nana’s makeup again?” Lacey responded with a nonchalant “No,” a casual toss of her head, and just the slightest pout on her Glazed Raspberry lips.

King Saul also tried to deny the evidence of his disobedience. God instructed him to completely destroy the Amalekites, including their animals, as punishment for that nation’s long history of wickedness. But Saul and his army kept the best of the cattle and sheep as plunder from the battle. When God sent Samuel to confront the king, Saul greeted the prophet by stating matter-of-factly, “I carried out the Lord’s instructions.”

Samuel knew better. “But what is this sound of sheep in my ears and this sound of cows that I hear?” he asked. Saul protested that sparing the animals had been the army’s idea; besides, they planned to offer them as sacrifices to God. His excuses didn’t work. Since Saul had rejected God’s Word by disobeying it, God now rejected Saul as Israel’s king.

It’s amazing how often we deceive ourselves about our disobedience to God’s instructions. Maybe we did something that really doesn’t seem all that bad. Or maybe we started out to obey but stopped short of full compliance with God’s will. Even when confronted with evidence of our sin, sometimes we still deny it or try to make excuses. How do we think we can hide anything from an all-knowing God? He doesn’t need external proofs of our disobedience like the color of our lips or the animal sounds ringing in his ears. God sees into our heart and there’s no way we can ever fool him.

You may be sure that your sin will find you out.

Numbers 32:23 NIV

Ask yourself: **Does God see any evidence of sin in my life that I’m pretending isn’t there?**

JULY

19

“How long will wicked people triumph?”

Psalm 94:1–13

Christopher fumed every time he thought about the promotion he didn’t get. *Maybe nice guys do finish last*, he told himself. He’d seen a lot of guys climb up the corporate ladder—while stepping on other people in the process. It seemed like his company rewarded kissing up, stealing other people’s ideas, and using sneaky business practices. Boy, just once he’d like to see those people get what they deserve.

The writer of Psalm 94 also wanted to see the wicked people around him get what they deserved. He longed for God’s righteous judgment on the arrogant people who crushed godly people and destroyed the needy and helpless. “How long, O Lord, will wicked people triumph?” he cried out. “How long?” While the wicked people scoffed that God didn’t see what they did, the psalmist reminded them that he sees, hears, and knows everything, including their thoughts.

It’s easy to grow cynical when we see evil people prospering, especially if their success causes godly people to suffer. Why should the wicked enjoy so many blessings when others trying to live for God face hardships and struggles? We may even wonder why we should bother trying to do the right thing. Instead of being bitter when we see such inequity, we can trust God to set things right someday.

The writer of Psalm 73 felt so troubled by the way the wicked were thriving that he almost lost his faith in God’s goodness. He discovered how to make sense of injustice in the world by thinking ahead to the final destiny of people. God will give ungodly people the punishment they deserve, but as believers we receive a much greater reward than we deserve, both now and in the future. Instead of asking “How long?” we can remember who will really triumph in the end.

> *Then I went into your sanctuary, O God, and I finally understood the destiny of the wicked.*
>
> Psalm 73:17 NLT

Ask yourself: **Do I struggle with bitterness when I see evil people succeed?**

JULY
20

"Who knows how the Lord thinks?"

Romans 11:33–36

Emma cringed as she heard her daughter's bedroom door slam. How long would these confrontations go on? Lately, it seemed that Gina questioned every decision that Emma and her husband made. They tried to explain their reasoning when it was appropriate, but some situations were impossible for a preteen to understand. Many times Emma wanted simply to wrap her arms around her rebellious daughter and say, "Just trust me on this."

Paul pointed out that we can't always understand God's reasoning, but we can always trust his decisions. After discussing God's choice of the Jewish people to reveal his salvation plan to the world, Paul burst out in praise. "God's riches, wisdom, and knowledge are so deep that it is impossible to explain his decisions or to understand his ways," he wrote. "Who knows how the Lord thinks?"

God often acts in ways that are beyond our understanding. He sometimes allows things to happen that make no sense from a human viewpoint. But God sees events from a different perspective. He has his own purposes and his own timetable; he sees the past, present, and future all at the same time. Since God possesses infinite wisdom and knowledge, our human brains are incapable of understanding his thoughts.

Someday everything that has happened to us will make perfect sense, but for now, we can't see the big picture. We won't always like the way God handles a situation; sometimes we'll wonder what he has in mind. When we can't understand what he's doing, God asks us to believe that he's working all things out for his glory and our good. Sometimes we need to let God wrap his arms around us and listen to him saying, "Just trust me on this."

> *"My thoughts are not your thoughts, and my ways are not your ways," declares the* LORD.
>
> Isaiah 55:8

Ask yourself: **How do I react when I don't understand what the Lord is doing in a particular situation?**

JULY

21

"Why did you doubt?"

Matthew 14:22–33

The disciples held on tightly as the wind and waves buffeted their boat. Suddenly they saw what looked like a man, walking on top of the water. Thinking it must be an evil spirit, the men cried out in terror. Then they heard a familiar voice. "It's me. Don't be afraid!" Impulsive Peter had an idea: Why shouldn't he join his master? "Come," Jesus invited.

Without hesitating, Peter stepped out of the boat. A thrill rushed through him as he walked across the surface of the sea toward Jesus. But then his eyes shifted to the raging waves whipped up by the wind, and he felt himself sinking like a rock. "Lord, save me!" he shouted. Jesus grabbed Peter at once. "You have so little faith! Why did you doubt?" Jesus asked.

Jesus still invites his followers to climb out of the boat and accomplish great things for God. Sometimes he calls us to an area of service way outside our comfort zone. Once we step out in faith and obedience, we'll know the exhilaration of doing something that would be impossible on our own. Many times God calls us to be a witness of his power by weathering a storm with grace and quiet confidence. As long as we keep our eyes fixed on him, he will hold us up.

Like Peter, there will be times when our faith will falter. If we focus our attention on our inadequacies or the impossibility of our circumstances, we'll start to sink like a rock. But Jesus still stands ready to reach out a helping hand when we call. When he lifts us back up, we need to ask ourselves, "Why did I doubt?" It may be scary to walk on water, but think of what we miss when we stay in the boat.

Let us fix our eyes on Jesus, the author
and perfecter of our faith.

Hebrews 12:2 NIV

Ask yourself: **How would my life be different if I kept my eyes on Jesus in the middle of a storm?**

JULY
22

"Do you understand what you're reading?"

Acts 8:26–39

This week I did it again—I went to the library and checked out *War and Peace*. I love old classics, and Tolstoy's epic novel always appears on lists of the world's greatest books. But I've tried and given up on this book two or three times. Maybe it was the long Russian names or the huge cast of characters, but I had trouble keeping track of who did what, when, and where. *This time will be different*, I thought. *I will use whatever reference works I need to understand this book.*

An Ethiopian man needed help with what he was reading. The Holy Spirit told Philip to get close to the high-ranking official's chariot. Philip heard him reading Isaiah and asked, "Do you understand what you're reading?" The official answered with another question: "How can I understand unless someone guides me?" Then he invited Philip to ride along with him. After Philip explained how Jesus fulfilled Isaiah's prophecies, the official believed in Christ and asked to be baptized.

The Bible includes many passages that are difficult to interpret. Sometimes a person more advanced in Bible study can help us with something we don't understand, as Philip did with the official. Commentaries and reference works can also prove helpful, but they shouldn't be our main source of edification.

After Jesus's resurrection, he helped the disciples understand the Scriptures that referred to his ministry, death, and resurrection. Today the Holy Spirit does the same thing for us, showing us how to interpret the Bible and apply it to our lives. Without the Spirit's help, Bible study turns into an academic exercise. When faced with a difficult verse or passage, our first step is to read it within its context. Then we can pray for the Spirit's help, knowing that God wants us to understand what we're reading.

Then he opened their minds to understand the Scriptures.

Luke 24:45

Ask yourself: **Where do I turn for help in understanding a difficult Bible verse or passage?**

JULY

23

"I know Jesus, and I'm acquainted with Paul, but who are you?"

Acts 19:11–16

It was a family business—of sorts. The seven Jewish brothers earned a living by traveling throughout the area and trying to free people suffering from demon possession. They used a variety of chants, ceremonies, and incantations. After seeing the miracles and healings associated with Paul, the brothers decided to try to duplicate his power, which was obviously greater than theirs. So they began using the same name that Paul invoked.

On one such house call, the brothers proclaimed, "I order you to come out in the name of Jesus, whom Paul talks about." To their shock, the evil spirit answered them. "I know Jesus, and I'm acquainted with Paul, but who are you?" Then the demon gave the possessed man supernatural strength and he beat up all seven brothers. The exorcists ran out of the house naked, wounded, and terrified.

Satan and his demons knew more about Jesus than the seven brothers did. They also know about everyone who is a true follower of Jesus. The moment we believed in him, we switched sides—we went from being God's enemy to being Satan's enemy. First Peter 5:8 urges us to be on guard because our enemy constantly prowls around looking for someone to devour. The devil does everything in his power to plant doubts and fears in our mind, to lure us into sin, and to keep us from prayer and Bible study.

The first order of protection against our enemy is to submit to God's authority and obey his commands. We also need to put on the spiritual armor that God has provided for us to fend off Satan's attacks (see Eph. 6:10–17). If we stay armed and rely on God's strength, we won't need to run from demonic powers like the seven brothers did; Satan will run away from us.

So place yourselves under God's authority. Resist the devil, and he will run away from you.

James 4:7

Ask yourself: **In what ways do I need to resist the devil today?**

"Why have you done this?"

Jonah 1

God's instructions to take a message to Nineveh horrified Jonah. The Assyrian city had earned a reputation for cruelty, brutality, witchcraft, sexual immorality, and atrocities committed during war. Jonah probably knew of Amos's and Hosea's prophecies that Assyria would destroy Israel. When Jonah got his marching orders, he took off. But he boarded a ship going in the opposite direction from Nineveh.

Jonah soon learned he couldn't run away from God. The Lord sent a violent storm that endangered the ship and terrified the crew. As the superstitious men threw dice to identify the person responsible for the disaster, God intervened and pinpointed Jonah. The crew drilled him with questions to find out how he had caused the terrible storm.

Jonah confessed that the God he had tried to run away from is the One who controls the sea. This news terrified the sailors even more. "Why have you done this?" they cried. Although these men worshiped pagan gods, they understood that Jonah's disobedience jeopardized their own lives. Reluctantly, the sailors complied with Jonah's suggestion to throw him overboard so that the storm would end.

We often do the same thing Jonah did—maybe not with our feet but with our heart or mind. God may give us an assignment that sounds unreasonable. Or we read a command in his Word that seems impossible to do. Or maybe God's will for our life clashes with our desires. So we turn the opposite direction from the one God is pointing us toward. Trying to run away from God's will is asking for trouble. We can only have a joyful, fulfilling life when we obey God's will for us. And that includes going in the right direction.

I run in the path of your commands,
for you have set my heart free.
Psalm 119:32 NIV

Ask yourself: **What happened the last time I tried to run away from God's will for my life?**

JULY
25

"Isn't this what I said would happen?"

Jonah 4:1–3

Spending three days and nights inside a huge fish motivated Jonah to obey God. When God gave him a second chance to carry out his assignment, Jonah walked through the great city of Nineveh preaching a simple message: "In forty days Nineveh will be destroyed." Amazingly, the people paid attention to Jonah's words and believed God.

As signs of repentance, they fasted and wore sackcloth. The king ordered the people to turn from their violent and wicked ways. He encouraged them to cry out to God in hopes that he would turn from his anger and spare the city. When God saw how the Ninevites responded, he decided not to destroy their city.

Jonah reacted in a surprising way. "Lord, isn't this what I said would happen when I was still in my own country?" he protested. Knowing that God is merciful, compassionate, patient, and forgiving, Jonah figured that God might change his mind and not judge Nineveh. He admitted that was the reason he hadn't wanted to deliver the message in the first place. Jonah didn't want the people of Nineveh to be saved; he wanted them destroyed.

Like Jonah, many Jews were reluctant to carry out their God-given mission to share God's love and mercy with the rest of the world. Many Christians today have the same mindset. It's easy to get so cozy in our own little Christian community that we forget our God-given mission to the world. Through us, God wants to extend his offer of salvation to others, even people who seem the least likely to respond. He never intended for us to keep the Good News all to ourselves. God wants help in harvesting his crops, even in cities like Nineveh.

Then he said to his disciples, "The harvest is large, but the workers are few. So ask the Lord who gives this harvest to send workers to harvest his crops."

Matthew 9:37–38

Ask yourself: **Am I willing to share the Good News with anyone, regardless of who they are?**

"What right do you have to be angry?"

Jonah 4:4–11

The fourth chapter of Jonah gives an account of one of the first anger management classes ever held. Jonah had hoped to see the evil city of Nineveh destroyed. God's decision to spare it made him mad—so mad that he didn't want to live anymore. God didn't kill Jonah as he requested, but he asked him a question: "What right do you have to be angry?"

Instead of answering, Jonah sat down outside the city to see what would happen to it. God provided a plant to shade him from the sun, which pleased Jonah. The next day God sent a worm to kill the plant, and also a hot, scorching wind. Once again Jonah wanted to die. And once again God asked him a question: "What right do you have to be angry over this plant?" Jonah protested that he had every right to be angry.

God pointed out that Jonah's anger was based on selfish interests. First, he got mad because he didn't get what he wanted when God spared Nineveh; then he reacted in anger over the loss of a plant that had made him comfortable. But Jonah showed no concern for the welfare of the thousands of people in Nineveh.

Anger is a natural human emotion, but it can lead us into sin if we don't let God help us handle it. When we evaluate the root cause of our anger, we'll usually find it stems from self-centered interests like Jonah's. Whatever triggers it, a failure to deal with our anger makes us miserable and unfit for God's work. It blocks our communication with God and can do a lot of damage in our relationships with other people. That's why the Bible urges us not to let the day end with unresolved anger. Thankfully, God's anger management classes are always open for enrollment.

Be angry without sinning. Don't go to bed angry.
Don't give the devil any opportunity to work.

Ephesians 4:26–27

Ask yourself: **Do I have any anger issues that need to be resolved?**

JULY
27

"But how can one person keep warm?"

Ecclesiastes 4:9–12

David and Jonathan enjoyed a close friendship with each other even in the face of King Saul's jealous rages against David. Mary, the mother of Jesus, and Elizabeth, John the Baptist's mother, encouraged each other as they faced the complications of miraculous pregnancies. Widowed Naomi had her daughter-in-law Ruth with her as she struck out on the road back to her homeland.

Solomon explained why "two people are better than one" by listing some practical benefits of having a companion versus going it alone. If we fall down, we have someone to help us get up. If someone attacks us, we have someone to help us defend ourselves. And when it's cold, another person comes in handy. "Again, if two people lie down together, they can keep warm, but how can one person keep warm?" Solomon wrote. He concluded by noting that three people are even better than two.

God designed us with a deep need for companionship. When we have friends to share our life, the good times are intensified and the hard times seem easier to bear. Christians can enjoy especially close fellowship because of the faith in Jesus we share. As we love and serve our Savior, we can offer each other mutual help and encouragement.

With today's busy, high-tech lifestyles, many people don't take the time to develop genuine friendships. As a result, they struggle with feelings of loneliness and isolation. Medical research indicates that people without close relationships suffer more frequent and serious illnesses and die at an earlier age. Lasting friendships demand a commitment of time and energy, but the rewards are worth it. Without the warmth of friendship, life can get pretty cold.

Two people are better than one. . . . A triple-braided rope is not easily broken.

Ecclesiastes 4:9, 12

Ask yourself: **How much time and effort do I invest in developing godly friendships?**

"Don't you know that a little yeast spreads through the whole batch of dough?"

1 Corinthians 5:6–11

The Jewish people celebrated the Festival of Unleavened Bread immediately after the Passover feast. For seven days, they ate bread made without leavening. On the first day of the festival, the families threw out all of their yeast, which symbolized sin. They even searched every nook and cranny of their houses with lights and swept the floors clean to make sure they didn't miss a crumb of bread made with yeast.

Paul used the analogy of yeast and sin when he addressed the church at Corinth. Although these believers boasted about their church, they had failed to reprimand members who openly lived a sexually immoral lifestyle. Paul warned that if they allowed this blatant sin to continue, it would spread and corrupt the entire church. "Don't you know that a little yeast spreads through the whole batch of dough?" he asked. He went on to urge them not to associate with people who claimed to be believers yet practiced blatant, deliberate sin.

Christ represents the perfect Passover lamb sacrificed for us. So in a sense, the rest of our life is a celebration of the Festival of Unleavened Bread. Our goal is to live a life of purity and obedience to God's commands. But just as a small amount of yeast diffuses itself through an entire mass of dough, a single sinful habit or wrong attitude can grow and spread corruption. God's Word and Holy Spirit provide light to search every nook and cranny of our life so we can make a clean sweep. With God's help, we can live like the new batch of dough he has made us to be.

Remove the old yeast of sin so that you may be a new batch of dough.

1 Corinthians 5:7

Ask God **to help you search the nooks and crannies of your life for any sins you've overlooked.**

JULY
29

"Why were things better in the old days than they are now?"

Ecclesiastes 7:7–10

Nostalgia is big business in America, as evidenced by magazines, movies, antique shops, museums, and historical attractions. Whenever I hear someone long for the simpler life of a century ago, I wonder if they're remembering some of the modern-day comforts and conveniences they would have to give up—like indoor bathrooms, air-conditioning, and medical cures. In a similar way, we often forget the bad things in the "good old days" of our personal lives.

The writer of Ecclesiastes noted that adversity often makes a person who is dissatisfied with their present circumstances yearn for "the old days" when things seemed better. But giving in to this temptation clouds our thinking and can fill us with despair over our present life and our future. Even as Judah suffered under Babylonian captivity, God urged the people to trust in his plans for them and look ahead to "a future filled with hope."

When we're going through difficulties, we may long for a time in our past when life seemed easier and more enjoyable. On the opposite end of the spectrum, we may be fixated on our past failures and missed opportunities. Either mindset can cause us to miss blessings in our present situation and lose sight of the fact that God has our future planned out.

Rather than yearning for a past we may or may not remember accurately, God wants us to move ahead toward his goals and purposes for us. We can trust that his plans include a closer relationship with him and new ways to experience his love and see his power revealed. Every day represents a fresh opportunity to step into that future.

I know the plans that I have for you, declares the
Lord. They are plans for peace and not disaster,
plans to give you a future filled with hope.

Jeremiah 29:11

Ask God **to help you look forward to the future of hope and purpose that he has planned especially for you.**

"Who has bloodshot eyes?"

Proverbs 23:29–35

When someone passed out glasses of wine during the neighborhood party, my husband and I politely declined. But I was surprised when one of my friends also declined. I knew that she and her husband kept liquor in their house and served it whenever they entertained. When I asked her about it, she told me that she never drank. "I grew up around a couple of relatives who were alcoholics," she explained. "I saw how it can ruin someone's life and I don't want to risk that."

The Bible has several warnings about drinking too much, but Proverbs 23 gets really graphic. "Who has trouble?" the writer asks. "Who has quarrels? Who has wounds for no reason? Who has bloodshot eyes?" He warns that although wine looks pretty and "goes down smoothly," later it "bites like a snake." The rest of the passage paints a picture of how drunkenness can impair a person's senses and judgment.

Christians may have different opinions about whether it's okay to drink alcohol, but the most important point is to not let it control us. Instead, we're to be filled with God's Spirit and controlled by him as described in Ephesians 5. The picture painted in this passage contrasts sharply with the one in Proverbs.

Alcohol clouds and degrades our judgment; the Spirit gives us godly judgment and discernment. Alcohol leads to loss of control; one of the fruits of the Spirit is self-control. A drunk person can't walk a straight line; a person filled with the Spirit is able to walk in obedience to God. The effects of alcohol are temporary; the Holy Spirit has a lasting effect on our life. God wants us to be intoxicated with him alone.

Don't be drunk with wine, because that will ruin your life. Instead, be filled with the Holy Spirit.

Ephesians 5:18 NLT

Ask yourself: **Do I live like someone who is filled with God's Holy Spirit?**

JULY

31

"Why are you amazed about this man?"

Acts 3:1–16

Pandemonium broke out as people rushed to see for themselves whether it was true or not. Every day they'd seen this lame man sitting and begging beside the gate at the temple where his friends had carried him. Now, this same man had entered the courtyard—not only walking but jumping around and praising God at the top of his lungs! Witnesses spread the word that the beggar had been healed at a command from the two men he now held on to so tightly.

Peter saw the crowd's astonishment and the awe and wonder they directed at him and John. He seized the opportunity to share the gospel. "Men of Israel," he began, "why are you amazed about this man? Why are you staring at us as though we have made him walk by our own power or godly life?" Peter reminded the crowd about Jesus's recent crucifixion and their part in it. Then he testified that the beggar had been healed solely by the power of Jesus.

God wants to give us the power to accomplish great things. But he does it for the purpose of pointing people to him, not to draw attention to us. All our achievements are useless if they merely bring glory to ourselves. Every success or accomplishment represents an opportunity to testify to God's goodness and power. God may choose to work through us in astonishing ways. But rather than let people stare at us in wonder, our goal is to get them to look at the One who deserves all the praise and glory. Then they'll really be amazed.

> *Glory belongs to God, whose power is at work in us. By this power he can do infinitely more than we can ask or imagine.*
>
> Ephesians 3:20

Ask yourself: **Do I always use my achievements and successes to point people to God?**

Ask God **to work in your life in ways that reveal his power to others.**

"What does God know?"

Psalm 73:1–11

Evan checked to make sure he'd closed the door to the basement. Then, safely out of his mom's hearing, he started telling Kyle about his big plans for Saturday night. After his parents went to sleep, he would sneak out of the house and wait at the corner for the other guys to pick him up. One friend's brother had already arranged for fake IDs, so getting into the club shouldn't be a problem. "Aren't you afraid of getting caught?" asked Kyle. Evan snorted. "Nobody will ever know." And that's when he noticed that the intercom at his elbow was still on.

Psalm 73 describes people with a similar attitude. Asaph complained about wicked people prospering in spite of their malice, violence, and oppression of others. Then they displayed the height of arrogance by asking, "What does God know? Does the Most High know anything?" These people felt free to live any way they pleased without worrying about God's reaction.

In Psalm 139 David expressed the opposite attitude. He acknowledged that God knew him intimately, inside and out. God knew every move he made, every thought he had, and every word he spoke before he ever opened his mouth. Because David trusted God completely, this knowledge comforted him.

Knowing that God is omniscient seems frightening if we're not in a right relationship with him, or if we're harboring sin in our life. But when we fully trust him, we don't mind being transparent before him. We find joy in the fact that God knows us so intimately and still loves us unconditionally. It also motivates us in our quest to live in a way that pleases him. Sometimes it's good to remind ourselves that the answer to "What does God know?" is "Everything!"

Even before there is a single word on my tongue, you know all about it, LORD.

Psalm 139:4

Ask yourself: **How do I feel about the fact that God knows even my thoughts?**

AUGUST

2

"Are you one of us or one of our enemies?"

Joshua 5:13–15

Joshua's eyes scanned the high, fortified walls of Jericho. How could the ill-equipped Israelite army move against such an invincible city? Now that they had crossed the Jordan River into Canaan, the next obvious step seemed to be the battle against Jericho. So far, God had not given specific instructions on how to proceed from this point. Joshua would consider the best military strategies while trusting God's promise to give Israel victory over the Canaanites.

Suddenly, Joshua was startled to see a man standing with a sword in his hand. He quickly approached the stranger. "Are you one of us or one of our enemies?" Joshua demanded. "Neither one!" the stranger responded. "I am here as the commander of the LORD's army." Joshua knew instinctively that he was in the presence of the Lord. He also now understood who was really in charge of the coming battle. God would lead the fight; Joshua would serve under him.

Children sometimes form cliques and ask a question similar to Joshua's: "Are you on our side, or are you one of them?" As we get older, animosity between rival groups becomes a more serious issue. Even though such thinking is out of place among Christians, we often let our differences prompt us to "choose sides." There are core beliefs we must defend without budging, but there's no reason to act like enemies over denominational distinctions or different viewpoints on nonessential issues.

When Jesus's disciples saw a man driving out demons in Jesus's name, they tried to stop him because he wasn't one of "them." Jesus told them that anybody who wasn't working against him was for him. Just because believers in Christ don't all look or think alike doesn't mean that we can't work together. Imagine what an impact we could have on the world if we remembered that we're all on God's side.

[Jesus said] "Whoever isn't against us is for us."

Mark 9:40

Ask yourself: **Do I ever treat other believers like enemies because of minor differences?**

"If salt loses its taste, how will it be made salty again?"

Matthew 5:13–16

I woke up during the night as thirsty as a person crawling across desert sands in search of water. Then I remembered the country ham my mom had served for dinner, which had been preserved and aged with salt. I also remembered how odd the flavor had seemed to my friend when she tried it for the first time. She didn't know country ham was supposed to be salty.

Jesus used the example of salt to illustrate the way his followers would impact the world. Perhaps Jesus meant that they would create a thirst to know God, or act as a preservative against the spread of evil in their culture. Either way, Jesus emphasized that in order to remain useful to God, we have to retain the characteristics of a disciple. "But if salt loses its taste," he asked, "how will it be made salty again?"

God intends for us to have a positive effect on the world. Testifying about our transformed life and sharing about God's offer of forgiveness will trigger a thirst in people to know more about him. By taking a stand against evil, promoting God's standards of right and wrong, and committing to intercessory prayer, we can help to preserve the good in our society and slow the spread of evil.

Just as the right amount of salt can bring out the best in certain foods, we can enhance the world around us. But to be effective, our life must retain the character of a devoted, disciplined follower of Christ. If we try to blend in with our culture, our witness becomes so bland that we aren't much use to God. People detect the presence of salt in their food, and they will notice the salt of the earth. Some of them might think we have an odd "flavor," but we can't forget that Christians are supposed to be salty.

You are salt for the earth.
Matthew 5:13

Ask yourself: **How is my faith having an effect on the world around me?**

AUGUST
4

"Do you know why I have come to you?"

Daniel 10

In his later years, Daniel still lived and worked in Babylon even though Israel's captivity had ended. His thoughts were often fixed on Jerusalem and the exiles who had returned there to rebuild the city. Recent news about the opposition they faced discouraged Daniel. When God gave him a vision about a great war involving Israel, Daniel spent three weeks mourning, fasting, and praying. Then he received a visitor whose majestic, brilliant appearance knocked all the strength out of Daniel.

The angel told Daniel that God had heard everything he said from the moment he decided to humble himself and pray for understanding. God had immediately dispatched the angel, but his arrival had been delayed for three weeks while demonic spirits tried to stop him. He was able to resume his mission when Michael, another chief angel, came to help him fight. "Do you know why I have come to you?" the angel asked. He assured Daniel that God had sent him in answer to his prayers, to explain what would happen to the Jewish people in the last days.

This passage in Daniel reveals the ongoing battle between angels serving God and the fallen angels that do Satan's bidding. If we caught a glimpse of that unseen realm, it would knock the strength out of us as it did Daniel. It's amazing enough to know that our prayers influence movements in the heavenly realm.

Prayer is both a privilege and a responsibility, but sometimes we forget how powerful it can be. If we let ourselves get complacent or lazy, our prayers turn into rituals or empty repeated phrases. Satan does everything he can to keep us from praying, and then he tries to oppose God's answer. But if we take prayer seriously, we can expect God's best answers in spite of Satan's best efforts.

He told me . . . "I have come in response to your prayer."

Daniel 10:12

Ask yourself: **How seriously do I take my prayer life?**

"Who despised the day when little things began to happen?"

Zechariah 4:1–10

Julia opened her day planner and once again felt amazement at how her home business had grown. Who would have predicted this when she attended her first scrapbooking party six years ago? Now, Julia not only held impressive sales records, but she also supervised nineteen other sales representatives and taught workshops. *I'm sure glad I listened to my family's encouragement to not give up during that first year*, Julia thought.

God encouraged Zerubbabel not to give up as he oversaw the rebuilding of the temple in Jerusalem. The leaders and builders faced severe harassment and opposition from outsiders. On top of that, some older Jews became discouraged by the fact that the new temple wouldn't measure up to the original one that Solomon built.

A mere remnant of the Israelites, a city that still lay in shambles, and the prospect of a lesser temple—it's no wonder some of the people felt that they lived in an insignificant time compared with Israel's past glory. But God knew their future. "Who despised the day when little things began to happen?" he asked. "They will be delighted when they see the plumb line in Zerubbabel's hand."

Some Christians live with the frustration of wanting to accomplish great things for God while feeling as though they never get the chance. Others are tempted to give up when they don't see tangible results from their ministry. God calls us to be faithful, even in the small details that may seem insignificant to us. Each one of us is surrounded by plenty of opportunities to join in his work. We may miss important assignments if we're only looking for the big projects. If we persevere and do our best when little things begin to happen, God will make something big out of it.

Whoever can be trusted with very little
can also be trusted with a lot.

Luke 16:10 *

Ask yourself: **Am I faithful in the little details?**

AUGUST
6

"What is this faithless act you have committed?"

Joshua 22:11–31

That little weasel. Ben took one look through the glass wall and knew what was going on. His supervisor was in there telling the boss about "his" great ideas for increasing production—except the ideas had come from Ben, over lunch that very day. Well, if that's the way Larry wanted to play, maybe a few scratches on his brand-new car were in order.

Later, Ben returned from the parking garage to find a note from his boss: *Larry tells me you have some great ideas for streamlining production. Can't wait to hear them.*

Misunderstandings can cause arguments, conflicts, broken relationships, and worse. When Israel heard that the tribes who had settled in Gilead had built an altar by the Jordan River, they prepared to wage war against their fellow Israelites. But first they sent a delegation to investigate, as God had instructed in Deuteronomy 13:12–18.

"What is this faithless act you have committed against the God of Israel?" the leaders asked. "Today you have turned away from following the LORD by building an altar for yourselves." The horrified leaders of the Eastern tribes explained that they built the altar to remind their descendants that they were a part of Israel. They never intended it as a place to offer sacrifices, which would have gone against God's commands.

We can avoid a lot of unnecessary conflict if we refrain from jumping to conclusions about what we see or hear. Some people automatically assume the worst about another person's actions without giving them a chance to explain. Since only God knows a person's true motives, it's best to avoid passing judgment until we learn all the facts. What seems to be a faithless or hurtful act on the surface may turn out to be something quite different from what we imagined.

O LORD of Armies, you judge fairly and
test motives and thoughts.

Jeremiah 11:20

Ask yourself: **Do I ever jump to conclusions about other people's intentions?**

“Don’t you realize that it is God’s kindness that is trying to lead you to him?”

Romans 2:1–4

Each time that I volunteered in my daughter’s first-grade classroom, her teacher amazed me. Mrs. Smith motivated her students with love and kindness rather than fear of punishment. For example, as we boarded a bus for a field trip, Mrs. Smith reviewed the rules but focused on her belief that her students would make her proud and be the best-behaved group at the event. She had very few problems in the classroom, because her students didn’t want to disappoint their teacher who cared so much about them.

God’s desire is that people would turn to him because of his love and kindness rather than out of fear of punishment. He holds back judgment, giving people time to repent of their sins. Paul pointed out that people sometimes treat God’s patience with contempt. “Do you have contempt for God, who is very kind to you, puts up with you, and deals patiently with you?” Paul asked. “Don’t you realize that it is God’s kindness that is trying to lead you to him and change the way you think and act?”

People risk eternal separation from God when they reject his kindness and offer of salvation. But it’s also dangerous for believers to presume on his patience. God doesn’t always punish a sinful action or habit immediately; he often gives us time to come to our senses and make things right. But a holy God can’t overlook sin in any form. There will always be consequences. The choice is up to us. We can either respond to his kindness and seek forgiveness now, or face correction and discipline later on.

> *The Lord isn’t slow to do what he promised, as some people think. Rather, he is patient for your sake. He doesn’t want to destroy anyone but wants all people to have an opportunity to turn to him and change the way they think and act.*
>
> 2 Peter 3:9

Ask yourself: **Am I taking God’s patience and kindness for granted in any area of my life?**

AUGUST

8

"Why is the king's decree so harsh?"

Daniel 2:1–19

The assortment of magicians, psychics, sorcerers, and astrologers had approached the king's throne with confidence; now they probably wished they could quit their jobs. In the past, they'd always been able to satisfy Nebuchadnezzar with their interpretations of his dreams. But this time he demanded that they also tell him *what* he had dreamed.

The men tried to convince the king that what he asked was impossible, but he only grew angrier. Finally, Nebuchadnezzar ordered the execution of all the wise men in Babylon. When Daniel heard about it, he knew that the decree included himself and his friends. He calmly asked the captain of the guard, "Why is the king's decree so harsh?"

Arioch explained the situation, prompting Daniel to make a risky move. Daniel asked the king to give him some time to figure out the dream and its meaning. Then Daniel enlisted prayer support from his friends. That night, God revealed the information to Daniel.

How could Daniel react so calmly to the news that the king's advisers were to be torn limb from limb? A normal human response would be to denounce the king as a madman or to be filled with terror. Instead, Daniel used tact and spoke to the royal official with "shrewd judgment." Instead of letting emotions control him, Daniel asked questions to learn the details.

Jesus warned his followers that they would need to be as cunning or shrewd as snakes. If we give in to our emotions, we'll have a hard time sensing the wisdom and guidance that God gives. Instead of the normal human reaction in a crisis, a better response would be gathering the information we need for prayer. Then we can trust God to give us the shrewd judgment of a wise man or woman.

Be as cunning as snakes but as innocent as doves.

Matthew 10:16

Ask yourself: **Are my reactions in times of crisis based solely on an emotional response or do I use God-given judgment?**

"Was God able to save you?"

Daniel 6:3–23

King Darius looked at the hard, cruel faces of his officials and inwardly admitted that there was no way out. He deeply regretted signing the decree that people could pray only to the king for thirty days. How could he have forgotten about Daniel and his faith in Israel's God? But his vanity had been flattered by the officials' suggestion; now the decree could not be revoked. He had considered putting Daniel in charge of the whole kingdom; instead he would be forced to throw his most trusted official into a den of lions.

Daniel faced certain death, and yet—Darius had seen his unshakeable confidence in Yahweh. Did he dare hope . . . ? "May your God, whom you always worship, save you!" the king told Daniel. After Daniel was shut up in the lions' den, Darius spent a wretched, sleepless night. At first light, he rushed to the den, hoping against hope.

Darius called out in an anguished voice, "Daniel, servant of the living God! Was God, whom you always worship, able to save you from the lions?" The king gasped as he heard Daniel's greeting, respectful as always. Then Daniel explained, "My God sent his angel and shut the lions' mouths so that they couldn't hurt me."

People around us watch to see if we really depend on God for help, especially when our safety is threatened. Like Daniel, our life can impact others if we display steadfast confidence in God's power and refuse to back down, even in the face of a king's decree. But we can't wait until we land in a lions' den to develop that kind of faith. If we stay committed to God's will in everyday matters, then we'll be better prepared to face wild animals or wild times.

He saves, rescues, and does miraculous signs
and amazing things in heaven and on earth.
He saved Daniel from the lions.

Daniel 6:27

Ask yourself: **Is it obvious to people around me where I place my trust?**

AUGUST
10

"What should we do?"

2 Kings 6:8–17

The king of Aram called his officers together and demanded to know who had been spying for Israel. Their surprise attacks had failed lately; obviously someone had been tipping off Israel about where the Aramean army camped. One of the officers informed the king that the prophet Elisha told the Israelite king even what the Aramean king said in his bedroom. "Find out where he is," the king ordered.

When the king found out where Elisha was staying, he sent a large army with chariots and horses to capture the prophet. They approached at night and surrounded the city. The next morning, Elisha's servant stepped outside and saw that enemy forces had hemmed them in. Terrified, he cried out, "Master, what should we do?"

Elisha calmly answered, "Don't be afraid. We have more forces on our side than they have on theirs." Then Elisha prayed and asked God to open his servant's eyes so he could see. Immediately, the servant saw a heavenly army of fiery horses and chariots filling the mountain around Elisha.

God allowed Elisha's servant to glimpse a force normally unseen—a host of angels ready to follow God's orders and protect his people. That army is still on active duty today. No matter what enemies come against us, we're surrounded by God's supernatural protection. Nothing can break through that barrier without his permission.

It's not easy to rely on the unseen. But God asks us to trust in what he says instead of what our eyes tell us. Whether we face a frightening situation or just feel hemmed in by our problems, we can ask God to open our eyes. Once we look through the lens of faith, we'll see the spiritual resources he's placed all around us.

Our lives are guided by faith, not by sight.

2 Corinthians 5:7

Ask yourself: **When I face problems, am I guided more by what I believe or by what I see?**

AUGUST
11

"Why did you deceive us?"

Joshua 9:3–23

Joshua and the Israelite leaders eyed the travelers with suspicion. These men claimed to have come from a distant country to request a peace treaty. But what if they really lived nearby? God had commanded Israel to destroy all the cities within the Promised Land. Under questioning, the men insisted that they had come from a great distance to ally themselves with Israel after hearing stories of what Yahweh had done for his people.

The travelers pointed out their dry, moldy bread, broken wineskins, and worn-out sandals and clothes. Joshua checked out this evidence, but he didn't check with God before making the decision. Three days after the Israelites ratified a formal treaty with the men, they discovered the scam. The "travelers" turned out to be their close neighbors.

Joshua asked the Gibeonites, "Why did you deceive us by saying, 'We live very far away from you,' when you live here with us?" Israel had disobeyed God by making the treaty, but his law forbade breaking a covenant based on an oath in his name. So Joshua spared the Gibeonites, making them servants in God's tabernacle.

The episode with the Gibeonites holds valuable lessons for us today. That nagging feeling that something isn't quite right may be a warning from God's Spirit. We can't always trust superficial evidence when making a decision. Even when the answer seems like a no-brainer, we need to seek God's guidance.

God promises to give us discernment, but it's our responsibility to ask for it. We can avoid serious mistakes by preceding every decision with prayer. When we fail to do this, we become vulnerable to deception from other people and to Satan's subtle attacks. Without God-given discernment we may find that we've fallen for a scam, even though the situation seemed so clear-cut.

Teach me good discernment and knowledge.
Psalm 119:66 NASB

Ask God **for discernment concerning whatever decisions you face today.**

AUGUST
12

"Did you come here to torture us before it is time?"

Matthew 8:28–34

Most travelers avoided that road, but not Jesus. As he and his disciples passed through a region southeast of the Sea of Galilee, two demon-possessed men confronted them. (Mark and Luke give a more detailed account, and focus on one of the men, possibly the more violent or well-known of the two.) Forced out of the city, these men lived among the tombs, wild, disheveled, and usually naked. Chains couldn't hold them because the demons gave them superhuman strength. The men posed a danger to other people and to themselves.

The evil spirits controlling the men recognized Jesus and his authority over them. They also showed an awareness of their final end—that one day God would condemn them to everlasting punishment. Afraid that Jesus would cut their time short, the demons shrieked, "Why are you bothering us now, Son of God? Did you come here to torture us before it is time?" Rather than become disembodied spirits when Jesus cast them out of the men, the demons begged to go into a nearby herd of swine. Jesus agreed, and the possessed swine rushed into the Sea of Galilee and drowned.

It seems natural to wonder why Jesus didn't use his power to destroy the demons. This incident reminds us that God has allowed a window of time for Satan to exercise limited power. Satan and his demons work furiously to influence believers and possess the minds of unbelievers. But it won't always be that way. Whenever we're discouraged or bewildered by the evil that goes on in the world, we can remember what Satan and the other fallen angels know full well: their day of judgment is coming.

The devil, who deceived them, was thrown into the fiery lake of sulfur, where the beast and the false prophet were also thrown.

Revelation 20:10

Ask God **to help you remember that a day of judgment is coming when he will vindicate all injustice and remove all evil from the world.**

"Why are you persecuting me?"

Acts 22:1–8

As Saul got closer to Damascus, a surge of adrenaline quickened his pace. He had important business—an errand for the God he served. The letters he carried gave him the power to capture any Christ-followers in that city and bring them to Jerusalem to face imprisonment and, hopefully, execution. Suddenly, a brilliant light flashed around him.

As Saul fell to the ground, a voice called out, "Saul! Saul! Why are you persecuting me?" Saul squinted in the direction of the voice and asked, "Who are you?" Never in a million years would he have expected the answer he received: "I'm Jesus from Nazareth, the one you're persecuting."

When Saul persecuted Jesus's followers, it was the same as if he had done those things to Jesus himself. This assurance that Jesus identifies so closely with Christians serves as both a warning and a comfort to us. Since Jesus defends all believers, we want to make sure we never mistreat one of his own. If we hurt a fellow believer, then we've hurt Jesus. We show our devotion to him when we treat his followers with love and respect.

The other side of this principle is that Jesus is our defender too. Whatever someone does to us, they've also done to him. Whether we endure petty criticism, unfair treatment, or outright persecution, he takes it personally. Whatever concerns our welfare also concerns him. Jesus wants us to come to him when we're mistreated in any way and trust him to take care of us. He can handle things far better than we ever could. There is great security and freedom in trusting our Defender when we're picked on or persecuted.

The Lord your God defends his people.
Isaiah 51:22

Ask yourself: **When someone picks on me, is my first response to run to my Defender?**

AUGUST
14

"What are you waiting for now?"

Acts 22:9–16

When the resurrected Jesus confronted Saul on the road to Damascus, he told him to go into the city and wait for further instructions. For three days Saul fasted and prayed. Then Jesus sent a disciple named Ananias to lay his hands on Saul. After the temporarily blinded man regained his sight, Ananias confirmed that God had chosen Saul to be a witness of the Good News to Jews and Gentiles.

Saul must have been weakened by the traumatic experience on the road, combined with three days of fasting, but Ananias urged him to action. "What are you waiting for now?" he asked. "Get up!" Saul got up, was baptized, and ate. For several days he stayed with the believers in Damascus. Saul immediately began preaching in the synagogues that Jesus is the Son of God (see Acts 9:19–20), shocking people by his about-face change in attitude and in actions.

Many of us struggle with habitual procrastination on a daily basis. We may feel overwhelmed by the list of responsibilities and demands on our time and by the people who need our attention. Sometimes our only alternative seems to be to let some things slide. Other times, our procrastination stems from a lack of desire, poor organizational skills, or simply bad habits.

It's harder to admit that we sometimes procrastinate with our spiritual responsibilities—and that's a much more dangerous habit. We may drag our feet if God asks us to make some change in our behavior that we're not thrilled about. We might hesitate if God urges us to speak to someone in a way that falls outside of our comfort zone. But by not following through right away, we risk letting our heart grow insensitive to God's communications. We can't afford to procrastinate in spiritual matters. Whenever we hear God's voice, that's the time to get up and take action.

If only you would listen to him today!

Psalm 95:7

Ask yourself: **When I sense God urging me to do something, do I immediately obey or do I tend to procrastinate?**

"Where is the one who led them through the deep water?"

Isaiah 63:7–16

Two years ago today, Dominic thought as he glanced at the calendar. Despite his prayers for his job, Dominic had gotten his pink slip the week after his second daughter's birth. And although his church had prayed fervently about his lab results, the cancer diagnosis had come the following week. That first year, Dominic had fought the feeling of being swept away by a flood of fears, disappointments, and mounting debts. Now, as he looked back, he knew who had carried him through to the other side.

Isaiah wrote to the Jewish exiles in Babylon who faced a situation that looked hopeless. He reminded them how God had protected and delivered them in the past, often in miraculous ways. "Where is the one who divided the water in front of them to make an everlasting name for himself?" Isaiah asked. "Where is the one who led them through the deep water?" Isaiah focused their attention on examples of God's faithfulness, such as when he divided the Red Sea and the Jordan River so they could cross to the other side.

God doesn't always remove every trial and obstacle in our path, but he does promise to lead us through them. Sometimes our problems surround us like rising floodwaters, threatening to sweep away our sanity and our faith. Thankfully, God won't leave us to "sink or swim." He's right there with us, holding us up. When our worst fears come true, we don't always sense his presence in our initial shock. Afterward we can look back and see how he led us safely through to the other side. We might get wet, but we can always trust God to keep our head above water.

When you go through deep waters and great trouble, I will be with you. When you go through rivers of difficulty, you will not drown!

Isaiah 43:2 TLB

Ask God **to help you sense his guiding presence when you feel as though you're drowning in problems.**

AUGUST

16

"How can we force them out?"

Deuteronomy 7:16–26

I knew that autumn had officially arrived when I walked into the utility room that morning. Asian lady beetles crawled across the walls and clustered in the corners. Later that day, I found smaller numbers in other parts of the house. Each fall these little bugs invade our home by the hundreds. Within an hour after vacuuming them up, the utility room would once again be filled. Getting rid of these pests seems like a losing battle until cold weather hits.

God commanded Israel to get rid of all the nations in Canaan, but Moses knew it might look like a losing battle to them. "You may say to yourselves, 'These nations outnumber us. How can we force them out?'" Moses said. He urged the people not to give in to their fear. Instead of looking at their enemies' strength, they needed to focus on God's power and the miracles he had already done on their behalf.

The Israelites faced a daunting task, but it was important to completely wipe out the inhabitants in Canaan. Otherwise, the people would trap Israel into sin and idolatry, cutting them off from God's promised blessings. In a similar way, believers are commanded to be ruthless about getting rid of sinful habits and attitudes. Any sin that we allow to remain will be a trap, and will rob us of blessings that we could enjoy.

Ephesians 4:25 and Colossians 3:8 command us to get rid of anger, hot tempers, hatred, cursing, loud quarreling, and obscene language. First Peter 2:1 includes more subtle sins such as "every kind of deception, hypocrisy, and jealousy." We can easily get overwhelmed and feel like we're fighting a losing battle. When we feel outnumbered, or temptation seems too strong for us, we can focus on God's power. Since he saved us from the penalty of our sin, surely we can trust him to help us force out our "enemies."

So get rid of all immoral behavior and
all the wicked things you do.

James 1:21

Ask yourself: **What enemy have I failed to force out of my life?**

AUGUST
17

“Do you love me?”

John 21:15–17

Peter’s life changed forever after he denied knowing Jesus three times, but not in the way he probably expected. Peter had meant it when he vowed to give his life for Jesus. He’d been sincere when he promised to stand by Jesus even if everyone else deserted him. Jesus had given him the name “Peter,” or “Rock,” yet he had crumbled easily in the face of fear. How could he have failed the Master so miserably?

Jesus knew Peter’s heart. He saw his shame and humiliation, but he also understood how Peter’s failure could strengthen his faith. In order to be an effective leader, Peter would need a fuller understanding of his own heart. “Simon, son of John,” Jesus asked, “do you love me more than the other disciples do?”

Peter was through with boasting. “Yes, Lord, you know that I love you,” he answered. Then Jesus simplified the question. Twice he asked, “Do you love me?” The third time Peter responded, “Lord, you know everything. You know that I love you.” With each affirmation, Jesus urged Peter to “feed” and “take care of” his sheep. Rather than being washed up, Peter had a new awareness of his weakness, which would make him a stronger leader.

When we feel as though we’ve let God down, we may be tempted to question whether he still loves us. At those times, it can be helpful to examine our own heart toward him. Failure represents an opportunity to affirm our love for God with a deeper understanding of our weakness, and to be comforted by the knowledge that he’s not through with us. Jesus’s questions required more than an answer from Peter; they required action. Rather than being sidelined by our spiritual failures, we can become more effective in our ministry to other believers. But first, we need to have a simple conversation with Jesus.

Peter said to him, “Lord, you know everything. You know that I love you.”

John 21:17

Ask yourself: **What is the condition of my heart toward God right now?**

AUGUST
18

"What seems best to you?"

Judges 9:1–6

Although our nation was founded on Judeo-Christian standards, today many people have adopted a worldview of moral relativism. Polls show that the majority of college professors teach that there is no such thing as right and wrong; rather, moral choices depend on the specific circumstances, the people involved, and the cultural context. Instead of asking, "What's the right thing to do?" the question becomes, "What seems best in this particular situation?"

Gideon's son Abimelech took advantage of such thinking to grab power for himself. When Gideon (or Jerubbaal) died, Abimelech went to Shechem and used his mother's family to spread a message. "What seems best to you?" he asked. "Do you really want all of Jerubbaal's 70 sons to rule you or just one man? Remember, I'm your own flesh and blood."

The people of Shechem decided to follow Abimelech, and gave him money that he used to hire thugs. His first act was to murder all but one of his seventy half brothers. Abimelech's violent three-year reign ended with the slaughter of the entire population of Shechem and the destruction of the city.

Our culture scoffs at the concept of absolute moral standards, telling us to "follow our heart" or "do what feels right." Basing decisions on such foolish advice can prove problematic—and even deadly. Many people live with broken relationships, financial ruin, or incurable sexually transmitted diseases because they made choices based on what seemed right at the time.

Human judgment is limited; we often don't perceive the long-term consequences of our actions. God's standards of right and wrong are designed for our protection and well-being. It's risky to base decisions on what seems best to us. A better guideline would be, "What does God say is the right thing to do?" We can't go wrong with that.

In those days Israel didn't have a king. Everyone did whatever he considered right.

Judges 21:25

Ask yourself: **Have I ever ignored God's standards and based any decisions on what seemed best to me at the time?**

"Did you bring us out into the desert to die?"

Exodus 14:1–12

At last, the deliverer promised by God had come, ending more than four hundred years of slavery. The Israelites walked out of Egypt as free people—and rich ones at that. Moses told them to ask their former masters for silver, gold, and clothing; God prompted the Egyptians to give the Israelites whatever they requested. Even more importantly, God promised to lead them to a rich land of their own. They began their journey with his very presence guiding them, visible as a column of smoke by day and a column of fire at night.

As the Israelites set up camp facing the Red Sea, their high hopes suddenly plunged into terror. They saw Pharaoh's immense army closing in on them. The people cried out to God and then turned on Moses. "Did you bring us out into the desert to die because there were no graves in Egypt?" they demanded. "Look what you've done by bringing us out of Egypt! It would have been better for us to serve the Egyptians than to die in the desert!"

We may wonder how the Israelites' faith could have wavered so soon after seeing God's miraculous protection during the plagues on the Egyptians. We understand better when we take a close look at our own life. Fear can make us forget how God has delivered and protected us in the past. When a crisis hits, we may feel like saying, "Look at what you've done by bringing me to this place!" But no matter what's closing in on us, God promises to guide us and to be with us through it all. He will never abandon us, and he always knows what he's doing.

The LORD is the one who is going ahead of you.
He will be with you. He won't abandon you or
leave you. So don't be afraid or terrified.

Deuteronomy 31:8

Ask yourself: **How do I react when a crisis hits and my faith wavers?**

AUGUST
20

"Why are you crying out to me?"

Exodus 14:13–28

The starter gun cracked and the pack of runners took off. Donna watched for several minutes until they disappeared over the rise and into the wooded area. Now it was time to move to a spot on the course where the spectators could watch the runners go by. Suddenly, Donna felt a tap on her shoulder. Turning around, she saw her adolescent son, wearing a sheepish look along with his cross-country uniform. "What happened?" she gasped. Her son admitted that he'd been talking to a girl and had missed the start of the race.

There's a time to talk and a time to get moving. When the Israelites found themselves trapped between the Egyptian army and the Red Sea, they wailed and railed at Moses. He told them to stand still and see what God would do to save them. Then God revealed his startling plan. "Why are you crying out to me?" he asked Moses. "Tell the Israelites to start moving." God opened up a path through the sea with walls of water on either side. While he protected them from behind, the people walked through to the other side on dry ground.

Crying out to God is an appropriate response when we're trapped by our problems. We also need to watch for his answer and be ready to move according to his plan. God will show us the way, but he may ask us to do something that seems uncomfortable, difficult, or even startling. Fear can paralyze us when we need to take action. We may even use prayer as a stall tactic when we don't really want to do what God has directed. God will show us the way to handle our problem if we cry out to him—and then stand by for his signal to get moving.

There is a right time and a right way to act in every situation.

Ecclesiastes 8:6

Ask yourself: **Is there a situation in my life that calls for action right now?**

AUGUST
21

"What is this?"

Exodus 16:11–26

When the Israelites worried about starving to death as they moved through the desert, God promised to rain down food from heaven for them. He outlined his plan for the people to go out each morning and gather only enough for that day. On the sixth day, the people could gather twice as much to cover their needs for the Sabbath. These limitations would test the Israelites' willingness to trust God to provide for their needs.

The next morning after the dew dried, a thin layer of flakes like frost covered the ground. "What is this?" the people asked. Moses told them it was the food the Lord had provided, and reminded them to gather only what they needed for that day and not save any. When some of them disobeyed, they found the hoarded manna spoiled the next morning.

God provided the manna six days a week for forty years, until the Israelites reached the border of the Promised Land. They sometimes longed for more variety in their diet, but this "bread from heaven" met their nutritional requirements perfectly. Each day the manna reminded the Israelites that God promised to take care of them on a day-to-day basis.

God still provides for his people on a daily basis. We don't always get what we expect; if we're not careful, we may miss his "manna" when it comes. We might not get as much as we'd like; God often meets our basic needs and ignores our "wants." There are dangers in having too much (pride, self-sufficiency, trusting in wealth) and in having too little (excessive anxiety, doing something to dishonor God). The writer of Proverbs 30:8 asked God to give him just enough to meet his needs. God wants us to trust him, day by day and moment by moment, to take care of us. Once we learn that lesson, we'll be satisfied with whatever he rains down.

Don't give me either poverty or riches.
Feed me only the food I need.

Proverbs 30:8

Ask yourself: **Do I trust God to meet my needs on a day-by-day basis?**

AUGUST
22

"Remember all the free fish we ate in Egypt?"

Numbers 11:1–6

How could I be such a fool? Mallory dropped her head into her hands and wondered why in the world she'd decided to make up with her old boyfriend. During the months of their separation, she'd missed the good times—nice restaurants, front-row seats at concerts and plays, boating trips. But after a few weeks of being back together, Mallory remembered why she'd broken it off before. The verbal abuse had started up again, and Mallory understood just how selective her memory had been.

The Israelites had selective memory about their former life back in Egypt. After the initial thrill of their miraculous deliverance wore off, they seemed to forget about the grueling labor under harsh, uncaring slave masters. When they faced hardships in their new life, all the people seemed to remember was the food. "Remember all the free fish we ate in Egypt and the cucumbers, watermelons, leeks, onions, and garlic we had?" they cried. "But now we've lost our appetite! Everywhere we look there's nothing but manna!"

God never promised that the Christian life would be problem-free. In the face of hardship and deprivation, our old life can actually start to look better in some ways. Maybe we enjoyed more material wealth or prestige. Maybe life seemed easier when we didn't try to live by God's standards. Our selective memory can make us forget what it was really like to live in slavery to sin.

The Israelites could have borne their hardships better if they had looked ahead to their future, focusing on God's promise to give them a wonderful land of their own. We'll be able to bear difficulties in our present life by looking ahead to our glorious future with God. Nothing in our past or present life could ever compare with that.

I consider our present sufferings insignificant compared
to the glory that will soon be revealed to us.

Romans 8:18

Ask God **to help you remember what life was like before he set you free from sin's control.**

"Is God unfair when he vents his anger on us?"

Romans 3:1–12

"But that's not fair!" Kayla shouted. Her parents had just laid out her punishment for sneaking off to the party. She could understand why they'd be upset about her lying to them, especially because of the underage drinking thing. But did they have to make such a big deal out of it? "I thought parents were supposed to be understanding and loving," she said, pouting. "We wouldn't be very loving if we skipped the discipline for wrongdoing," her dad answered.

Our human nature has a hard time seeing the fairness of discipline and punishment, no matter how guilty we are. When Paul wrote about the sinfulness of man, he anticipated an objection in the minds of his readers. He knew that some would ask why they should be held accountable if their unbelief served to exhibit God's faithfulness.

"Is God unfair when he vents his anger on us?" Paul asked them. He answered with an emphatic, "That's unthinkable!" If it was unfair for God to judge the unbelieving Jews, wouldn't it be unfair for him to judge the rest of the world? If that were true, then all evil behavior would go unpunished. No one would call that fair.

Most people prefer to focus on God's love and avoid talking about his anger. But Scripture makes it clear that his holiness requires him to judge sin. God's love has two sides—mercy and discipline. We can expect our heavenly Father to deal with any sin that we allow in our life. Rather than accuse him of being unfair, we need to think how unfair the world would be if he never judged any wrongdoing. And we can be thankful that his anger lasts but a moment while his favor lasts a lifetime (see Ps. 30:5).

The Lord is merciful and gracious, slow to anger, and abounding in mercy.
Psalm 103:8 NKJV

Ask yourself: **Do I accept God's right to be angry at sin in my life?**

AUGUST
24

"If God is for us, who can be against us?"

Romans 8:28–32

As the PE teacher tossed the coin in the air, Aiden held his breath. *Tails—thank you!* he thought. Everyone knew if you wanted to win the basketball game, you had to go first in choosing guys for your team. And everyone also knew whose name would be called first. "Scott!" Aiden said. With a few extra inches in height and great coordination, Scott was unstoppable on the court. Having him on your side meant a sure victory.

Paul explained that having God on our side means a sure victory for believers. God is taking everything that happens in our life and working it together for our ultimate good, with the goal of conforming us to the image of Christ. "What can we say about all of this?" Paul wrote. "If God is for us, who can be against us?" Since God gave up his Son to die for us, how can we doubt that he will provide whatever we need to live a victorious life?

That doesn't mean we won't have adversaries. From the moment we decide to follow Christ, we become hated enemies of Satan and his demons. Sometimes unbelievers hostile to the faith will lash out against us. While we may have to face some tough battles, our ultimate victory is assured since God controls the outcome.

God doesn't want us to live like defeated people. When disappointments and troubles make us feel beaten down, we can go to the Bible and ask our Coach for a pep talk. Meditating on what God has done for us in the past and what he's promised for our future will transform our attitude no matter what we're up against. If we're a child of God, we can never be a loser—because we're on the winning side.

The victory for righteous people comes from the LORD.

Psalm 37:39

Ask yourself: **Do I face challenges with a sense of victory, knowing that God is on my side?**

“How could such an evil thing happen among you?”

Judges 20:1–14

Just how low can a society sink when its people reject God’s truth and try to live by their own standards? An incident near the end of the book of Judges shows what resulted from each person doing whatever seemed right to them. When a Levite spent the night in Gibeah, some of the local men surrounded the house and demanded that he come out and have sex with them. The Levite gave them his concubine, and they abused her all night until she died. The next morning, the Levite cut her body into twelve pieces and sent them throughout Israel.

At a special gathering, the Levite told his story, leaving out the fact that he had pushed his concubine out the door to save his own skin. As immoral and sin-hardened as Israel was, the news of this crime outraged the people. Men were sent to confront the tribe of Benjamin. “How could such an evil thing happen among you?” they asked. The Benjamites’ refusal to hand over the guilty men led to civil war and their tribe’s near-annihilation.

When people reject God’s standards, they begin a downward spiral into sin and degradation. This process may be gradual and can go unnoticed at first, but one compromise with the truth leads to another. Eventually, the culture becomes so hardened to sin that it takes something horrific to shock people and make them ask, “How could such an evil thing happen among us?”

It’s dangerous to rely on our own reasoning and judgment rather than God’s Word. Our minds and emotions are easily deceived. Our thinking can become so distorted that we have a hard time recognizing evil. How much better our lives—and our country—will be if we choose to be ruled by God rather than our own deceitful minds.

The human mind is the most deceitful of all things.
Jeremiah 17:9

Ask God **to reveal any area of your life where you’ve drifted away from his standards.**

AUGUST
26

"What will we get out of it?"

Matthew 19:21–30

Cherie sat across from the successful businessman and shared the need for corporate sponsors to support her after-school programs. She described the recreational activities, job skills training, and homework help. Then she showed him statistics that pointed to improved grades and lower dropout rates. "Do you have any questions?" she asked. "Just one," the man answered. "What do I get out of this?"

Peter wanted to know the same thing. When a rich young man asked Jesus about inheriting eternal life, Jesus told him to sell his possessions, give away the money, and follow him. The man seemed unwilling to comply and went away sad. Peter thought about how he and the disciples had walked away from their former lives when Jesus called them. "Look, we've given up everything to follow you," he said. "What will we get out of it?"

Jesus explained that the disciples would be given special honor in his future kingdom, sitting on thrones alongside him and judging the tribes of Israel. In addition, anyone who has given up family or home to follow him will be repaid a hundred times as much in this life, along with eternal life in the world to come.

God promises future rewards for those who serve him, but should that be our primary motivation? Jesus temporarily left the glories of heaven to take on a human body, suffer, and die an agonizing death. Instead of thinking about himself, his actions were motivated by what his sacrifice would offer us. The more we come to understand how much Jesus gave up for us, the less we'll think about what we'll get for serving him. Our question will change to "What can I give to you?"

Although he was in the form of God and equal with God, he did not take advantage of this equality. Instead, he emptied himself by taking on the form of a servant, by becoming like other humans.

Philippians 2:6–7

Ask yourself: **What is my primary motivation for serving God?**

“Would you like to get well?”

John 5:1–9

Tracy looked at her watch as she checked the man’s heart rate. Mr. Woods had been in the nursing home when she first started her job twelve years ago. He’d had bouts of illness before but had always bounced back, ready for outdoor walks and any activity offered by the staff. This time was different. Although the doctors had given him a clean bill of health, Mr. Woods stayed in bed, listless and uninterested in the world. Tracy understood the situation; she’d seen the signs before—Mr. Woods had lost his will to get better.

The man in today’s passage may have given up all hopes of getting well after 38 years of being an invalid. He lay beside a pool that people believed would heal the first person to enter it after the water was stirred up. Jesus looked into the man’s heart and saw that his hope needed to be stirred up. “Would you like to get well?” Jesus asked. When the man explained that he had no one to help him into the water, Jesus instructed him to get up and walk. The man obeyed and his paralysis instantly left him.

Sinful habits, addictions, and dysfunctional relationships can become a way of life after so much time passes. We can get so used to living with a problem that we don’t recognize our need anymore. Or we may simply despair of ever finding a solution and accept things as they are. Jesus died so that we can be whole and healthy in every area of our life. But he can’t relieve our suffering until we recognize our need for healing. When we feel like giving up, we can remember the “hopeless” case of the paralyzed man by the pool.

Heal me, O Lord, *and I will be healed. Rescue me,*
and I will be rescued. You are the one I praise.
Jeremiah 17:14

Ask yourself: **What situation in my life have I accepted as hopeless?**

Ask God **to stir up your hope for healing and restoration in that area.**

AUGUST

28

"Hasn't God turned the wisdom of the world into nonsense?"

1 Corinthians 1:18–25

The school's website showcases a sprawling campus and faculty bios that indicate a well-rounded team of reputable professors. Such good prices too. For only $1200, you get a bachelor's *and* master's degree. Throw in an extra $75 in tuition and you can graduate *magna cum laude*. This "university" is just one among hundreds of online diploma mills offering fake degrees. Degrees can often be "earned" within days, and sometimes shipped overnight. Some diploma mills even offer options such as having your diploma postdated or choosing your GPA at the time of purchase.

We can all agree that the idea of "earning" a higher education within days is pure nonsense. Paul wrote that what the world considers wisdom is pure nonsense from God's viewpoint. Jewish scholars and Greek philosophers found it hard to accept the message of Christ because it conflicted with their thinking. But in God's eyes they looked foolish if their idea of wisdom kept them from accepting his gift of salvation. "Hasn't God turned the wisdom of the world into nonsense?" Paul asked.

Christians are often labeled as dumb by the rest of the world. They accuse us of not using our brains, and wonder how we can believe such old-fashioned nonsense as the Bible. Meanwhile, much of what passes as higher education among bona fide universities has become downright absurd. More often, the world promotes slightly distorted versions of truth.

There's nothing wrong with the pursuit of knowledge or wanting to be well-educated. But we want to guard against trying to fit in with the world's way of thinking, which is worth about as much as an overnight degree.

If any of you think you are wise in the
ways of this world, you should give up that
wisdom in order to become really wise.

1 Corinthians 3:18

Ask yourself: **Am I letting the world's wisdom influence my attitudes rather than God's Word?**

"How can the Messiah come from Galilee?"

John 7:40–52

The late Paul Harvey attracted millions of listeners to his weekly radio broadcasts. His segment called "The Rest of the Story" grew in popularity until it became a separate series in 1976. During these broadcasts, Harvey related factual stories with a twist or surprise thrown in at the end. He always concluded with the familiar tagline: "And now you know . . . the *rest* of the story."

Some of the Jews knew that Jesus had been raised in Nazareth, but they didn't take the time to find out the rest of the story. Some people called Jesus the Messiah; others asked, "How can the Messiah come from Galilee?" They knew that Old Testament prophets had predicted the Messiah would be a descendant of David, born in Bethlehem—not in Nazareth. But if they had really wanted to know the truth, they would have discovered that Jesus fit both of these qualifications.

Ironically, the Pharisees accused the crowds of being too ignorant of the Scriptures to recognize Jesus as a deceiver. All the while, they ignored the many prophecies that identified Jesus as the Messiah. From our perspective, we wonder how they could have been so blind. Yet all of us can fall into error if we aren't thoroughly familiar with the Bible as a whole.

It can be dangerous to pull verses or passages out of context, or to concentrate on certain teachings while ignoring others. If we take a selective approach, we end up with a distorted view of who God is. Living a life pleasing to God requires a dedication to studying the Bible from beginning to end, throughout our life. We want to do our best to correctly interpret and apply the Scriptures until we go to live with their Author. Then we'll *really* know the rest of the story.

Do your best to present yourself to God as one approved, a workman who does not need to be ashamed and who correctly handles the word of truth.

2 Timothy 2:15 NIV

Ask yourself: **Am I careful to interpret the Scriptures accurately?**

AUGUST
30

"Why do you see the piece of sawdust in another believer's eye and not notice the wooden beam in your own eye?"

Matthew 7:1–5

Years ago I read a true anecdote that stuck in my mind. When a young wife moved to a new neighborhood, the woman next door came over to introduce herself. The newcomer was dismayed, however, when the older woman leaned forward and confided, "Let me just warn you about one of your neighbors." After rattling off a list of annoying traits and shortcomings, she sat back and smiled. "Now that you understand some of my faults," she said, "I hope that we can become good friends."

Most of us don't have that keen of an awareness of our own shortcomings, because we're too busy looking through a magnifying glass at others' imperfections. Jesus used a memorable hyperbole to expose this tendency. "So why do you see the piece of sawdust in another believer's eye and not notice the wooden beam in your own eye?" he asked. Jesus went on to explain that we need to deal with our own wrongdoing before confronting another believer with theirs.

It's easy to have impaired vision when it comes to our own faults and shortcomings. The habits and character traits that annoy us the most in others are often the very ones we're guilty of. Other times, we rush to point out minor offenses in another person without seeing the big ones we commit.

There are times when we do need to confront a fellow believer about their sin, but our first step is to examine our own life. Without a proper assessment of our personal struggle with sin, we can't have the humility and compassion to help others. Before we judge another person's habits and actions, we'd better follow Jesus's advice to turn the magnifying glass around and inspect our own life.

First remove the beam from your own eye.

Matthew 7:5

Ask yourself: **Do I tend to magnify others' faults while ignoring my own?**

“Where can I run to get away from you?”

Psalm 139:5–18

In Margaret Wise Brown’s picture book, *The Runaway Bunny*, a little bunny announces that he plans to run away. His mother tells him that she will follow him because he’s her little bunny. The bunny says that if she follows him, he’ll become a fish. The mother says that if he becomes a fish, she’ll become a fisherman. The bunny will become a rock on a mountain; she’ll become a mountain climber. After several more ideas, the bunny decides that he may as well stay home and be her little bunny.

David asked hypothetical questions about running away from God as he marveled at God’s omnipresence. “Where can I go to get away from your Spirit?” he wrote. “Where can I run to get away from you?” Even if David could climb the rays of the sun or land on the most distant seashore, even there God’s hand would hold him and guide him. Even if total darkness covered David, he would be seen by the same God who had witnessed his conception in his mother’s womb.

This beautiful psalm reminds us that we are never out of God’s reach. There is no place in the universe or beyond so remote that he wouldn’t be there to guide and care for us. We’ll never face a situation so dark that God can’t see our need and offer his comfort and help. No matter where we go, his presence surrounds us.

Unconfessed sin can make us feel alienated from our heavenly Father. Adopting worldly attitudes can dull our sense of his presence. But if we belong to God, he will never leave us. We have his Spirit inside us and his presence around us. Who would ever want to run away from such a love?

You are all around me—in front of me and in back of me. You lay your hand on me.

Psalm 139:5

Ask God **to give you a sharper sense of his loving presence surrounding you as you go through the day.**

SEPTEMBER
1

"Why should you go with me?"

Ruth 1:6–18

As a widow with no living sons, Naomi faced a bleak future. So when she heard that the famine had ended in Judah, she decided to return home. She and her two daughters-in-law struck out on the road together, but on the way, Naomi had second thoughts. Surely it would be in the girls' best interests to stay in Moab. What chances of remarriage would they have in Israel?

Naomi blessed Orpah and Ruth and kissed them farewell. As they cried and clung to her, three times she urged them to return home. "Go back, my daughters," she said. "Why should you go with me?" Finally, Orpah relented and turned back. But Ruth refused to leave Naomi, vowing that "Wherever you go, I will go. . . . Your people will be my people, and your God will be my God."

Ruth had grown up in a pagan culture that practiced human sacrifice. Her relationship with Naomi's family had opened her eyes to the true God and a better way of life. Naomi's faith and her unselfish kindness to her daughter-in-law prompted Ruth to follow her, even though it meant facing an uncertain future in an alien country.

In his letter to Titus, Paul summed up his life's purpose: to proclaim the Good News that leads people to faith in Christ and to the knowledge of truth that leads to godly living. As a believer, we share that same purpose. When we demonstrate God's love in our relationships, people will want to know him. If we're living an obedient lifestyle, it will serve as an example for people to follow. We may have the desire to lead others to Christ, but the real question is: Do we give them a reason to go there with us?

I was sent to lead God's chosen people to faith and to the knowledge of the truth that leads to a godly life.

Titus 1:1

Ask yourself: **Am I leading people to Christ by my relationships and lifestyle?**

"Why are you so helpful?"

Ruth 2:8–15

Our newspaper's editorial section occasionally includes a letter from someone expressing amazement and thanking a stranger for an act of kindness. Maybe the other person stopped to help when they had car problems, or returned a lost wallet with all the money and credit cards intact. I find these letters encouraging, but also sad in a sense. How does it reflect on our society when people find simple acts of decency and kindness so astonishing?

Ruth found Boaz's kindness and concern astonishing. To provide food for herself and Naomi, she took advantage of the Israelite law that allowed poor people to gather stalks of grain left behind by the reapers. Boaz invited her to work alongside his servant girls during the entire harvest season. He assured Ruth that she would be safe and could drink the water provided for his workers instead of having to draw her own.

Gratitude flooded Ruth, but she wondered why she had been singled out for special treatment. "Why are you so helpful?" Ruth asked. "Why are you paying attention to me? I'm only a foreigner." Boaz responded that he'd heard of Ruth's kindness and loyalty to her mother-in-law. Later, he shared his own food with Ruth and ordered his harvesters to make her work easier.

In our cynical, jaded culture, an act of simple kindness can attract a lot of attention. But unselfishness should be a hallmark of the Christian life. Paul wrote that we should be just as concerned about others' needs as our own. Our goal is to develop the attitude of humility that Jesus demonstrated when he performed the supreme act of kindness by dying for us. Since this attitude goes against the world's thinking, we can expect people to be astonished when we follow Christ's example.

> *Don't be concerned only about your own interests,*
> *but also be concerned about the interests of others.*
>
> Philippians 2:4

Ask God **to give you genuine concern for others' needs and opportunities to surprise them with kindness.**

SEPTEMBER

3

“Where did you gather grain today?”

Ruth 2:17–23

Ruth put in long hours picking up barley left behind by the harvesters. At the end of the day, she beat out the grain from the stalks. Ruth had gleaned about half a bushel of barley, enough to feed her and Naomi for many days. This unusually generous amount was due to her diligence—and also to Boaz’s instructions for his workers to deliberately drop stalks in her path.

When Ruth carried her bundle back to town, the amount of grain astonished Naomi. “Where did you gather grain today?” she asked. “Just where did you work?” Ruth replied that a man named Boaz owned the field. Naomi immediately saw God’s hand in their circumstances. She explained to her daughter-in-law that Boaz was a close relative, in line to act as a kinsman-redeemer for the two widows. Although Naomi had returned to Judah destitute and bitter, God now made it clear that he would provide for her.

God had established laws about gleaning to give poor people a way to feed themselves, but they had to be willing to do the work. In a similar way, God has provided his written Word to make sure we have all the spiritual nourishment we need. But we have to be willing to put in effort to study it, meditate on it, and apply its principles to our life.

It’s a good idea to periodically evaluate the sources of our spiritual nourishment. Are we involved with a church that promotes biblically based teaching and trains people to be disciples of Christ? Do the Bible studies, small groups, and special events that we attend focus on the Word or solely on entertainment and fellowship? Since God’s Word is the source of spiritual growth, we want to make sure that we gather “grain” in the right field.

I delight in your decrees; I will not neglect your word.

Psalm 119:16 NIV

Ask yourself: **Am I making sure that my spiritual nourishment comes from the right source?**

"Could it be that you're failing the test?"

2 Corinthians 13:5–9

Kyesha sat down at her kitchen table. Timer, check. Pencils, check. Practice LSAT, check. Law school had been her dream ever since she could remember. She'd scraped together the money for the study course for the entrance exam and had spent every weekend for months preparing herself. Kyesha took a deep breath. She had a lot riding on this self-test. Would she score high enough, or would the test reveal that she needed to put in more study time?

Paul invited the believers at Corinth to take a self-test. After defending himself and his ministry, Paul urged them to examine themselves. "Don't you recognize that you are people in whom Jesus Christ lives?" he wrote. "Could it be that you're failing the test?" Then Paul expressed hope that the Corinthians would grow and mature as believers.

Some people believe that Paul challenged the Corinthians to test themselves to see if they were true Christians; others believe that he wanted them to examine their lives to see if they truly lived like Christians. Both kinds of tests are beneficial to take on a regular basis. It's wise to periodically examine our faith to make sure that it's genuine. Have we trusted in Christ alone for our salvation? Do we see evidence that God's Spirit lives in us?

Even if we pass that major exam, we all need to perform spiritual self-checks from time to time. Are we growing closer to God and learning more about him through his Word? Do we engage in consistent, meaningful prayer and worship times? Are our attitudes and behavior becoming more Christlike? Do we share the gospel with others and bear fruit for God's kingdom? It's easy to get complacent and neglect to nurture our spiritual growth, so Paul's instruction to examine ourselves is sound advice. A pop quiz every now and then will do us good.

Test yourselves!
2 Corinthians 13:5

Ask yourself: **If my spiritual growth were tested, would I get a passing grade?**

SEPTEMBER

5

"Do you see a person who is efficient in his work?"

Proverbs 22:29

As the owner of a small company, James does his best to provide good benefits and job security for his employees. Some days, though, he wonders if it's worth the trouble. Pilfering of supplies is a problem, along with employees using time on the job for personal phone calls, online surfing, and computer games. A few employees routinely come in late; he suspects that others call in sick when they simply want time off. Along with the lack of productivity, James has to deal with the complaints of workers who feel that certain tasks are "beneath" them.

The Bible addresses the topic of a proper work ethic. The writer of Proverbs 22 asks, "Do you see a person who is efficient in his work? He will serve kings." This wise saying reminds us that the best way to get promoted in our job is to be dependable, hardworking, and diligent about the quality of our work. What a far cry from the attitude of many people today, who focus on getting by with doing as little work as possible.

Paul's letter to the Colossian Christians explains that no matter what we're doing, we're ultimately working for Jesus Christ. Whether we have a blue or white collar job, or mostly change diapers all day, God wants us to give our best. As believers in Christ, we should be the most conscientious workers in any environment.

If our aim is to obey and please God, there's no such thing as a dead-end job or a chore that's beneath us. As we serve our employer with excellence and integrity, our work setting will be transformed and we will honor God. We'll begin to see any work that comes our way as another opportunity to worship him.

Whatever you do, do it wholeheartedly as though you were working for your real master and not merely for humans.

Colossians 3:23

Ask yourself: **Do I honor God by working hard and always giving my best?**

"What makes your beloved better than any other beloved?"

Song of Songs 5:9–16

Vanessa watched her husband eating the dinner she'd spent so much time preparing. She wondered if he liked the new recipe, but why bother asking? He pretty much gave the same stock answer whether she asked about food, clothes, her hair, or the arrangement of furniture: "It's alright." Vanessa had tried explaining that she needed to hear some positive feedback and affirmation once in a while, but he just shrugged and said he wasn't into that sort of thing.

The couple in Song of Songs really got into pouring on the compliments. When the bride went searching for her husband, the women of Jerusalem asked her, "What makes your beloved better than any other beloved?" The girl proceeded to list his physical characteristics that made him stand out "among 10,000 men." She ended her description by declaring that "Everything about him is desirable!" Her bridegroom had earlier praised her traits and said, "You are beautiful in every way, my true love."

We're all hungry for words of affirmation from people we care about. Giving compliments doesn't come naturally to some people because of their personality or childhood. As time passes, even verbally supportive spouses, parents, and friends often drop the habit of complimenting each other. Developing the habit might be uncomfortable at first, but it's amazing how sincere praise can build up a relationship.

God likes to hear words of praise from his children. But sometimes we skip that element of prayer, rushing straight into our list of needs and requests. When we meditate on God's many praiseworthy qualities, it helps our faith grow and strengthens our relationship with him. Our problems seem smaller and we find it hard to be negative when we're affirming why our God is better than any other.

No god is like you, O Lord. No one can do what you do.

Psalm 86:8

Ask yourself: **What words of affirmation do I need to speak to my family, my friends, and my God?**

SEPTEMBER
7

“How can they hear if no one tells the Good News?”

Romans 10:12–17

Anna settled in at her neighbor’s kitchen table for their usual Monday morning coffee and prayer time. *Who would have dreamed that we would ever wind up being sisters in Christ*? Anna marveled. Anna had hesitated to share her faith with this woman who strictly adhered to the religion of her home country, especially after reading about the rarity of conversions among certain populations. But God had nudged Anna time after time. Now she thanked him for letting her be the one to share the Good News that her neighbor had been waiting to hear.

Paul confirmed that God’s offer of forgiveness and eternal life extends to everyone, with no qualification other than faith in Christ. He then posed several rhetorical questions to illustrate the process of a person being saved, and our role in it. “But how can people call on him if they have not believed in him? How can they believe in him if they have not heard his message? How can they hear if no one tells the Good News? How can people tell the Good News if no one sends them?”

As believers, we have the most wonderful news that anyone could ever hear. Why do we so often hesitate to broadcast it? Sharing the gospel can be intimidating, especially with some people, but we never know how God has already prepared someone’s heart. If we consider the role that Christ played in the gospel, then our responsibility will seem easy. Instead of wimping out, we can ask God to give us the courage and wisdom to share about him with the right person at the right time. The results are in his hands, but we just might wind up with a new brother or sister in Christ.

As Scripture says, “How beautiful are the feet of the messengers who announce the Good News.”

Romans 10:15

Ask yourself: **What person has God brought into my life who needs to hear the Good News today?**

SEPTEMBER

8

"Why couldn't we force the demon out of the boy?"

Matthew 17:14–20

The nine disciples saw Jesus walking toward them with a mixture of relief and humiliation. While Jesus had been away with Peter, James, and John, they'd been struggling to heal a severe case of demon possession. They had cast out demons before in Jesus's name, but this time their efforts failed. Kneeling before Jesus, the distraught father begged him to have mercy on his son. "I brought him to your disciples, but they couldn't cure him," the father said.

Jesus's rebuke seemed directed at everyone present: "You unbelieving and corrupt generation!" When the demon saw Jesus, it threw the boy to the ground in convulsions (detailed in Mark 9). One command from Jesus brought instant healing. "Why couldn't we force the demon out of the boy?" the disciples asked Jesus later. "Because you have so little faith," he answered. Then he used a familiar Jewish metaphor for doing what seemed impossible. "If your faith is the size of a mustard seed, you can say to this mountain, 'Move from here to there,' and it will move."

Did the disciples' faith waver because of the severity of this particular case? Did their earlier success shift their focus from God's power to their own ability? Or did they give up too soon? We may not fully understand, but we can easily identify with their feelings of failure and frustration.

When we have "mountains" in our path that refuse to budge, it's time to examine our prayer life. Jesus promised that if our mind is saturated with his Word, then our desires will be transformed and our prayers will align with God's will. Then we can persevere in prayer, certain that we'll get a positive answer. Even if the mountain doesn't move, God will show us a way over or around it.

If you live in me and what I say lives in you, then ask for anything you want, and it will be yours.

John 15:7

Ask yourself: **What mountain do I need moved?**

SEPTEMBER

9

"Don't you know that love for this evil world is hatred toward God?"

James 4:1–8

Claire sat in stunned silence as her husband walked away. She had no idea her relationship with Ethan upset Stephen so much. Of course she and Ethan liked spending time together—their friendship went way back, before she'd ever met Stephen. Claire never dreamed that her close relationship with Ethan would endanger her marriage. But now Stephen had told her how he felt in no uncertain terms, challenging her to choose between himself and Ethan.

James told his readers that they had to choose between a relationship with the world and a relationship with God. "You unfaithful people!" he wrote. "Don't you know that love for this evil world is hatred toward God?" Then James laid down a challenge in no uncertain terms: "Whoever wants to be a friend of this world is an enemy of God."

God's first and foremost commandment is to love him with all our heart, mind, soul, and strength. Our human nature pulls in the opposite direction, feeling the seductive call of the world and all that it offers. We're engaged in an ongoing battle to resist things that easily draw our heart away from God: earthly pleasures, wealth, material possessions, the world's approval, self-pride.

God allows no middle ground. He has made it clear that we can't love him and the world at the same time. God challenges us to examine our life to see where our heart lies. What preoccupies our thoughts? Do our goals reflect a desire for his approval or the world's? Are we pursuing a lifestyle that's more obedient to God or more admired in the world's eyes? If we truly understood God's love for us, we would never hesitate to give up anything that hinders our relationship with him. That would always be an easy choice.

> *Don't love the world and what it offers. Those who love the world don't have the Father's love in them.*
>
> 1 John 2:15

Ask yourself: **In what areas am I easily seduced by the things of this world?**

"What are all the angels?"

Hebrews 1:4–14

I strolled down the aisles, surrounded by merchandise with an angel theme. T-shirts, tote bags, calendars, nightlights, and framed prints bore images of what looked like beautiful women dressed in flowing gowns and sporting wings. A buyer could also find statues of angels in any size and price range. I decided that instead of being in a Christian gift shop, I'd stepped into Angels R Us.

People have always been fascinated with angels, sometimes to the point of obsession. In the early churches, false teachers claimed that God could only be approached through levels of angels. Some people revered angels and invoked their protection. Some even considered Jesus as God's highest angel. The writer of Hebrews dedicated two chapters to setting the record straight. "What are all the angels?" he wrote. "They are spirits sent to serve those who are going to receive salvation."

The Bible portrays angels as having active roles in God's work. The only two named in the Bible, Gabriel and Michael, battled demonic spirits. Angels announced Jesus's birth and resurrection, and ministered to him during his wilderness temptation. Other angels brought messages and released Peter from prison. When John got a glimpse of heaven and future events, he fell down to worship his guide. But the angel rebuked John and called himself a fellow servant with the believers. "Worship God!" he said.

With so many magazines, books, and movies that describe purported encounters with angels, it's no wonder so many people have a distorted view. We must never let our curiosity or interest in angels draw our attention away from what's really important. God created angels for important roles, but those pale in comparison to what Jesus did for us. Instead of hoping for a Hollywood-type spiritual encounter, we're better off focusing on our Savior.

The Son has become greater than the angels since he has been given a name that is superior to theirs.

Hebrews 1:4

Ask yourself: **Do I have the proper attitude toward angels?**

SEPTEMBER
11

"Why do you brag about the evil you've done?"

Psalm 52

It's hard to stomach the thought of suicide bombers and other terrorists bragging about their crimes. Who can comprehend the distorted thinking that leads them to believe they're actually serving God by committing mass murder—and what's more, he will reward them in a special way for their heinous actions? Their self-deception blinds them to the reality that they are breaking God's standards and committing abominable sins, which he will judge.

When David wrote Psalm 52, he aimed it at Doeg, a man who committed atrocities in the name of serving the king (see 2 Sam. 22:9–19). While David was fleeing from Saul's murderous jealousy, he requested food from Ahimelech. Later Doeg reported the incident to Saul, describing the priest's hospitality in such a way that Saul accused Ahimelech of treason. Saul's men refused his order to kill Ahimelech's family, but Doeg slaughtered 85 priests and their entire city. Remembering Doeg's treachery, David asked sarcastically, "Why do you brag about the evil you've done, you hero?"

People who commit atrocities will face God's wrath someday, whether or not they claim to be acting in his name. His Word makes it clear that he despises people who call evil good. We see examples of such perverted values in our own culture. The evil of abortion is labeled as a "choice" or a "right." Men boast about how many babies they've fathered; men and women brag about how many sexual partners they've had. Some take pride in getting money by questionable means.

As believers, we want to saturate our minds with God's Word so that others' distorted values won't infiltrate our thinking. People today may have more relaxed attitudes toward such things as extramarital sex, materialism, and dishonesty, but God hasn't changed his mind. It's never a good idea to call evil good.

How horrible it will be for those who
call evil good and good evil.

Isaiah 5:20

Ask yourself: **In what ways have cultural influences dulled my sense of good and evil?**

"What will we eat in the seventh year?"

Leviticus 25:1–7, 18–22

As Israel prepared to enter the Promised Land, God instructed them to let the land take a Sabbath rest every seventh year. The Israelites were to work the fields and vineyards for six years and then allow the land to lie fallow. During that year, there would be no planting, pruning, or harvesting for the purpose of selling the produce. Whatever the land produced on its own would be what the people ate.

God anticipated that this scenario would naturally prompt a question in their minds: "You may ask, 'What will we eat in the seventh year if we do not plant or bring in our crops?'" In answer to their concerns, God promised to give them an abundant harvest in the sixth year that would carry them through to the ninth year's harvest. There would be plenty of food for the Israelites and foreigners in the land, as well as the domestic and wild animals.

Although letting the soil rest is a wise agricultural principle, God also had other purposes. The Sabbatical year honored God and reminded the people of his provision. It helped guard against greed and materialism. It also reinforced the idea that God really owns the land; people are stewards of his resources.

Today some people use the term "sabbatical" to refer to a paid leave from their job; that hardly fits the Sabbatical principle in Leviticus. God may call us into a situation that forces us to totally depend on him for our basic needs. Leaving a job to serve him or working as a self-supported missionary is naturally scary. God understands our concerns and promises to cover our basic needs when we're following his will. As we trust and obey him, we can depend on his promises and provision every year of our life.

I will give you my blessing in the sixth year so that
the land will produce enough for three years.

Leviticus 25:21

Ask yourself: **Is God asking me to give up some area of financial security in order to serve or trust him in a new way?**

SEPTEMBER
13

"Why are your disciples doing something that is not permitted on the day of worship?"

Mark 2:23–28

If we're honest, many of us would have to admit that we sometimes struggle to concentrate on the Sunday morning message because we're thinking about what we want to get done that afternoon. Others have a list of specific activities to avoid doing on Sundays that are acceptable on other days, such as playing cards, pursuing hobbies, or going to movies. It's easy to forget the real reason why we have a special day of the week.

The Pharisees often criticized Jesus for his Sabbath activities. One day he and his hungry disciples passed through a field, picking heads of grain to eat. This practice was perfectly acceptable under the law (see Deut. 23:25). The Pharisees accused the men of harvesting on the Sabbath, which the law had forbidden. "Why are your disciples doing something that is not permitted on the day of worship?" they asked. By reminding them of how David and his hungry men ate the consecrated bread reserved for the priests, Jesus showed that God does not place rules above human needs.

God never intended the Sabbath concept to burden people by forcing them to follow strict rules while ignoring their needs. He gave it as a gift so that we can be refreshed in body, mind, and spirit. Setting aside a day to focus on worship, rest, and family prepares us for the rest of our week. It also sets us apart from the rest of the world. Although we don't live under the old law, the principle of a Sabbath rest still holds value for us. No matter what activities we plan for Sunday, we can use the day to honor God. We just want to make sure we have a day of rest in him, not a day of rules.

Then he added, "The day of worship was made for people, not people for the day of worship."

Mark 2:27

Ask yourself: **Do I honor God with the way I spend my Sundays?**

"Why do you break the commandment of God because of your traditions?"

Matthew 15:1–9

After the service ended, I turned around to introduce myself to the visitors seated behind me. When they explained that they were looking for a church to attend, I offered to answer any questions. The young couple had plenty. Although they loved the people in their former congregation, the couple had realized that the church leaders had based their teachings on human traditions rather than on God's Word. The emphasis was on rules and regulations instead of a relationship with Christ.

Substituting manmade religion for God's Word has been a problem since the beginning. When the religious leaders asked Jesus why his disciples broke their ancestors' tradition of ceremonial washing, he answered with a question to them: "Why do you break the commandment of God because of your traditions?"

Jesus quoted the words that Isaiah spoke when he confronted similar hypocrisy centuries earlier. The Pharisees' worship lacked any meaning because they focused on observing and teaching rules and regulations instead of God's law. They sometimes ignored or sidestepped one of God's direct commands to adhere to one of their traditions.

Many churches follow practices and traditions that are hundreds of years old. While religious traditions can enhance our worship, they become idolatrous when they're given equal standing with divine teachings. Sometimes churches promote their own rules, rituals, and programs more than a life of discipleship. Teaching the Bible takes a backseat to fellowship, social causes, or even entertainment. In such an environment, the church becomes more like a club than the body of Christ gathering to worship God. Genuine worship is based on the foundation of God's Word and our personal relationship with him. Even the most cherished traditions can never replace that.

Their worship of me is pointless, because their teachings are rules made by humans.

Matthew 15:9

Ask yourself: **Is my worship of God based more on human traditions and rules or on his Word?**

SEPTEMBER

15

"How can we recognize that the Lord didn't speak this message?"

Deuteronomy 18:9–22

Many years ago I tried wallpapering for the first time. I spent a lot of time smoothing out that first strip, pushing out every single air bubble and pressing the top and bottom edges firmly against the woodwork. Standing back to check it out, I thought I'd done a great job. Then my husband pulled out a handy gadget. As he held the level in front of my beautiful work, it revealed something that my naked eye couldn't detect: the strip of paper wasn't exactly straight.

God gave Israel a way to check out the messages of people who claimed to speak for him. Rather than imitate the despicable Canaanite practices for revelation, the Israelites were to listen to the line of prophets whom God promised to send. God instructed them to put false prophets to death. He anticipated their natural question: "How can we recognize that the Lord didn't speak this message?" God gave two criteria for a genuine prophet: their predictions would come true, and they would speak in God's name and promote worship of him alone (see Deut. 13:1–3).

Today we're bombarded with all sorts of spiritual messages. Some are obviously wacky and contrary to God's commands. Many appear to be biblically sound, while in reality they mix truth with subtle errors. Fortunately, we're blessed to have something the Israelites didn't have—the complete revelation of God in written form, including the life and words of the ultimate Prophet, Jesus Christ.

Precept Ministries, for example, uses the symbol of the plumb line to illustrate how inductive Bible study can help us evaluate what we read and hear to make sure it lines up with what God says. The combination of Scripture, prayer, and the Holy Spirit will help us recognize when someone claiming to speak for God is actually distorting his words.

They want to distort the Good News about Christ.

Galatians 1:7

Ask yourself: **Do I evaluate every message I hear to make sure it aligns with God's written Word?**

"Who will stand by my side against troublemakers?"

Psalm 94:14–23

The elderly woman rose stiffly as the judge entered the courtroom. How glad she would be when this nightmare ended! For the hundredth time, she wished she'd never signed a contract that she didn't fully understand. Her savings had almost evaporated and now she faced the possibility of losing her home to this unscrupulous company. She'd had no idea where to turn—until her neighbor connected her with an attorney willing to represent her case for free. Now she breathed a silent prayer of thanks that this tall, confident man stood beside her.

Despite the way evil people prospered, the writer of Psalm 94 expressed confidence that God would not abandon his people in times of oppression and persecution. "Who will stand up for me against evildoers?" he asked. "Who will stand by my side against troublemakers?" The psalmist trusted God to hold him up, soothe his soul with assuring words, and even use his enemies' own wickedness against them.

During Paul's preliminary hearing before his trial in Rome, no one spoke up in his defense (see 2 Tim. 4:16–18). Even his friends abandoned him. But Paul said that the Lord stood by him and strengthened him, enabling him to continue spreading the Good News. We can also trust God to stand by our side even if circumstances drive our friends to desert us.

Whether we face persecution, prosecution, false accusations, or dangers of a life-and-death nature, God will be there holding us up. He may provide people or resources to help us, or he may soothe our soul with assuring words. But he will give us the strength we need to stand. No matter how our case turns out, we can be confident that God will stay right by our side.

King David said this about him: "I see that the Lord is always with me. I will not be shaken, for he is right beside me."

Acts 2:25 NLT

Ask God **to help you sense his presence when you face troubles or troublemakers.**

SEPTEMBER

17

"Shouldn't I hate those who hate you?"

Psalm 139:19–24

David's passion for God fueled a fervent desire to see people who opposed God punished. In Psalm 139 he cried out against people who said evil things about God and misused his name. "Shouldn't I hate those who hate you, O LORD?" he asked. "Shouldn't I be disgusted with those who attack you?" David declared that God's enemies had become his own enemies.

The writers of the Psalms never hesitated to honestly express their feelings to God. During times of personal suffering or national persecution, they often cried out for God to destroy their enemies. Sometimes they gave graphic suggestions about how to carry out their punishment. But these outbursts are typically followed by declarations of trust in God's justice.

These passages sound strange to those of us who are familiar with the New Testament teachings to love our enemies and to refrain from paying back evil for evil. But even in the heat of their emotions, the psalmists acknowledged that God claims the sole right to take vengeance on his—or their—enemies. When Saul sent men to kill David out of jealousy and spite, David cried out for God to have no pity on such traitors (see Psalm 59). But more than once David refused to take Saul's life when he had the chance, even though Saul wanted to murder him.

If we love God, we naturally feel anger toward someone who hates him or who actively opposes his purposes. The closer we are to God, the more passionately we'll hate sin. But God wants us to share his desire for his enemies to come to understand and accept his offer of salvation. He also wants us to remember that he's the one who will deal out punishment to his enemies, not us.

We know the God who said, "I alone have the right to take revenge. I will pay back."

Hebrews 10:30

Ask yourself: **Do I pray for God's enemies to have a change of heart?**

"Why do you bring this terrible disaster on yourselves?"

Jeremiah 44:1–10

Most people have heard some variation on this quote from George Santayana: "Those who cannot remember the past are condemned to repeat it." Through the prophet Jeremiah, God applied this principle to his own people. Jeremiah gave a history lesson to the exiled Jews living in Egypt. He reminded them that their cities lay in ruins because the people had worshiped and burned incense to other gods. Even though God had repeatedly warned them to stop, they refused to listen. Finally, he judged their sin.

In spite of the disaster brought on by their idolatry, the Jews who had fled to Egypt had already started worshiping the gods of that land. They acted as though they had forgotten what happened to them and their ancestors. God warned that if they repeated their sins, they would face repeated punishment. "Why do you bring this terrible disaster on yourselves?" God asked. "Why do you make me angry by burning incense to other gods in Egypt, where you have come to live?"

Each one of us has our own personal history that includes some parts we're proud of and other parts we'd prefer to forget. It's important for us to acknowledge our past mistakes so we can learn from them. Reviewing our failures can pinpoint areas of personal weakness and vulnerability. Remembering the painful consequences of our sinful actions helps us to be on our guard and resist temptation.

God disciplines us and allows us to experience natural consequences of our sin in hopes that we will learn to live a more godly life. If we forget those lessons, we'll be condemned to repeat the same mistakes over and over. On the other hand, if we keep a teachable spirit and listen to God's warnings, we can avoid a lot of self-made disasters.

But whoever listens to me will live without worry
and will be free from the dread of disaster.

Proverbs 1:33

Ask yourself: **What mistakes do I keep repeating?**

SEPTEMBER

19

"Shouldn't people ask their God for help instead?"

Isaiah 8:19–22

When Haley began struggling with financial problems, a friend recommended a source for advice on managing money and making wise investments. But after several weeks of lengthy phone consultations, Haley decided that her friend had steered her in the wrong direction. She still had the same old problems—with the addition of a new debt. Now she had to find a way to pay hundreds of dollars to a telephone psychic.

Through the prophet Isaiah, God criticized the people of Judah for going to the wrong source for help. God had forbidden his people to dabble in the occult practices of the pagan nations around them. Yet the people of Judah had consulted mediums and psychics who tried to contact the dead through whisperings and mutterings.

"Shouldn't people ask their God for help instead?" Isaiah asked. "Why should they ask the dead to help the living?" God told the people they should have gone to his written Word instead, where they would have found all they needed to know about their nation's future. Their actions only pulled them further into spiritual darkness. When they faced judgment, they even blamed God for their troubles.

Even though we may not seek help from psychics or the occult, we may have other sources we turn to in our difficulties. Our first response may be to seek advice from a trusted friend or adviser, or to try to solve the problem with our own intellect. God wants to be the One we think of first when we face a need or dilemma. The psalmist called God an "ever-present help in times of trouble." God stands ready to respond to his children when we call out to him. Why shouldn't he be the first one we ask for help?

God is our refuge and strength, an ever-present help in times of trouble.

Psalm 46:1

Ask yourself: **When I face trouble, do I automatically turn to God for help?**

"Who has directed the Lord or instructed him as his adviser?"

Isaiah 40:12–17

I'll sure be glad when this job is over, Nathan thought as he sighed and stepped down from his truck. As a remodeling contractor, he had no problem with clients asking a lot of questions. It seemed logical that they would keep a close eye on the progress. But this guy was ridiculous—questioning every choice of material and technique, constantly offering advice on a "better way." Apparently, all those home makeover shows had made him an expert. *He's the one who hired me*, Nathan thought. *Why can't he trust that I know what I'm doing?*

Isaiah asked a series of rhetorical questions to show that God knows what he's doing and doesn't need our advice. "Who has directed the Spirit of the Lord or instructed him as his adviser? Whom did he consult? Who gave him understanding? Who taught him the right way?" All of the questions in Isaiah's list have the same obvious answer: no one. God didn't need any help when he created the world; he doesn't need any help now to oversee it.

We know in our head that God doesn't need our advice, but sometimes our prayers reveal a different attitude. When we talk with him about matters that concern us, do we focus on seeking his will and discerning what our response should be? Or does our prayer end up being a one-sided conversation as we tell him how we think he should handle the situation?

God wants us to pour out our worries and fears, but he also wants us to trust his promise to work everything out for good. That includes everything from world problems to personal troubles that affect us and our loved ones. God doesn't need how-to books or consultants, and he certainly doesn't need us to be his adviser.

Let your will be done on earth as it is done in heaven.

Matthew 6:10

Ask yourself: **Do my prayers sound like I'm trying to give advice to God?**

SEPTEMBER
21

"What good does it do if someone claims to have faith but doesn't do any good?"

James 2:14–26

Anne looked across the table at her husband—or more accurately, at the back of the sports section. *Looks like this evening will be the same as usual*, she thought, and sighed. Newspaper during dinner, television on all evening, then Jim would fall asleep in the recliner. He showed no interest in doing things with her or for her, or even in a simple conversation. Whenever she asked if he still loved her, he always answered "Of course." *Then where's the evidence*? she wondered.

That's a question that can also be asked about our faith. James wrote that if our claim of faith is not backed up by action, it's worthless. Genuine faith will always reveal itself in good deeds and acts of service; otherwise, it's as dead as a body without breath. If we see someone lacking food and clothing and only give them our good wishes, our words are useless. In the same way, claiming we believe in God doesn't mean anything if our life doesn't display the evidence.

Faith is not just an intellectual agreement with the basic tenets of Christianity, it's a commitment that results in a transformed life characterized by good deeds. These works are not the basis of our salvation but rather the product of it. Our acts of kindness and obedience to God's commands make our faith visible to the world and prove that it's genuine.

Sometimes we're called to demonstrate our faith in dramatic ways, like Abraham offering his son on the altar or Rahab risking her life to hide Israelite spies. But every day we have opportunities to act out our faith in acts of loving service to God and others. The important thing is to show that our faith is alive and breathing.

Faith by itself is dead if it doesn't cause you to do any good things.

James 2:17

Ask yourself: **How does my life show visible evidence of my faith in God?**

"Why do you ignore the king's command?"

Esther 3

6:10 a.m.: Josiah shut off his alarm. It hadn't been easy moving to this small town, especially within the first weeks of a new school year. He hadn't had time to make friends yet. *Maybe I should just skip this . . .*

6:45 a.m.: Josiah climbed into the van beside his mom and remembered what a big deal "See You at the Pole" had been in his old school. He hadn't really seen it promoted here. *Will I be the only one there?*

6:58 a.m.: Josiah shifted his backpack and strode toward the empty area under the flagpole.

Mordecai knew how it felt to stand alone. When King Xerxes elevated Haman to the highest possible position, he also ordered the royal officials to bow down and honor Haman whenever he passed by. Everyone obeyed except Mordecai. Day after day the king's advisers asked him, "Why do you ignore the king's command?" Day after day Mordecai refused to comply, infuriating Haman. When the king's advisers told Haman that Mordecai was Jewish, he decided to destroy every single Jew in the kingdom of Xerxes.

We all face situations that force us to choose between going along with the popular view or standing up for what we believe. In some cases, taking a stand for God means standing alone. We may be tempted to keep our faith a secret if we fear the consequences of going against the status quo. Standing up for what's right can make us the target of ridicule, hostility, or even hatred. But God will give us the courage and strength to be a witness for him even when the rest of the world bows down to his enemies. When we're honoring God, we'll never really be standing alone.

This I know: God is on my side.

Psalm 56:9

Ask yourself: **Am I prepared to take a stand for God even when it means standing alone?**

SEPTEMBER
23

"What is troubling you?"

Esther 5:1–8

Queen Esther found herself in a desperate situation—with more than her own life at stake. Haman had persuaded the king to set a date for the extermination of the Jews in Persia. Esther's adoptive father had urged her to approach the king and intercede for her people. But anyone who entered the inner court without being summoned by the king received the death penalty, unless Xerxes chose to hold out his scepter to them. Since Xerxes had not called for Esther for thirty days, she had no idea how he would react to her bold action.

When Xerxes saw Esther standing in the doorway, he felt pleased and stretched out his gold scepter for her to touch. "What is troubling you, Queen Esther?" he asked. "What would you like?" Instead of sharing the burden that weighed so heavily on her, Esther invited the king to attend a dinner she had prepared for him and Haman. During the dinner, Xerxes repeated his question; once again, Esther held back. She promised to make her request at another dinner the next day.

Esther knew she walked a fine line in dealing with this temperamental tyrant. The lives of all the Jews depended on Xerxes' mood and how Esther handled herself. What a contrast to the relationship we have with our heavenly Father! God invites us to approach his throne boldly, in full assurance that he's always ready to hear us.

Sometimes we feel reluctant to approach God, but we never need to worry about his reaction. He wants us to pour out whatever is troubling us and trust that he understands even better than we do. What a privilege to have a standing invitation to draw near to the King of kings anytime we want. When he asks, "What is troubling you?" we never need to hold back.

Trust him at all times, you people. Pour out your hearts in his presence.

Psalm 62:8

Ask yourself: **Have I held back from talking to God about something that's troubling me?**

"How did I reward Mordecai for this?"

Esther 2:19–23; 6:1–3

The night before Esther's second dinner, King Xerxes suffered from insomnia. As a diversion, he had a servant read to him from the official records of daily events. The text chosen by the servant recounted an earlier incident when two of the king's eunuchs who guarded the palace entrance planned to assassinate him. Mordecai had overheard and told Esther about the plot, and she had passed the information to the king. "How did I reward and promote Mordecai for this?" Xerxes asked. To his astonishment, the king discovered that nothing had been done for the man who had saved his life a few years earlier.

What happened with Xerxes never happens with the God who promises to reward those who seek him (see Heb. 11:6). Being his child brings great blessing in itself, and living by God's standards assures a fulfilling life. Still, we often don't see any rewards for our good deeds. But that doesn't mean that God has forgotten or overlooked them. Our real rewards for the work we do for God will come at the judgment seat of Christ.

According to 1 Corinthians 3:10–15, the quality of our work will be tested by fire. To pass the test, our acts of service must have been done with the right motives (for God's glory, not for personal gain or selfish reasons), through God's power (not our human strength), and according to God's plan (not our own agenda). Anything that fails this test will be burned up.

We never have to worry about missing out on rewards that are due us. God has already given us so much more than we deserve. As we live for Christ and try to follow his will, our focus should be on whether our work for God is fireproof.

If what a person has built survives, he will receive a reward.

1 Corinthians 3:14

Ask yourself: **Will the work I've done for God bring rewards, or will it burn up?**

SEPTEMBER

25

“Who is in the courtyard?”

Esther 6:4–14

As Loren frowned at his watch, the tow truck driver asked, “Missing something important?” Loren explained about his job interview and how the recruiter had stressed that this employer didn’t give anyone a second chance. When Loren mentioned his degree, the driver chuckled. “What a coincidence! I just happen to have a brother in that field, and he’s looking for an assistant right now.” Two weeks later, Loren started his new job.

Some interesting “coincidences” also took place in Persia. The servant reading the official records to the king happened to pick the account of Mordecai saving his life. When Xerxes learned that Mordecai’s good deed had not been recognized, he decided to ask someone’s advice. “Who is in the courtyard?” Ironically, Haman had just dropped by to ask the king’s permission to hang Mordecai.

When Xerxes asked him what should be done for someone the king wanted to reward, Haman assumed Xerxes was talking about him. After suggesting several things that his inflated ego desired, Xerxes ordered Haman to apply them to Mordecai. Haman suffered the humiliation of having to publicly honor the man he wanted to kill. But God wasn’t through—he had more “coincidences” planned.

It may not be obvious to human eyes, but God is always working on behalf of his children, even using the actions of evil people to accomplish his purposes. Sometimes events in our life seem to have no reason or rhyme. At other times, a series of coincidences line up and our problems work out better than we dared hope. Either way, we can rest assured that God is orchestrating the details of our life, overruling anything that would thwart his plans for us. For the believer, unusual circumstances simply mean that God is at work as usual.

The Lord works out everything for his own ends.

Proverbs 16:4 NIV

Ask yourself: **What "coincidences" have shown God's hand moving in my own life?**

"What is your request?"

Esther 7

A date had been set for the slaughter of every Jewish man, woman, and child in the Persian Empire. Queen Esther was in a position to intercede for her people—but she had to deal with a king known for flying into rages. Despite the urgency of the situation, Esther controlled her emotions and impulses. She approached the king after three days of fasting and prayer. Instead of pleading her case at the first opportunity, Esther held back. The third time Xerxes asked, "What is your request, Queen Esther? And what would you like?" Esther sensed the time was finally right.

God had set the stage so Esther could play her part. He had arranged for Xerxes to rediscover Mordecai's act of saving his life, and the king had been flattered by the two special dinners Esther planned. Now she asked Xerxes to spare her life and the lives of her people. Xerxes was enraged when Esther identified Haman as the perpetrator. When Haman fell on Esther's couch as he begged her for mercy, Xerxes thought he was assaulting the queen. He ordered Haman to be hanged from the very pole Haman had erected for Mordecai's execution.

In our hurry to solve a problem, it's easy to rush headlong into actions that only make matters worse. Rather than act on our impulses, we need to first take time to pray for God's help and guidance. He may want us to hold back and give him time to arrange events for a favorable outcome. But we also need to be ready to play our role when we sense his timing is right. When dealing with an uncertain situation, we want to be certain when and how God wants us to take action.

Don't act thoughtlessly, but understand
what the Lord wants you to do.
Ephesians 5:17 NLT

Ask yourself: **Do I tend to act impulsively, or do I put a lot of thought and prayer into my decisions?**

SEPTEMBER
27

"Isn't life more than food and the body more than clothes?"

Matthew 6:25–34

I picked up the Sunday paper and a flurry of sales flyers spilled out on the floor. As I gathered them up, I noticed that the majority of the ads involved food or clothing—grocery store weekly ads, restaurant coupons, department store sale flyers featuring the latest fashions. Add to that all the magazine advertisements, television commercials, and weekly shows focused on how to cook and what to wear, and it's no wonder that these two things take up an awful lot of our time, thought, and money.

In Jesus's day, most people simply desired to have their basic needs for food and clothing met. But even then, he urged his listeners not to be overly concerned about these things. "Isn't life more than food and the body more than clothes?" he asked. Jesus pointed out that birds don't grow crops, yet God feeds them. The flowers don't make clothes, but God dresses them more beautifully than King Solomon in his finery. God knows our needs and has promised to meet them when we put him first.

Our affluent society has driven our desires way beyond our needs. As the fashion industry makes us dissatisfied with our wardrobe, we forget that the basic purpose of clothing is to cover our body. With an abundance of food stores and restaurants to try, food becomes something more than physical nourishment. We can easily cross the fine line between enjoying God's blessings and falling into greed.

Always wanting more demonstrates a lack of trust in God to provide for us. How would our life be different if we spent less time thinking about what we're going to eat and wear, and more time thinking about living a godly life?

> *First, be concerned about his kingdom and what has his approval. Then all these things will be provided for you.*
>
> Matthew 6:33

Ask yourself: **How much of my time is consumed with thoughts of food or other material needs?**

"What should I ask for?"

Mark 6:14–28

The teenage girl finished her dance and listened to the lavish praise from her stepfather, Herod, and his party guests. Caught up in the moment, King Herod swore an oath: "I'll give you anything you ask for, up to half of my kingdom." Technically, Herod had no kingdom to give, but the girl understood the expression—Herod was prepared to grant her almost any request. She ran out to her mother for advice. "What should I ask for?" she said.

Herodias had her answer ready. At last she saw the opportunity to get rid of John the Baptist. How she hated that man for his public denunciations of her unlawful marriage to Herod! Although Herodias had talked Herod into throwing John in prison, her husband had some strange fascination with the prophet and refused to execute him. "Ask for the head of John the Baptizer," she instructed her daughter. The girl obeyed. Herod deeply regretted his rash promise, but to save face he immediately ordered John's beheading.

Chances are we won't ever ask God for the head of an enemy, but the Bible says that sometimes we do ask for things based on selfish motives. God encourages us to bring our requests to him in prayer (see Phil. 4:6); however, he won't answer if we request the wrong things or if we're motivated solely by our personal desires.

Sometimes our prayers need a checkup to see if they're focused on honoring and glorifying God, or if they're self-centered. If our prayer life doesn't pass the test, we can ask God to remove any desire that's not pleasing to him. Once our requests line up with his perfect will, we can be sure that we're asking for the right things with the right motives.

When you ask, you do not receive, because you ask with wrong motives, that you may spend what you get on your pleasures.

James 4:3 NIV

Ask yourself: **Do my requests in prayer usually stem from self-centered motives or from a desire to glorify God?**

SEPTEMBER
29

"Who do you say I am?"

Matthew 16:13–19

When Jesus asked his disciples what people were saying about his identity, they told him what they'd heard. Some people thought he was John the Baptist; others said he was Elijah, Jeremiah, or one of the other earlier prophets of Israel. Then Jesus made the question more personal to his disciples. "But who do you say I am?" he asked.

Peter responded for the group. "You are the Messiah, the Son of the living God!" he proclaimed. Peter did more than acknowledge Jesus as the long-awaited Messiah; he testified to Jesus's deity. Jesus commended Peter's answer and pointed out that he hadn't figured this out on his own. God the Father had revealed it to him.

Opinions about Jesus's identity are still varied today. Some call him one of the greatest teachers or philosophers who ever lived. Others believe he was nothing more than a good man. These answers can't be squared with the biblical account of Jesus's life, which shows him claiming to be God and the only way to find salvation. Some people who are familiar with Jesus's claims label him as either a deceiver or self-deceived.

Jesus still puts his question to each one of us: "But who do *you* say I am?" Our answer determines the foundation of our life. If we accept everything that Jesus said about himself, we will submit to his total control over our life. We'll still have struggles with our old sinful nature, but our goal will be to live a holy life as Jesus did. Instead of living for selfish desires or pleasure, we'll imitate his example of self-denial and loving service to others. If we truly believe that Jesus is who he claims to be, then we'll claim him as our Lord and Master.

But in your hearts set apart Christ as Lord.

1 Peter 3:15 NIV

Ask yourself: **Does the testimony of my life match what I claim to believe about Jesus's identity?**

“Will you go with this man?”

Genesis 24:34–57

Abraham’s chief servant grew more excited as he shared his story with his host. His master had sent him to his former homeland to find a wife for his son from among his relatives. Eliezer had prayed for a specific sign that would lead him to God’s choice. When Rebekah fulfilled the sign perfectly and then turned out to be from Abraham’s family, the servant praised God and gave her gifts of gold jewelry.

Rebekah’s family listened intently and agreed that God had directed Eliezer’s steps. Her father and brother gave permission for Rebekah to become Isaac’s wife. The next morning, her family urged Eliezer to wait at least ten days before taking Rebekah back, but he insisted on leaving that day. So they called Rebekah and asked, “Will you go with this man?” Rebekah answered, “Yes, I’ll go.” That same day Rebekah left for her new life—in a land she had never seen with a man she had never met.

We all have to answer the same question that Rebekah did. When we accept Jesus as our Savior, he wants to know if we will go with him wherever he leads. Jesus called his disciples with the words, “Come, follow me!” Like those twelve men, he asks us to demonstrate our faith by walking away from our old way of living to follow him into a new life. Can we answer “Yes, I will go” as Rebekah did?

Following Jesus can be scary since we can’t see what lies ahead. Are we willing to venture into the unknown to follow his plan for our life? Do we trust his leadership even when he takes us down a path of sacrifice and suffering? We won’t always understand the exact route that our faith journey is taking. But if Jesus is leading us, then we know what our final destination will be.

Jesus said to them, “Come, follow me!”

Matthew 4:19

Ask yourself: **Am I committed to following Jesus wherever he leads me?**

OCTOBER

1

"Do you believe that I can do this?"

Matthew 9:27–31

Larissa fought back tears as she drove from her mother's house. She'd done her best to assure her mom that the prognosis looked good. Her mom's cancer had been caught early and was one of the more treatable types. Larissa tried to convince her that she had a good chance of being cured by the combination of chemotherapy and radiation. But her efforts had not been successful. Would the treatments work if her mother was already convinced they wouldn't help at all?

Jesus often emphasized the role of faith in his healing and other miracles. Two blind men cried out for Jesus to have mercy on them. When he didn't immediately respond, they followed him into a house. "Do you believe that I can do this?" he asked them. "Yes, Lord," they answered. Touching their eyes, Jesus declared, "What you have believed will be done for you!"

One of the conditions of effective prayer is belief that God will grant our request. He's not pleased when we pray with an underlying attitude that our prayers won't do any good. As long as we live an obedient lifestyle and pray according to his will with godly motives, a forgiving spirit, and a willing submission to his sovereignty, we can trust we will receive what we have asked for.

That kind of unwavering faith is not something we can summon up on our own; it's a gift from God. If our prayers are mixed with heavy doses of doubts, and if we can't answer a definite "Yes!" to Jesus's question, we need to ask for help. We can confess our weakness and ask God to strengthen our faith. How could we doubt that God would gladly grant that request?

Therefore I tell you, whatever you ask for in prayer,
believe that you have received it, and it will be yours.

Mark 11:24 NIV

Ask God **to strengthen your faith concerning your heaviest prayer burden.**

OCTOBER
2

"Will you bow down?"

Daniel 3:1–15

The movie *Chariots of Fire* dramatizes Scottish missionary Eric Liddell's participation in the 1924 Summer Olympics and his desire to run for God's glory. When he sees that his 100-meter race is scheduled for a Sunday, Liddell insists that participating would be against his convictions. The British Olympic committee and the Prince of Wales try to pressure Liddell into changing his mind. Despite their argument that he owes it to his country to run, Liddell refuses to bend. The problem is solved when a fellow teammate gives Liddell his spot in the Tuesday race.

The third chapter of Daniel tells the story of three other men who refused to bend—or to bow. King Nebuchadnezzar ordered the people to fall down and worship a huge gold statue whenever they heard the musical signal. When someone reported to the king that "certain Jews" did not obey his decree, Nebuchadnezzar angrily summoned Shadrach, Meshach, and Abednego.

"When you hear the sound of the rams' horns, flutes, lyres, harps, and three-stringed harps playing at the same time with all other kinds of instruments, will you bow down and worship the gold statue I made?" the king demanded. Even when he reminded them of the horrible penalty for disobeying, the three young men replied that they would never worship the statue.

It's never easy to live by our Christian convictions when they clash with the culture. Even our family or friends may sometimes try to convince us to just "go with the flow." If we give in and compromise our beliefs, we may come up with excuses that sound reasonable. But God wants us to resist the temptation to conform to the thinking of the world around us. Even when faced with serious consequences, we honor him when we refuse to back down or bow down.

Don't become like the people of this world.

Romans 12:2

Ask yourself: **In what ways am I pressured to bow down or bend my convictions?**

OCTOBER

3

"Didn't we throw three men into the fire?"

Daniel 3:16–30

King Nebuchadnezzar clenched his teeth in rage. How dare these Hebrew captives refuse his order to bow down and worship the gold statue—especially after he had elevated them to positions of authority! The king ordered the furnace to be heated as hot as possible, then had soldiers tie up Shadrach, Meshach, and Abednego. Flames from the blazing furnace killed the soldiers as the three young Hebrews fell into the fire.

A moment later, Nebuchadnezzar sprang to his feet. "Didn't we throw three men into the fire?" he cried. "That's true, Your Majesty," his advisers answered. The king looked again. Through the opening in the furnace, he clearly saw the Hebrew men walking around in the middle of the fire, untied and unharmed. He also saw that a fourth man accompanied them, one who had the appearance of a heavenly being.

When the king examined Shadrach, Meshach, and Abednego, he saw that the blazing fire had not harmed the men's bodies or clothes, singed their hair, or even deposited a smell of smoke. We're not guaranteed such a happy ending when we go through trials and suffering. God has the power to rescue us from any situation, but sometimes he chooses to work in other ways to accomplish his purposes. The young Hebrews had made the decision to worship God alone regardless of whether or not he chose to rescue them.

We can't be sure whether the "extra man" in the furnace was a physical appearance of Christ before his earthly birth, or an angel sent by God to strengthen the young Hebrews. But we can know for certain that God has promised to never leave those who trust and obey him, no matter what we go through. When we feel like we're in a fiery furnace, we can be comforted by the fact that Someone is walking with us.

He won't abandon you or leave you.

Deuteronomy 31:6

Ask God **to help you see his presence as you go through trials and suffering.**

OCTOBER

4

"Are they ashamed when they do disgusting things?"

Jeremiah 6:6–15

Politicians seemed to be in the headlines a lot that summer. One ousted governor raced around to talk shows promoting his book, even while facing serious charges of corruption. Another governor toured his state, trying to gain support after his yearlong extramarital affair was made public. A congressman chairing a committee entrusted with writing tax laws ignored calls to step down, even after evidence surfaced that he failed to report thousands of dollars in income. I wondered why these men weren't ashamed to show their faces on television.

During Jeremiah's day, God wondered something similar about Judah's leaders. Every level of society had become corrupt and refused to listen to God's warnings. At the head of the pack were the prophets and priests who deceived and lied to the people. Instead of setting an example, these leaders encouraged Judah in her sins. "Are they ashamed when they do disgusting things?" God asked. "No, they're not ashamed. They don't even know how to blush."

God's observation in Jeremiah doesn't apply only to leaders and politicians. We're all in danger of becoming insensitive to sin unless we make a conscious effort to live a disciplined, obedient life. The more we compromise with sin, the less we'll notice when our behavior strays from God's standards of right and wrong. Our human nature is vulnerable to self-deception, even when personal wrongdoing is exposed.

It's good to periodically gauge our attitudes: Do we feel comfortable doing or saying things that would have embarrassed us a few years ago? When we realize that we've done wrong, do we try to ignore it or does a sense of shame prompt us to seek forgiveness and restitution? If we stay attuned to God's Holy Spirit, he'll let us know when blushing—or shame—is appropriate.

No, they're not ashamed. They don't even know how to blush.

Jeremiah 6:15

Ask yourself: **Do I ever treat personal sins lightly instead of feeling appropriately ashamed?**

OCTOBER

5

"And now, our God, what can we say after all this?"

Ezra 9

As Christians, we know that we bear the responsibility to pray for our country, our government, and our leaders (see 1 Tim. 2:2). But sometimes it's hard to know where to begin. As television, movies, and newspapers remind us of how far our culture has rejected God's truth and embraced sin, it can leave us speechless. When we've strayed so far from his standards, what is there to say to the God whose name we put on our currency?

Ezra had similar emotions when confronted with his nation's sin and disobedience. Even after God used Babylon to judge Judah, the people still intermarried with people from pagan nations. As a result, idolatry and immorality saturated the culture. Ezra ripped his clothes and knelt before God. He admitted Israel's sinful past and acknowledged God's mercy in restoring a remnant to the land. "And now, our God, what can we say after all this?" he prayed. "We have abandoned your commandments!"

Ezra's heartfelt prayer provides guidelines as we pray for our own country. Some people react to our nation's sin with condemnation and self-righteousness. Even though Ezra wasn't personally guilty of intermarriage, he used the word "we" throughout his prayer. None of us are sinless; we all share the burden and consequences of our country's sin.

We can't afford to ignore national sins as though they have nothing to do with us. No one sins without affecting others. The condition of our country impacts the lives of each one of us. On the other hand, we want to avoid an attitude of hopelessness, thinking that there's nothing we can do. Like Ezra, we can intercede for our nation on the basis of God's mercy, acknowledging his goodness in the past. If we take that approach, we won't ever be at a loss for words.

> *We are not requesting this from you because we are righteous, but because you are very compassionate.*
>
> Daniel 9:18

Ask yourself: **How do I react when I'm reminded of my country's sin and disobedience?**

"What is this babbling fool trying to say?"

Acts 17:15–18

The 1994 movie *Nell* tells a story about a girl who grew up in an isolated, wooded area with no human contact other than her mother and twin sister. A local doctor discovers Nell after her family dies. At first, the doctor and a psychology student think that Nell doesn't have the intelligence to communicate. But as they spend time with her, they find that Nell speaks a unique, garbled language developed by her and her twin.

Some of the people in Athens had a similar reaction to Paul after listening to him share his faith. "What is this babbling fool trying to say?" they asked. Paul didn't let their reaction discourage or intimidate him. He used every opportunity to boldly talk about Jesus and eternal life in this intellectual capital of the world. After Paul spoke before the city council, some of the Greeks became believers.

We shouldn't be surprised if people act like we're talking nonsense when we share the gospel or other biblical truth. A person who doesn't have God's Spirit living inside will be incapable of fully understanding God's wisdom. Regardless of intellectual capacity or education, they will lack the discernment that only the Holy Spirit can give. But that doesn't give us an excuse to refrain from sharing our faith.

We never know when God will open someone's mind to understand his truth. Just because a person's initial reaction is negative doesn't mean that God isn't speaking to them through our words. Whether our listeners think we're brilliant or babbling makes no difference. With God's help, we just need to keep saying what they need to hear.

The man without the Spirit does not accept the things that come from the Spirit of God, for they are foolishness to him, and he cannot understand them, because they are spiritually discerned.

1 Corinthians 2:14 NIV

Ask yourself: **Have I ever let someone's negative reaction keep me from speaking God's truth to them?**

OCTOBER
7

“How can this man be so educated when he hasn’t gone to school?”

John 7:14–18

Today Frank Abagnale is a sought-after security consultant, lecturer, and author who has worked with the FBI for more than 35 years. But between the ages of 16 and 21, Abagnale was a sought-after con man. Besides cashing fraudulent checks worth $2.5 million, he posed as a college professor, airline pilot, pediatrician, and attorney. Amazingly, Abagnale succeeded in his impersonations for lengthy periods of time despite his lack of formal training for these professions.

The Jewish leaders knew that Jesus lacked formal Rabbinic training in the Scriptures and the traditions of their elders. Yet his teaching often amazed the leaders and the people. After Jesus taught in the temple courtyard during a festival, the leaders asked, “How can this man be so educated when he hasn’t gone to school?”

They didn’t see how Jesus could possibly display such penetrating insights and deep understanding of the Scriptures and their application. Jesus responded that what he taught came from God the Father. He didn’t seek to draw attention to himself but to glorify God. That made him a true teacher with honest motives.

The world respects degrees, credentials, and certain titles before and after a person’s name. But the most valuable education comes from our relationship with God. In Christ, we have an infinite reservoir of spiritual knowledge and godly wisdom. When we tap into that source, our thinking becomes transformed as we see the world and other people from God’s perspective. Our life is transformed as we gain insights about his Word and how to apply it. Formal education and training can be wonderful opportunities that are worth our time, but our first priority is to enroll in the life-changing education that only God can give.

God has hidden all the treasures of wisdom and knowledge in Christ.

Colossians 2:3

Ask yourself: **Am I tapping into God’s storehouse of knowledge and wisdom found in Christ?**

"Who can find someone who is really trustworthy?"

Proverbs 20:6–7

Four-year-old Jennifer looked out at the stormy night and pulled off her party hat. "He's not coming," she pouted. "Daddy has a long drive," her mom soothed. "But he promised to get here in time to kiss you good night on your birthday."

After Jennifer's father tucked her in bed later that night, he told his wife about the business trip. "What about the $500 bonus?" she asked. "Oh, that," he answered. "They only awarded that to salesmen who stayed through to the end of the conference."

Someone who consistently keeps their word is a rare commodity, as the writer of Proverbs 20 noted. "Many people declare themselves loyal," he wrote, "but who can find someone who is really trustworthy?" In Ecclesiastes 5:5, Solomon warned that it's better not to make a promise than to make one and not keep it.

Many people in our society make promises at the drop of a hat, then don't seem to think twice about breaking them. Sometimes it's tempting to take the easy way out instead of sticking to our word. We may feel like walking away from our marriage rather than staying and working through difficult issues. Our selfish nature may buck at a relationship that requires us to provide long-term care for a loved one. Friends may advise us to find any means to avoid paying our debts.

God expects us to keep our promises—even when it's inconvenient, costly, or painful. As someone called to reflect his character, we're bound to do everything in our power to honor our commitments, unless circumstances beyond our control make it impossible. When it seems too hard to follow through, we can stop and think: "Where would I be if God treated his promises as lightly as I treat mine?"

Who may live on your holy mountain?. . . The one who makes a promise and does not break it, even though he is hurt by it.

Psalm 15:1, 4

Ask yourself: **Am I known as someone who can be trusted to keep my word and honor my commitments?**

OCTOBER

9

"Do you realize that when the Pharisees heard your statement they were offended?"

Matthew 15:10–14

When I saw the message from my website pop up, I expected it to be positive feedback. *Good—I could use some encouragement today*, I thought. It wasn't to be, though. A man had written to tell me that my first book was garbage and promoted ignorance. He called me an obstacle to reason and demanded that I stop spreading lies. The man seemed especially offended by a devotional based on Jesus's statement that no one comes to the Father except through him (see John 14:6). He ended by expressing his hope that I would die soon.

Jesus knew what it was like for people to get offended at his words. As he addressed a crowd, Jesus contradicted the religious leaders' teaching that ceremonial washing rituals could make a person spiritually clean. "Do you realize that when the Pharisees heard your statement they were offended?" his disciples asked. Jesus told the disciples to ignore the Pharisees, whom he called "blind guides."

It shouldn't come as a surprise when unbelievers hate us. After all, Jesus gave us a heads-up on the treatment his followers could expect. Since the world hated him, it will hate us (see John 15:18). We'll be called intolerant and narrow-minded when we take a stand for core ideas of Christianity: faith in Christ is the only way to heaven, those who reject him will go to hell, and God has set absolute standards of right and wrong.

We can't let other people's responses cause us to shirk our responsibility to share God's message of salvation. Better to risk offending people with the truth than to repeat the world's lies.

A time will come when people will not listen to accurate teachings. Instead, they will follow their own desires and surround themselves with teachers who tell them what they want to hear.

2 Timothy 4:3

Ask yourself: **Do I hold back from sharing God's truth because I'm worried about offending someone?**

OCTOBER
10

"Do you want to leave me too?"

John 6:61–69

What a dirty trick! Jerry thought as he watched the crowd dwindle. As a mayoral candidate, Jerry was anxious to share his thoughts on the serious issues affecting their town. He'd been pleased at the turnout for his rally this morning. But just as he began speaking, his opponent had set up camp on the opposite end of the park. It didn't take long to lose the people's attention once the free food and rock music got started. Jerry felt even more frustrated when he saw his own teenage son slip away.

Jesus watched his crowd of supporters dwindle when his teachings became hard to understand. Many people had been attracted by the miracles he performed; others expected Jesus to set himself up as a political ruler. When Jesus called himself the bread of heaven that gives eternal life to those who eat of it, it was too much for many of his followers. Many deserted him and returned to their former lives. Jesus asked the twelve disciples, "Do you want to leave me too?" Speaking for the group, Peter acknowledged Jesus as the only source of eternal life.

We all face situations when we're forced to choose between following Jesus and following the crowd. Sometimes being a Christian means taking an unpopular stand on an issue when it would be easier to go along with the general consensus. Sometimes living the Christian life just seems too hard and we feel like walking away. And there are times when it looks like we're missing out on a party.

Even if our faith is genuine, we'll occasionally stumble in our spiritual journey. But knowing that Jesus is the only source of eternal life will help us resist the temptation to follow the crowd. Nothing the world offers compares with the party that waits for Jesus's followers someday.

Never follow a crowd in doing wrong.
Exodus 23:2

Ask yourself: **In what ways am I tempted to follow the crowd instead of Jesus?**

OCTOBER

11

"How long are you going to waste time conquering the land God has given you?"

Joshua 18:1–10

God had kept his promise to give Canaan into the hands of Israel. Much of the area had been conquered; now it was time for Israel to obey God's command to completely wipe out the remaining Canaanites. But seven tribes had yet to possess an inheritance of land. Perhaps they were weary of fighting, or they found it hard to break the nomadic lifestyle they'd always known. In any case, Joshua knew that the longer they waited to occupy the land, the more time it gave their enemies to return or to gain strength.

Joshua rebuked the tribes for their procrastination in finishing the mission God gave them to do. "How long are you going to waste time conquering the land which the LORD God of your ancestors has given you?" he asked. Then Joshua made careful preparations for the job ahead. He sent representatives from the seven tribes out to survey and write descriptions of the land. Through the sacred lots, God matched each tribe with its individual inheritance of land.

We all act like the Israelites sometimes. We procrastinate when God tells us to do something hard. We put off doing things we know we need to do. We avoid facing unpleasant issues or problems we need to address. Our inaction results in wasted time and missed opportunities, and often allows a pressing situation to get worse.

In addition to our future inheritance in heaven, God has also called us to a life filled with spiritual blessings. But we have to move forward in faith and obedience to claim his promises. It cost God the life of his Son to open up our Promised Land. Why would we wait around instead of moving in to occupy our rightful place?

Fight the good fight for the Christian faith. Take hold of everlasting life to which you were called.

1 Timothy 6:12

Ask God **to show you where you have failed to claim your rightful inheritance of spiritual blessings.**

"Where were you when I laid the foundation of the earth?"

Job 38

Almost twenty years ago, Ken Ham brought his Answers in Genesis seminar to our area. I took my first-grade daughter to the children's program. After reviewing the Genesis account of creation, Ken talked about science "facts" (such as molecules-to-man evolution) that contradict the Bible. The kids loved it when Ken periodically stopped to let them shout out the logical response to such claims: "Were you there?"

God asked Job a similar question when he responded to Job's complaints about his suffering. "Where were you when I laid the foundation of the earth?" God began. "Tell me if you have such insight." God listed more than seventy questions that made his point clear: If Job couldn't even explain events in the natural world, how could he ever understand God? Since Job didn't comprehend the principles that God set in place to govern heavenly bodies, what right did Job have to pass judgment on God's dealings with people?

God has given humans the intellect and ability to make amazing scientific discoveries about the natural world, but we will never comprehend all the mysteries within our universe. People respond to the complexity and wonders of nature in different ways: What one person interprets as proof of a loving Creator prompts another person to reach the opposite conclusion.

Although God has revealed much about himself through his written Word, we'll never fully understand his thoughts or his ways. But we can have a relationship with him through Jesus. There's no need for Christians to feel intimidated by those who reject the Bible as the source of truth and try to replace it with human reasoning and theories. After all, we personally know the One who *was* there.

God's riches, wisdom, and knowledge are so deep that it is impossible to explain his decisions or to understand his ways.

Romans 11:33

Ask God **to give you a deeper sense of his majesty as Designer, Creator, and Sustainer of the universe.**

OCTOBER
13

“How could I do such a wicked thing?”

Genesis 39:1–12

Glenda believes that whatever goes on between “two consenting adults” can’t be considered immoral. Bill calls his addiction to pornography a “victimless crime.” Many people claim that any behavior is okay “as long as no one gets hurt.” Even Christians tend to rank sins according to their degree of seriousness. Joseph knew better.

Day after day, Potiphar’s wife tried to entice the handsome Hebrew slave to sleep with her; day after day, Joseph refused. Potiphar had put Joseph in charge of his entire household and all his possessions. To sleep with his master’s wife would be a violation of Potiphar’s trust in him. Joseph also understood that such behavior would ultimately be an offense against God. “How could I do such a wicked thing and sin against God?” he asked Potiphar’s wife.

Some sins, such as murder, theft, fraud, slander, or adultery, have obvious victims. We may believe that such behaviors as gluttony, drug addiction, drunkenness, or pornography only have the potential to harm ourselves. But regardless of who gets hurt, all sinful behaviors represent an offense against God. Whenever we do something against his commands, we rebel against his right to have authority over our life.

We may try to categorize some sinful behaviors as less serious than others, but there is no such thing as a harmless sin. All sins hurt us or other people and carry consequences. Willful disobedience of God’s commands creates a barrier in our relationship with him since his holiness requires him to judge all sin. When we’re tempted to downplay some immoral behavior, or when we’re struggling against a sin that entices us day after day, we need to ask Joseph’s question: “How could I do such a wicked thing and sin against God?”

I have sinned against you, especially you.

Psalm 51:4

Ask yourself: **Are there sins that I tolerate in my life because I consider them harmless?**

OCTOBER
14

"Why should it use up good soil?"

Luke 13:6–9

When we bought our house in a country subdivision, my husband immediately planted several fruit trees. For the most part, they've flourished. Every spring we have more cherries than I can pick, and in the fall we usually gather at least some apples. But the peach tree never produced enough fruit for a single pie. Our "harvest" usually amounted to no more than two or three pitiful looking objects. Finally, my husband cut the tree down.

Jesus told a parable about a fig tree that failed to produce fruit. After a few years, the owner got tired of waiting. "Cut it down!" he told the gardener. "Why should it use up good soil?" The gardener talked the owner into giving the tree one more year to produce figs. Jesus's story served as a warning: if Israel didn't produce fruit that demonstrated repentance of sin, she would be judged. Like the owner in the parable, God had been willing to wait, but there was a limit to his patience.

Jesus used an illustration of a vine to explain that believers are expected to produce fruit. Like branches growing from a vine, we have to stay connected to Jesus so that his life flows through us. We can only receive the nourishment we need to grow and be fruitful by making sure we stay in a close, personal relationship with the true Vine.

A fruitful life will demonstrate Christlike character traits such as joy, peace, kindness, humility, and self-control. We'll have an effective prayer life and will actively share the Good News with others. Sometimes God will do a little pruning. It may be painful when he cuts away something that holds us back, but God doesn't want occasional fruit—he wants to see a bumper crop year after year.

You give glory to my Father when you produce a lot of fruit and therefore show that you are my disciples.

John 15:8

Ask yourself: **What kind of fruit has my life been producing lately?**

OCTOBER
15

"How often do I have to forgive a believer who wrongs me?"

Matthew 18:21–35

Isabella looked over the guest list for her cookie exchange. *Oops—I forgot to take Cheryl's name off!* she thought. She'd always invited Cheryl to things like this, but after that comment she made last week . . . Then there was the time Cheryl had picked her own child for the solo in the church musical, and last summer when she had let Isabella do most of the work for their Vacation Bible School class. *Three strikes and you're out, honey!* Isabella made a large X across Cheryl's name.

During New Testament times, Jewish rabbis taught that a person needed to forgive someone who wronged them, but only three times. One day Peter felt especially generous and asked Jesus, "Lord, how often do I have to forgive a believer who wrongs me? Seven times?" Jesus answered, "I tell you, not just seven times, but seventy times seven." Then Jesus told a parable about a servant whose master canceled his huge debt. That servant went out and showed no mercy to someone who owed him a much smaller amount.

Jesus introduced a new principle for his followers: forgiveness without limits. As long as someone is penitent, we are expected to forgive them no matter how many times they hurt us. We can only do this when we remember how much God has forgiven us, and how much we continue to depend on his mercy.

When we withhold forgiveness from another believer, we can't be in a right relationship with God or with the body of Christ. And we're acting like the first servant in Jesus's parable. Since God forgave all of our sins, how could we refuse to extend forgiveness to someone who has wronged us, even if they do it 490 times?

Put up with each other, and forgive each other if anyone has a complaint. Forgive as the Lord forgave you.

Colossians 3:13

Ask yourself: **Have I been withholding forgiveness from a fellow believer?**

"Why did she waste it like this?"

Matthew 26:6–13

Andrew grew more agitated as he read the newspaper obituary. He'd lost touch with Darlene soon after graduation. He had no idea she'd gone off to be a missionary in the slums of India—until he read of her death at age 48. Andrew remembered her years as a cheerleader, a homecoming queen, and a top student. He shook his head in amazement. *No husband or children, and a life spent living under who-knows-what conditions*, he thought. *How could she just waste her life like that?*

Jesus's disciples asked a similar question about a woman in Bethany. During a dinner party, Mary, sister of Martha and Lazarus (see John 12:1–3), poured expensive perfume over Jesus's head and feet. The disciples were indignant. That jar of nard cost the equivalent of a year's wages for the average laborer. "Why did she waste it like this?" they demanded. "The money could have been given to the poor."

Jesus defended Mary's actions because he knew her motivation. He also knew his time on earth would end in a matter of days. He reminded the disciples that there would always be plenty of opportunities to help the poor, but they had limited time to express love for him. Jesus referred to Mary's act of devotion as "a beautiful thing" that would be remembered.

Some people might call it a waste when we spend our money, time, and energy in serving God. But everything we do out of pure love and devotion to God is worth it, regardless of the cost. We may or may not see earthly results, but we can be sure that such actions will reap eternal rewards. Each one of us has a brief window of time to live for God. We can't afford to hold back. No matter how much it costs us, doing something for Jesus is never a waste.

[Jesus said] "She has done a beautiful thing for me."

Matthew 26:10

Ask yourself: **Am I holding back from doing "beautiful things" for Jesus?**

OCTOBER
17

"Couldn't this man keep Lazarus from dying?"

John 11:33–44

Twenty years ago, my mom called to tell me that a close friend from high school had been diagnosed with cancer. I immediately sent Libby's name to our church's prayer chain. Later I talked with her on the phone and made plans for a visit when I returned to Tennessee for Christmas. In early December I received word that Libby had died. I felt heartbroken at her death, and also that I had not been able to see her in time.

Mary felt heartbroken that Jesus had not arrived in time to heal her brother. The tears and sorrow of Mary and other mourners deeply moved Jesus. As he cried along with them, some remarked about his love for the dead man. Others remembered how he had healed the sick. "Couldn't this man who gave a blind man sight keep Lazarus from dying?" they asked. Jesus went on to perform an even greater miracle by restoring life to Lazarus after he'd been dead for four days.

When an acquaintance or loved one is sick, we naturally pray for their healing. Even though God has the power to restore anyone's health, he doesn't always work that way. Sometimes he chooses to set the person free from more than their illness—he releases them from the earthly restraints that hold them back from fully knowing him. He takes them home to an environment free from pain, suffering, and sadness.

God understands our disappointment when our prayers don't bring the outcome we'd hoped for; he understands our struggle to accept his decision. God wants us to trust his love and believe that he's right there sharing our grief and crying with us. As we gradually let go of our desires and learn to submit to his control, we might find ourselves being set free from our sorrow.

Jesus told them, "Free Lazarus, and let him go."

John 11:44

Ask yourself: **Do I trust God even when he chooses not to heal a loved one?**

"How can you believe when you accept each other's praise and don't look for the praise that comes from God?"

John 5:41–44

Alex sat in the pew, waiting for the meeting to start and hoping to get some reassurance. He wasn't the only one concerned about the direction the church was headed—and these business meetings didn't help. Instead of addressing the issues, the pastor and elders treated the meetings like a sort of Mutual Admiration Society in which they complimented and applauded each other. Alex got the feeling that these church leaders were more interested in standing ovations than in spending time on their knees before God.

Jesus accused some religious leaders of desiring the praise of people while being unconcerned about having God's approval. "How can you believe when you accept each other's praise and don't look for the praise that comes from the only God?" he asked. The leaders basked in the prestige and honor that their positions afforded, and they concentrated on keeping things that way. In contrast, Jesus made it clear that he wasn't in a popularity contest. His only goal was to please God and do God's will.

The world's praise and accolades are temporary, but a compliment from God lasts forever. God called David a man after his own heart—not because he was perfect but because he wholeheartedly desired to obey God (see Acts 13:22). Jesus told a parable about a man whose master praised him as a "good and faithful servant" for wisely investing what he had been given (see Matthew 25).

We can't live the Christian life focused on winning other people's admiration. Our choice is clear: Will we let our behavior be dictated by what would attract the world's praise, or will we concentrate on being a good and faithful servant whose heart beats in tune with God's?

A person with a changed heart seeks praise from God, not from people.

Romans 2:29 NLT

Ask yourself: **Am I more concerned about winning other people's praise or God's?**

OCTOBER
19

"Men, what are you doing?"

Acts 14:8–18

As the weeks passed, Jordan remained in shock over the youth pastor's arrest. All the kids had adored their leader, but since Jordan didn't come from a Christian home, he especially depended on the support and guidance of the man who had introduced him to Christ. Now Jordan saw no reason to go to church, to pray, or to open his Bible. He wasn't sure what he believed anymore.

It's always dangerous to put someone up on a pedestal, no matter how godly they are. In Lystra, Paul and Barnabas had the experience of people literally worshiping them. After they healed a lame man, the people concluded that they were two Roman gods come down to visit. The priest of Zeus's temple brought bulls to sacrifice to them. Paul and Barnabas were horrified. "Men," they cried, "what are you doing? We're human beings like you." Then they seized the opportunity to introduce the people in the pagan city to the one true God.

In our culture we don't physically bow, but we do treat certain people like royalty. Even Christian circles can have their own "superstars." Like Paul and Barnabas, we should be horrified if someone tries to put us on a pedestal. Being the object of great admiration makes us more vulnerable to the sin of pride. Even worse, it can take other people's focus off of Jesus.

We should also be careful not to give a spiritual leader or mentor the kind of devotion that rightly belongs to Christ. While we do owe our leaders respect and honor, there's a fine line that shouldn't be crossed. If our faith depends on another human being, we'll eventually be disappointed. As the angel in Revelation 22 told John, there is only One who is worthy to be worshiped.

He told me, "Don't do that! I am your coworker. I work with other Christians, the prophets, and those who follow the words in this book. Worship God!"

Revelation 22:9

Ask yourself: **Is there anyone that I'm elevating higher than I should?**

"Shouldn't we place ourselves under the authority of God?"

Hebrews 12:4–11

Tyrone dropped his skateboard on the playground's smooth asphalt and looked back at his hesitant friend. "Are you sure this is okay?" Robbie asked. "I mean, the school board made such a big deal about the new rule. What if we get caught?"

Tyrone laughed. "Are you forgetting who just got hired as the new principal? Let's just call this one of the perks of my dad's new job." Later, Tyrone learned that his father called it breaking the rules; he received two weeks in detention.

The writer of Hebrews explained that just because we're God's children doesn't mean we can get away with wrongdoing. Just as earthly parents discipline their children out of love, God disciplines us for our own good. "Shouldn't we place ourselves under the authority of God, the father of spirits, so that we will live?" Nobody enjoys being disciplined, because it seems painful at the time. But later on we can look back and appreciate how the discipline trained us to do the right thing.

One way our heavenly Father shows his love for us is by correcting and training us to live a godly life. He may use our circumstances to teach us lessons or send other believers to confront us with some truth that we need to hear. We may experience a relentless nagging in our spirit that doesn't let up until we repent of a sin. Or God may temporarily remove a sense of his presence.

When we're under God's discipline, our best response is to ask what he wants to teach us. Becoming angry or resentful, or denying that we deserve the correction, only prolongs the pain. It's easier to have a submissive attitude by remembering that God's discipline proves we're his child, and he loves us too much to let us get away with something.

Endure your discipline. God corrects you
as a father corrects his children.

Hebrews 12:7

Ask yourself: **How do I react when God disciplines me?**

OCTOBER
21

"As you teach others, are you failing to teach yourself?"

Romans 2:17–24

Olivia fumed as she listened to her parents' lecture on lying. How could they be so self-righteous? Didn't her dad call in sick when he wanted to play golf? And more than once she'd overheard her mom make up some lame excuse to get out of helping with school activities. But it didn't do any good to point out discrepancies between the rules they laid down for her and their own behavior. They always responded the same way—with a shrug, a laugh, and those familiar words: "Do as I say, not as I do."

Paul confronted Jewish people who took pride in their responsibility to teach God's law to the Gentiles but whose lifestyle didn't match their words. "As you teach others, are you failing to teach yourself?" Paul asked. Then he asked questions to point out specific areas of disobedience and immorality. Their failure to practice what they preached had caused God's name to be blasphemed among non-Jewish people.

James wrote that teachers will be judged more strictly because of their great responsibility. Even if we're not in a formal teaching role, we serve as an example to others. Someone out there is watching our life to see if we really mean what we claim to believe. If our actions contradict our words, it dishonors God's name and turns people away from wanting to know him.

It's easier to tell people how to do the right thing than to live out Christian principles. God wants us to practice what we preach. As in all things, Jesus serves as our perfect role model. His life never revealed a discrepancy between what he taught and how he acted. We'll never be perfect, but as we imitate him our life will become a better example for others to follow.

Imitate me as I imitate Christ.

1 Corinthians 11:1

Ask God **to point out any discrepancies between what you say and what you do.**

"How did you get in here without proper clothes?"

Matthew 22:1–14

Invitations used to specify proper attire for the event, with phrases such as "black tie required." As society grew more casual, the idea of a dress code fell out of favor. Today, however, many people believe that the "anything goes" attitude has gone too far. Some public schools are instituting a dress code for students. These requirements often include a minimum length for skirts and the requirement that waistbands be located at the waist instead of near the thigh.

Jesus told a parable about a dress code that caused trouble for one man. In the story, a king prepared a wedding banquet for his son, but the invited guests refused to come. So the king sent his servants out into the streets to invite anyone they could find. During the festivities, the king noticed a man not wearing the clothes he had provided for his guests. "Friend," the king asked, "how did you get in here without proper wedding clothes?" The guest had no explanation for the way he had insulted his host, and was summarily thrown out.

God has a spiritual dress code for those who want to enter his kingdom. We can't get in by dressing ourselves in religious rules or our own efforts at goodness. Admittance is given only to those who choose to put on the robe of righteousness God has provided through Christ's sacrifice.

One day God will summon us to a very special banquet. In the meantime, he wants us to clothe our spirit by imitating the attitudes and character traits Jesus modeled. Sometimes we choose to throw on ragged remnants of our old sinful nature instead of the clothing God bought for us at such a high price. Why wouldn't we want to wear our best every day?

Clothe yourselves with the Lord Jesus Christ, and do not think about how to gratify the desires of the sinful nature.

Romans 13:14 NIV

Ask yourself: **Do I make sure to clothe myself with Christ every day?**

OCTOBER
23

"Who says that you are any better than other people?"

1 Corinthians 4:1–7

Can't say I'm sorry to see him go, Denise thought as she and her husband dropped off their guest at the airport. She'd been thrilled to snag a nationally known speaker for her church's daylong retreat. But the man had disgusted the committee members by acting like a movie star favoring his fans with his presence. Denise couldn't help wondering what effect his pompous behavior had on the unbelievers visiting the services.

The apostle Paul had a highly visible and productive ministry but he often stressed the importance of humility. He described himself and other church leaders as servants of Christ. Using rhetorical questions, Paul encouraged all believers to examine their own attitudes: "Who says that you are any better than other people? What do you have that wasn't given to you?"

A "diva" attitude is never appropriate, whether we're relating to other believers or interacting with those outside the church. The world often portrays Christians as self-righteous people with a holier-than-thou attitude. Nothing could be further from the life God calls us to live and the attitudes modeled by Jesus. Philippians 2:5–11 describes how Jesus voluntarily gave up his equality with God for a period of time. Taking on human form, Jesus humbled himself to the point of dying a shameful death on the cross.

The Bible challenges us to have an honest estimate of ourselves, including our strengths, weaknesses, abilities, and gifts. When we ponder the questions that Paul asked, there's no way we can have an inflated opinion of ourselves or our position in the body of Christ. Remembering that everything we have comes from God makes us think more highly of him—not ourselves.

> *Because of the kindness that God has shown me, I ask you not to think of yourselves more highly than you should.*
>
> Romans 12:3

Ask yourself: **Does my self-perception ever contain a hint of superiority over others?**

OCTOBER
24

"What miracle are you going to perform so that we can believe in you?"

John 6:22–34

After a boat ride to Capernaum, the crowd finally found Jesus. The day before, he had turned a little boy's lunch into enough food to feed several thousand people. They couldn't wait to see what Jesus would do next. Knowing their hearts, Jesus pointed out that they didn't look for him because they had witnessed miracles but because their stomachs had been filled.

Jesus challenged the people to take the food that lasts through eternity. They would find this food by believing in the One whom God had sent. "What miracle are you going to perform so that we can see it and believe in you?" the crowd demanded. "What are you going to do?" They reminded Jesus of the miracle of manna given to their ancestors, seeming to forget the miraculous nature of the previous day's feeding of the crowd.

Many people today want God to perform a miracle so they can believe in him. Those people are missing the obvious. The world around us proves the existence of the Creator (see Rom. 1:20). God gave the rainbow as a sign of his promise to never again destroy the earth by a flood (see Gen. 9:11–13). He promised Israel the sign of a virgin giving birth to a son named Immanuel (Isa. 7:14). During his time on earth, Jesus performed many miracles, culminating in his resurrection and ascension into heaven.

Besides these signs recorded in Scripture, each believer is a walking miracle. God has placed his Spirit in us so that his life and power flow through us. He's broken sin's power over us. And he's using our life to accomplish his purposes. If we look around and don't see miracles, it's because we're overlooking the obvious.

Meditate on all the miracles he has done.

1 Chronicles 16:9

Ask God **to open your eyes to his miraculous works that surround you and permeate your life.**

OCTOBER

25

"Don't you know me yet?"

John 14:6–11

As a newlywed, Nicole often thought about her grandparents' relationship. After 48 years of marriage, they knew each other like a book, one often finishing the other's sentences. Sometimes it seemed as though they even shared a secret code between them. Nicole and her husband struggled simply to adjust to a shared bathroom. *Will we get to know each other that well as the years pass?* Nicole wondered.

Jesus had been with his disciples for three years, but sometimes they seemed to understand little about him. When Jesus told them that the only way to the Father was through him, Philip said, "Lord, show us the Father, and that will satisfy us." Jesus responded, "I have been with all of you for a long time. Don't you know me yet, Philip?" Then Jesus repeated that anyone who had seen him had seen the Father.

If we are a believer, we should be getting to know Jesus more and more intimately as time passes. The Gospels paint a portrait of his character and his earthly life. Other New Testament books offer insights into his ministry and how to apply his teachings to our life. Through Bible study, prayer, and obedience to his words, we can grow in our understanding of Jesus and our relationship with him.

Still, our human perception will always be limited. Right now we can only have an imperfect view of Jesus, like a reflection in an ancient metal mirror. But we can look forward to the day when we will see Jesus face-to-face and know him as fully and completely as he knows us. What joy it will be when nothing obscures our view of the One we love.

Now we see but a poor reflection as in a mirror; then
we shall see face to face. Now I know in part; then
I shall know fully, even as I am fully known.

1 Corinthians 13:12 NIV

Ask yourself: **How can I make sure I am getting to know Jesus better as time passes?**

“Why did you make us leave Egypt?”

Numbers 21:4–9

Shannon grimaced as she put dinner on the table. The mashed potatoes had lumps and the gravy looked a little thin. Two of her children didn't care for roast beef and all of them hated broccoli. *If they complain about this meal, so help me . . .* she thought. As a customer service rep, Shannon had already heard her fill of grumbling for the day. She called her family to the table with an announcement: “The first person who makes a negative comment gets to clean up the kitchen tonight.”

The Israelites faced severe consequences for their continued grumbling. Despite the way God had rescued and protected them, they refused to trust him. Whenever things got tough, they acted like God didn't care about their welfare. “Why did you make us leave Egypt—just to let us die in the desert?” they cried. “There's no bread or water, and we can't stand this awful food!”

This is the eighth recorded incident of the Israelites grumbling, and this time God decided to punish them. He sent poisonous snakes that caused many deaths, until the people admitted their sin and asked Moses to intercede. Then God provided a way for the people to be healed from snake bites: looking up at a bronze snake on a pole.

When we're not happy about something, our natural response is to grumble and whine. But constant complaining only reinforces our disappointment and dissatisfaction. It also affects the attitudes of people around us and spreads discontent within a group setting. And it gives a negative impression of the Christian life to unbelievers. Since God controls our circumstances, our complaining is really against him. To break this destructive habit, we need to first confess that our negative attitude is sinful. Then, as we focus on praising and thanking God, we'll see that we don't have that much to complain about after all.

Do everything without complaining or arguing.
Philippians 2:14

Ask yourself: **How much grumbling and complaining does God hear from me?**

OCTOBER
27

"How old are you?"

Genesis 47:5–10

Teresa overheard her daughter's voice in the next room. "How old are you, Grandma?" Bailey asked. Teresa smiled at her mother-in-law's answer: "I'm just a little older than your mom." Not satisfied with the answer, four-year-old Bailey asked the question again. "Just a little bit older than your mom," Grandma insisted. After two more tries to get a different answer, Bailey finally gave up.

Many people today avoid revealing their age, but at one time an advanced age was something to take pride in. When Joseph moved his family to Egypt so they could escape the famine in Israel, he presented his father to Pharaoh. "How old are you?" Pharaoh asked. "The length of my stay on earth has been 130 years," Jacob proudly answered. Then he added, "The years of my life have been few and difficult, fewer than my ancestors' years."

No one can deny that we live in a society obsessed with youth. We're constantly bombarded with the message that we need to make ourselves look younger—at any expense. The desire to stay healthy and physically fit sometimes gets distorted into a battle to reverse the clock. Instead of respecting the years of experience and wisdom that age brings, our cultural attitudes influence many to hide or even lie about their age.

For God's people, aging is nothing to fear. He promises to take care of us even when we're old (see Isa. 46:4). He also promises we can still have fruitful lives in our old age. The Bible shares stories of many people whose later years included some special assignment or reward from God, such as Caleb, Anna, Miriam, Elizabeth, Abraham, and Sarah. If we stay faithful to God, there's no reason to dread aging. Besides, who knows what surprise he has planned for our later years?

They shall still bear fruit in old age; they shall be fresh and flourishing.

Psalm 92:14 NKJV

Ask yourself: **Have I let the culture around me influence my attitude toward age?**

OCTOBER
28

"What do your sacrifices mean to me?"

Isaiah 1:10–15

Samantha signed for the package and closed the front door. Even though the delivery had come from the most expensive jewelry store in town, Samantha felt no desire to open it. *Just another attempt to buy me off*, she thought. Each time Neil broke their wedding vows, he promised to never do it again. He always followed up his apology with an outrageously expensive gift. Samantha's friends envied her for having a husband who had once surprised her with a new car. She longed to tell them how meaningless Neil's gifts were, since they came from an unfaithful heart.

In Isaiah's day, God found the Israelites' offerings and sacrifices meaningless because the people were unfaithful to him in their hearts. They thought they could follow the prescribed rituals of sacrifices to get clean before God—and then go out and live however they wanted. "What do your many animal sacrifices mean to me?" God asked. He also expressed displeasure with their offerings, their festival observances, and even their prayers. Their outward expressions meant nothing because of their inward spiritual condition.

When our heart isn't right with God, there's nothing we can do to "buy him off." Big bucks in the offering plate won't impress him. Generously giving our time and service doesn't compensate for unfaithfulness. Following rituals or traditions is no substitute for obedience to God's standards. The main things God wants from us are a heart that's broken over our sinfulness and a desire to change. These are the starting points of true worship. Once we come to God in humility and repentance, we can be sure our sacrifices and offerings will please him.

The sacrifice pleasing to God is a broken spirit. O God,
you do not despise a broken and sorrowful heart.

Psalm 51:17

Ask yourself: **Do I have a heart attitude that makes my sacrifices and offerings pleasing to God?**

OCTOBER
29

"Who has determined the course of history?"

Isaiah 41:1–10

Wars and threats of wars, rumors of nuclear missiles being built, broken diplomatic relationships between formerly friendly nations, acts of terrorism, and guerrilla warfare—the evening news can be frightening. At times, it looks as though the world is spiraling out of control with no way to stop it.

Through the prophet Isaiah, God gave all the people of the earth a reminder of who controls world events. "Who has determined the course of history from the beginning?" he challenged. "I, the LORD, was there first, and I will be there to the end. I am the one!"

As an example of how leaders and world empires unknowingly carry out his plans, God referred to a ruler he would raise up from the east. In Isaiah 44, he named this person as Cyrus of Persia, who would come to power more than a hundred years later. Despite changing world events, God urged his chosen people not to be intimidated. He promised to be with them and support them with his "victorious right hand."

Even when the news seems to be a string of random, senseless events, God has everything under control. World events are influenced by the presence of evil and people's sinful choices, but God is sovereign. He governs governors, presides over presidents, and dictates how far dictators can go. People who don't know him carry out his will without realizing it.

We may struggle to understand the purpose of historical or current events, but we can trust that God knows what he's doing. We can also take comfort in knowing that he will be with us in the midst of a world that sometimes seems out of control. Someday everything will make sense, when we meet the One who directs the course of history from beginning to end.

I, the LORD, was there first, and I will be there to the end. I am the one!

Isaiah 41:4

Ask yourself: **Do world events ever make me forget who controls history?**

"Are only a few people going to be saved?"

Luke 13:22–30

Mavis pushed open the door to her office building and froze when she realized that it would lock behind her. She'd forgotten to bring her key to work, and everyone else had left for the day. Mavis really needed to bring in that box of files from her car. Then she had an idea. Slipping off her shoe, she used it as a wedge to hold the door open. *Brilliant!* she thought. A few minutes later, Mavis stood holding her cardboard box, staring at the closed door.

Jesus told about another door that would not stay open permanently. As Jesus traveled toward Jerusalem, someone asked, "Sir, are only a few people going to be saved?" Instead of answering the question directly, Jesus urged his listeners to make sure they entered through the narrow door while they had the chance. He told a parable about a homeowner who closed his door and didn't open it again. Some of the people outside knocked and called to get in, but it was too late.

It's disheartening to think that most people who hear about God's offer of forgiveness and eternal life choose not to accept it. Many people waste time looking for another door, refusing to believe that Jesus is the only way. God freely offers salvation to every single human being, but there will eventually come a time when the opportunity to trust Christ is taken away.

God desires for everyone to come to an understanding of his offer and enter into a relationship with him. When we pray for someone's salvation, we know we are praying in accordance with God's will. But there's only a window of time when the door will stay open. Jesus's parable reminds us to grab every opportunity to point people toward the narrow door—before it's too late and they're left standing outside.

He wants all people to be saved and to learn the truth.

1 Timothy 2:4

Ask yourself: **Am I doing my best to point others toward the narrow door before it closes?**

OCTOBER
31

"What's your verdict?"

Matthew 26:57–66

After Jesus's arrest, the Jewish council frantically searched for some legal basis to condemn him to death. Many volunteers came forward to give false testimony and distort Jesus's teachings. Finally, the chief priest called for Jesus to answer a question under oath: "Are you the Messiah, the Son of God?" Jesus answered calmly, "Yes, I am." He added that in the future, he would occupy the highest position in heaven.

At this point, the Jewish leaders only had two choices in how to respond: they could believe Jesus was telling the truth and worship him as the Messiah, or they could reject his claim and sentence him to death for blasphemy as required by their law. The high priest tore his robes in horror. "You've just heard him dishonor God! What's your verdict?" he asked. "He deserves the death penalty!" they agreed.

When a judge asks for a jury's verdict, the foreman answers "guilty," "not guilty," or else explains that the jury is hung and unable to reach a decision. When voting on legislation, politicians vote "aye" or "nay." In most states, they also have a third option: they can avoid taking a stand with a vote of "present." But when it comes to spiritual matters, there is no third option. We can't avoid taking a stand on Jesus's claim to be divine.

Either we accept the gospel as truth and choose to become God's child, or we refuse to believe it and remain his enemy. As believers, God calls us to reaffirm our commitment to him each day. Will we worship him or ourselves today? Will we be controlled by his Spirit or by our own desires? Each one of us must answer God's question: "What's your verdict?" And there are only two possible answers.

If you don't want to serve the LORD, then
choose today whom you will serve.

Joshua 24:15

Ask yourself: **Does my lifestyle make it obvious to others what my verdict is?**

"Is there a limit to the Lord's power?"

Numbers 11:18–23

Darrell drove home from the interview feeling pleased with himself. Not only did the manager offer him the job on the spot, but he agreed to Darrell's request for a modest increase in salary and five more vacation days. Several weeks later, however, Darrell wasn't quite as satisfied with his new position. His new friend in management had shared some inside information: the personnel manager had been prepared to go quite a bit higher on his salary. Darrell had underestimated his bargaining power.

Moses needed a reminder not to underestimate God's power. When the Israelites complained about having nothing but manna to eat, God promised to provide a month's worth of meat. Moses had witnessed God's miraculous power and provision, but he had trouble believing this promise. He questioned how God could accomplish such a feat for the vast multitude of people. "Is there a limit to the LORD's power?" God responded. "Now you will see whether or not my words come true."

Paul wrote that God's power can do "infinitely more than we can ask or imagine" (Eph. 3:20). Yet sometimes our thinking puts limits on God's power. We may let a lack of faith make us timid in how we pray, or we may not bring a request to him at all. A failure to trust God can inhibit his working in our life.

We never have a reason to underestimate God's infinite power. It's at work in us, in other people, and in the world around us. God wants us to dream big and expect miracles. He loves to answer our prayers in ways that help our faith grow. Since his power is unlimited, why should we expect only limited blessings from him?

> *You will also know the unlimited greatness of his power as it works with might and strength for us, the believers.*
>
> Ephesians 1:19

Ask yourself: **How have I been placing limits on God's power in my attitudes and in my prayers?**

NOVEMBER
2

"Who is greatest in the kingdom of heaven?"

Matthew 18:1–5

There he goes again! The father sighed in exasperation as he watched the soccer field. He knew Jeremy was only seven, but if he wanted to excel he needed to get serious about the game. How could he become the team's best player if he kept stopping to offer his hand to every player who got knocked down? *This kid needs to be a little less compassionate and a little more competitive*, he thought.

Jesus's disciples displayed a competitive spirit as they argued over who would be greatest in the kingdom of heaven. Jesus answered their question with a paradox: In order to be important in God's eyes, a person has to take the last place and be a servant to other people (see Mark 9:35). Then Jesus used a child as an illustration of faith. "Whoever becomes like this little child," he explained, "is the greatest in the kingdom of heaven."

We tend to associate greatness with strength, impressive achievements, or positions of power. God evaluates us from a different perspective. To be "great" in his eyes, we must dedicate our lives to serving others. Rather than seeking status or prestige, we should look for opportunities to meet people's needs. Instead of elevating ourselves, we must build others up. And we should never consider ourselves above doing tasks that seem unimportant or menial.

God values childlike faith. Salvation requires us to move from an attitude of self-sufficiency to one of humility and implicit trust, depending on God to do what we cannot do for ourselves. As our understanding of God deepens, we learn to let go of our pride and rely on him for everything. Like a child, we instinctively run into our heavenly Father's arms in times of need or trouble. The more we mature spiritually, the more comfortable we feel with the knowledge that God controls our life. In God's kingdom, growing up means becoming more childlike.

Whoever becomes like this little child is the greatest in the kingdom of heaven.

Matthew 18:4

Ask yourself: **How can I develop a more childlike trust in God?**

"Should we pay taxes or not?"

Mark 12:13–17

Questioning the government's right to tax individuals is nothing new. In the United States, the movement to repeal the Sixteenth Amendment grew more radical in the 1960s and 1970s. Many people in today's tax protest movement are accused of activities such as failure to file, tax fraud, and racketeering. Some factions resort to threats, harassment, or even violence.

In New Testament times, the Jewish people hated paying taxes to their Roman oppressors. Two different groups, who also hated Jesus, decided to use this thorny issue to trap him with a trick question. After flattering him, they asked, "Is it right to pay taxes to the emperor or not?" A "yes" answer would make it easier to turn people against Jesus; a "no" answer could get him in trouble with Rome.

Holding up a coin, Jesus asked whose name and image it bore. Then he instructed his listeners to "give the emperor what belongs to the emperor, and give God what belongs to God." The simplicity and wisdom of his answer left no room for rebuttal. Our citizenship on earth requires us to pay for the benefits of civil government; since we bear the image of God, we owe him our obedience and devotion.

We may not like it, but the Bible tells us to submit to all earthly authorities and manmade laws, as long as they don't conflict with God's commands. That doesn't mean we have to agree with our nation's laws and leaders. But we can respect their position of authority over us even when we can't respect the individual. Since governments are ordained by God, we are really submitting to him. It helps to remember that when civil obedience taxes our strength.

Place yourselves under the authority of human governments to please the Lord.

1 Peter 2:13

Ask yourself: **Do I display the proper attitude toward human authorities?**

NOVEMBER

4

“Why have you let the boys live?”

Exodus 1:15–21

The Hebrew midwives recoiled from Pharaoh’s words with horror. In spite of harsh treatment, the enslaved Hebrews had kept growing in number. So the king of Egypt ordered the two principal Hebrew midwives to kill any boys born, while allowing the girls to live. Shiphrah and Puah had a choice to make: Would they follow Pharaoh’s order or risk their lives to obey God’s law, which forbade the taking of innocent life?

These two courageous women decided to follow God’s higher law and let the boys live. Pharaoh confronted them about their disobedience. “Why have you done this?” he demanded. “Why have you let the boys live?” Puah and Shiphrah excused their behavior by saying that the Hebrew women tended to deliver their babies before the midwives arrived.

Puah and Shiphrah may have exaggerated or even lied to protect themselves from Pharaoh’s anger, or the midwives may have instituted a policy of responding late to calls from women about to deliver. But God rewarded them for obeying him rather than Pharaoh. He increased the numbers and strength of the Hebrews, and especially blessed Puah’s and Shiphrah’s family life.

While Scripture instructs us to obey the governing authorities, there may be times when doing so would cause us to sin. Whenever man’s laws conflict with God’s commandments, our allegiance to God takes precedence. We are not bound to earthly authority if it would involve us in fraud, theft, harming others, or anything that forces us to break one of God’s commands or deny our Christian faith. Choosing to disobey civil laws in order to follow God may bring serious consequences, but he will reward our faithfulness. When we can’t obey both God and people, we know who comes first.

We must obey God rather than people.

Acts 5:29

Ask God **to give you the courage to obey his laws even when it conflicts with earthly authorities.**

“When may I come to see God’s face?”

Psalm 42:1–4

The soldier stepped off the airplane and anxiously scanned the crowd. The balloons, signs, and even the local celebrities held little interest for him. After spending a year in Afghanistan, he looked forward to many things. But right now he only had one goal in mind. Finally his eyes lighted on what he most longed to see—the faces of his wife and little boy.

The writer of Psalm 42 compared his longing for God to a deer craving the water it needed to sustain its life. Feeling separated from the God he loved, he asked, “When may I come to see God’s face?” Cut off from formal worship at the sanctuary in Jerusalem, the psalmist tearfully recalled participating in special services. He yearned to regain the closeness to God he had felt during those times.

No human being can ever know true satisfaction until they form a relationship with their Creator. We find purpose and meaning through knowing him and understanding that he loves us unconditionally. Many people search for fulfillment through all the world offers, without realizing that what they really long for is God.

After becoming God’s child, we’re still separated from him to a certain extent by our physical body and our old sinful nature. We live with the underlying dissatisfaction of wanting to know him more intimately, to have a deeper prayer life, and to live a holier life. One day all our desires will be satisfied when we get our eternal body, perfect and completely free from the effects of sin. Then we can enter into God’s presence with nothing between us. When we see Jesus face-to-face, we’ll get what we’ve longed for all our life.

Dear friends, now we are God’s children. What we will be isn’t completely clear yet. We do know that when Christ appears we will be like him because we will see him as he is.

1 John 3:2

Ask yourself: **Do I long to see God’s face? Why or why not?**

NOVEMBER

6

"What have I done compared with that?"

Judges 8:1–3

As soon as Rosemary answered the phone, Megan launched into an angry tirade. She demanded to know why the committee had met secretly behind her back, and threatened to call the pastor. "You're all trying to get rid of me—right before the fall banquet, which you know is my favorite event!" Rosemary cleared her throat and explained that the members had gathered spontaneously after church. They didn't want to bother Megan while her son had pneumonia. "But we voted unanimously to ask you to plan the fall banquet, if you want to."

Gideon's gracious words diffused a potentially explosive situation when the leaders of Ephraim confronted him. They demanded to know why Gideon didn't call them when he fought against the Midianites. Instead of reacting to their anger in self-defense, Gideon insisted that their tribe had accomplished more than his own clan had. Ephraim had come from behind and taken care of the escaping Midianites, including the two army commanders. "What have I done compared with that?" Gideon asked. His response dissolved the Ephraimites' resentment.

In the face of confrontation, it's hard to exercise self-control, especially if the other person is being unreasonable. But lashing out in self-defense or retaliation only provokes more anger and can escalate the situation into something worse than an argument. A gentle, gracious answer tends to soothe the other person's emotions and allow for a rational discussion.

When we find ourselves in a tense situation, the best way to stay calm is to send up a quick prayer before we open our mouth. If we let him, God will help us control our emotions so we can answer with a soft voice and carefully chosen words. The choice is ours: Will we give a response that turns away anger, or one that stirs it up and makes it burn even hotter?

A gentle answer turns away rage, but
a harsh word stirs up anger.

Proverbs 15:1

Ask yourself: **During tense situations, do my words escalate anger or help to dissolve it?**

“Do any of you have wisdom and insight?”

James 3:13–18

We’ve all met people who pride themselves on their intelligence or educational background but who live a life plagued by foolish decisions. Television programs often interview people considered experts in their field, or who have written textbooks in a specific branch of knowledge. What often comes out of their mouths is sheer stupidity. As I once heard an older person put it, “That boy might have plenty of book-learning, but he sure doesn’t have any smarts.”

James had a lot to say about true wisdom. “Do any of you have wisdom and insight?” He challenged his readers to examine their character and actions to see if their lives showed evidence of the world’s wisdom or God’s wisdom. Earthly wisdom inspires jealousy and self-centered ambition, resulting in disorder and rivalry. In contrast, the wisdom that comes from God is pure, peaceful, gentle, submissive, and considerate of others. A life based on heavenly wisdom demonstrates mercy, sincerity, righteousness, and humility.

Wisdom is far more than intellectual knowledge; it involves understanding and practical application of knowledge. Even if we could acquire all the knowledge and truth in the world, it would have little value if it didn’t impact our life. Our character, attitude, and behavior reveal the source of our wisdom. If we lean toward the world’s wisdom, our life will be plagued with conflicts and self-centeredness. If we’re seeking God’s wisdom, we’ll be developing godly character traits.

The world often elevates knowledge and intelligence above true wisdom, but God values a humble spirit much more than an impressive IQ. “Do any of you have wisdom and insight?” We would all love to answer James’s question in the affirmative, but God challenges us to prove it by our life.

Do any of you have wisdom and insight? Show this by living the right way with the humility that comes from wisdom.

James 3:13

Ask yourself: **Do my behavior and lifestyle display more characteristics of earthly wisdom or heavenly wisdom?**

NOVEMBER

8

"Who is my mother, and who are my brothers?"

Mark 3:31–35

Early in our marriage, my husband's job change moved us several hundred miles away from our families. Loneliness overwhelmed me as soon as the last boxes came off the truck. When Sunday came, we picked a church to visit. A couple named Bud and Jackie Taylor insisted on taking us out for lunch. They told us about the church, asked questions about our move, and showed interest in our two little boys. I was touched when I learned that this couple's children and grandchildren lived in the same town, yet they spent their Sunday with us. Their kindness helped us choose our new church family.

Jesus never downplayed family obligations, but he also stressed the importance of spiritual kinship. When his family became concerned about his welfare, they came to take him away. "Who is my mother, and who are my brothers?" Jesus asked. He explained that whoever followed God became part of his family. While family ties are important, the bond between forgiven sinners is even stronger.

Once we make the decision to follow Christ, we become a member of the largest family in the world. Whether we come from a large close-knit family or grew up as an only child, we're related to every other believer in the world. We can find more experienced Christians to mentor us as spiritual parents, and brothers and sisters in Christ to love and support us.

In today's megachurches it's easy to remain anonymous, slipping in and out of worship services. If we attend church that way, we miss out on a large part of the Christian life. Small groups, Bible studies, and ministry opportunities not only nurture our spiritual growth, they help us get to know people while learning and serving together. There's no reason to be lonely when we're part of God's family.

God places lonely people in families.

Psalm 68:6

Ask yourself: **Am I nurturing the relationships I have in God's family?**

“Must we bring water out of this rock for you?”

Numbers 20:1–12

The Israelites’ forty years of aimless wandering in the wilderness had almost come to an end, but their complaining had not. When they arrived back at Kadesh and found the usual water sources dry, they turned on Moses once again. And Moses, as usual, turned to God. For the second time, God promised to bring water from a rock for the people. In the earlier incident (see Exod. 17:6), God had told Moses to strike the rock; this time God gave Moses slightly different instructions.

God commanded Moses to take his staff and his brother Aaron, gather the people, and speak to the rock. But as Moses faced the assembly, his exasperation with the people came out. “Listen, you rebels,” he exclaimed, “must we bring water out of this rock for you?”

Although God caused water to gush out of the rock, he rebuked Moses for drawing attention to himself and his authority instead of making it clear that the miracle was an act of God’s provision. Because of their disobedience, Moses and Aaron would not be allowed to enter the Promised Land.

God’s decision may seem harsh, but it underscores an important spiritual principle. God gives us gifts, opportunities, and privileges to bring glory to him—not to draw attention to ourselves. The more he gives us, the more he demands from us. When God puts us in a position of authority, it’s especially important to guard against lapses in judgment that would dishonor him in front of others. When people look at us, we want to redirect their eyes toward God. Even if we find ourselves in the limelight, it’s just another chance to shine the spotlight on him.

Our message is not about ourselves. It is about Jesus Christ as the Lord.

2 Corinthians 4:5

Ask yourself: **Do I use every opportunity to point people to my Father?**

NOVEMBER
10

"When did we see you hungry and feed you?"

Matthew 25:31–46

In 1885, Leo Tolstoy published a story called "Where Love Is, God Is There." In the tale, one night an old cobbler dreamed that Jesus promised to visit him. While he worked and watched for his guest the next day, he offered hospitality, warmth, and food to strangers who passed by his window. But Jesus didn't visit. That night, the disappointed man's Bible fell open to Matthew 25. Then he understood that Jesus had indeed visited him that day, and he had welcomed his Savior.

One day Jesus will sit on his throne and judge the nations. He will invite his true followers, the sheep, to enter the kingdom prepared by God. Along with the invitation, the king will commend them for their acts of compassion toward him: providing food, drink, clothing, and housing when he needed it; taking care of him during illness; visiting him in prison.

These people will express surprise at his words. "Lord," they will ask, "when did we see you hungry and feed you or see you thirsty and give you something to drink?" After they ask similar questions about each act of service, the king will explain that whenever they showed kindness to one of his brothers or sisters, it was the same as doing it for him.

Scholars have long debated the identity of the "brothers and sisters" but the principle clearly applies to us. Each time we perform a practical act of kindness for a believer, Jesus counts it as though we did it for him. If we view an opportunity to serve the needy as a chance to serve Jesus himself, it will transform our attitude—and also help change the way the world sees Jesus.

The king will answer . . . "Whatever you did for one of my brothers or sisters, no matter how unimportant they seemed, you did for me."

Matthew 25:40

Ask God **to give you opportunities to show compassion to others in Jesus's name today.**

NOVEMBER
11

"Are you going to stay here while the rest go to war?"

Numbers 32:1–19

The sergeant leaned back and took a long drink. Now that his men had secured their assigned area, they could relax. The sergeant couldn't remember such an easy operation—not much resistance from the insurgents. From the sounds of heavy gunfire, he could tell that the adjacent area wasn't giving up as easily. Well, he wished his fellow soldiers good luck, but that wasn't his responsibility. His battle had already been won.

This ridiculous scenario gives an idea of what Moses assumed about some of the Israelites. Before Israel entered the Promised Land, the tribes of Reuben, Gad, and part of Manasseh asked to settle on the east side of the Jordan River. Their request shocked Moses, and he accused them of trying to evade their duty to help conquer Canaan.

"Are you going to stay here while the rest of the Israelites go to war?" he asked. The leaders from Reuben, Gad, and Manasseh assured Moses that after securing the area for their families and livestock, their fighting men would cross the Jordan. They would not return until every other tribe had conquered their land.

For believers, living in this world means that we're engaged in ongoing spiritual warfare. Ephesians 6:10–18 details our enemy and the weapons God has provided for us. Besides defending ourselves from Satan's attacks, we have the duty to battle on behalf of fellow believers. We can't afford to drop our weapons and relax—and going AWOL is not allowed. This deployment won't end until our Commander sends for us. Then we can look forward to an honorable discharge.

For we are not fighting against flesh-and-blood enemies,
but against evil rulers and authorities of the unseen
world, against mighty powers in this dark world,
and against evil spirits in the heavenly places.

Ephesians 6:12 NLT

Ask yourself: **Do I live like I'm on active duty in God's army?**

NOVEMBER

12

“Can light have anything in common with darkness?”

2 Corinthians 6:14–18

Matthew looked at the invitation and tossed it in the trash can. He just didn’t enjoy getting together with his old fraternity brothers anymore. Now that he had become a Christian, he felt out of place with the language, the jokes, and the steamy entertainment the other guys thrived on. Matthew didn’t want to lose touch with his former friends—he just didn’t want to be associated with that organization when he no longer had anything in common with them.

Paul warned believers to avoid inappropriate ties with unbelievers. “Can right and wrong be partners?” he asked. “Can light have anything in common with darkness?” Although Paul was addressing the issue of false apostles within the Corinthian church who opposed him, the principle applies to all of us. Any time we become involved in a relationship or situation where we could be strongly influenced or controlled by an unbeliever, we risk compromising our faith.

The Bible makes it clear that we’re not expected to avoid all contact with unbelievers or leave an unbelieving spouse if we’re already married (see 1 Cor. 5:9–10; 7:12–13). Instead of living in isolation, God calls us to be his witness to the world while avoiding entanglements that could weaken our effectiveness and make us vulnerable to sin.

God rescued us from the kingdom of darkness and transferred us to the kingdom of his Son, who is the Light of the world. He wants us to avoid any relationship, behavior, habit, or attitude that would weaken our allegiance to this kingdom. We can’t shine as brightly when we allow something to dim the light of God’s truth in our life.

God has rescued us from the power of darkness and has brought us into the kingdom of his Son, whom he loves.

Colossians 1:13

Ask yourself: **Have I allowed anything in my life that’s not compatible with someone living in the light of God’s truth?**

"Why did I come out of the womb?"

Jeremiah 20:7–18

Jasmine raced up the steps. What a morning to be late—just when she'd been so pumped up about her first marketing presentation. But she'd had to rush back home when she noticed that she'd forgotten her purse when she tried to pay for the store-bought cookies for her daughter's class, which they couldn't bake themselves last night because the electricity had gone off. Plopping down at her desk at last, she found a phone message from her son's teacher, saying that she needed to come in and sign a permission form for today's field trip. *Why did I bother getting out of bed?* Jasmine wondered.

Jeremiah took the question a step further. He'd faithfully delivered God's messages to the people; in return, they ridiculed, persecuted, and imprisoned him. As Jeremiah expressed confidence in God despite his circumstances, his emotions suddenly plunged into despair and self-pity. Cursing the day of his birth, Jeremiah cried out, "Why did I come out of the womb? All I've seen is trouble and grief."

When God called Jeremiah to be his prophet, he told him, "Before I formed you in the womb, I knew you. Before you were born, I set you apart for my holy purpose" (Jer. 1:5). God also set us apart for his purposes before our birth. Even before he formed us in our mother's womb, he knew what our future would hold—the good days when we're riding high, and the bad ones that threaten our sanity.

God knows there will be times when our emotions take a turn and we struggle with self-pity and even despair. But he wants us to remember that while our emotions change, he never does (see James 1:17). His love and care for us hold fast even on the worst of days. And that's always reason enough to get out of bed—or to be glad that we came out of the womb.

The Lord made you, formed you in
the womb, and will help you.

Isaiah 44:2

Ask yourself: **How do I handle my emotions when I have a bad day?**

NOVEMBER

14

"What do you want me to do for you?"

Mark 10:46–52

Just another beggar, sitting beside the road outside Jericho—a common sight in those days. But this blind beggar's life was about to change. Bartimaeus couldn't be an eyewitness to Jesus's miracles, but he had heard about them, and he believed.

As Jesus and his disciples drew near, Bartimaeus called out, addressing Jesus as the Messiah: "Jesus, Son of David, have mercy on me!" The annoyed crowd frowned and ordered him to be quiet. But Bartimaeus would not, could not, waste this opportunity. He cried out even louder, "Son of David, have mercy on me!"

Suddenly, Jesus stopped and called for Bartimaeus. The blind man jumped up. "What do you want me to do for you?" asked Jesus. This time Bartimaeus used a more personal term identifying Jesus as his Lord and Master. "Teacher, I want to see again." In an instant, the blind man received his sight and started following Jesus on the road.

Why did Jesus ask Bartimaeus what he wanted? Since Jesus was all-knowing, he didn't need to find out the answer. But his question had a significant purpose. It gave Bartimaeus the chance to verbalize his need and demonstrate the faith that had led him to call out to Jesus. This approach strengthened Bartimaeus's trust and made his interaction with Jesus more personal.

Jesus said that our Father knows what we need before we ask him (see Matt. 6:8), but he still wants us to tell him. Repetitions of generic phrases asking for blessing are a far cry from the genuine prayer described in Philippians 4:6. God wants us to demonstrate our trust in him by asking for specific things. Then, when we receive specific answers, we'll be like Bartimaeus and will see him more clearly.

In the morning I lay my needs in front of you, and I wait.

Psalm 5:3

Ask yourself: **Do I ask God for answers to specific needs?**

"Why are you doing such things?"

1 Samuel 2:12–25

Alan finally admitted to himself that the rumor must be true. More than one acquaintance had seen his son going into a nearby town's strip club with his friends. *Why in the world would he do such a thing?* Alan wondered. He'd taken his son to church. They'd talked about sex and healthy relationships. But each time Alan questioned his son about his "extracurricular activities," Todd would shrug off his father's concerns—until the day he admitted that he'd contracted a sexually transmitted disease.

Eli also asked "Why?" when he should have yelled "Stop!" Hophni and Phinehas had been treating their priestly duties with contempt, stealing the people's sin offerings instead of following God's instructions. They even had sex with the women who served near the tent of meeting. Although Eli was a moral man, he failed to control his sons, who were priests serving under his supervision.

By the time Eli confronted his sons, everyone had heard about the sins they were committing. "Why are you doing such things?" he pleaded. "I hear about your wicked ways from all these people." Although Eli warned Hophni and Phinehas about the seriousness of their sins, they refused to listen. Their hearts had hardened and God had decided to put a stop to their rebellion.

Sometimes we wait too long to speak out against evil. It may be helpful to understand someone's motivations for sinful behavior in order to help them change. During an examination of our own life, we may be able to trace the root causes of our struggle with a particular sin to past events. But analyzing sinful behavior doesn't excuse it, and may even delay repentance and change. There comes a time to stop asking why and simply say, "Don't do that," whether we are warning ourselves or someone else.

Come back to the right point of view, and stop sinning.
1 Corinthians 15:34

Ask yourself: **Am I aware of any situation that calls for me to speak out against sin?**

NOVEMBER

16

"Why do you honor your sons more than me?"

1 Samuel 2:27–36

As the other committee members filed into the room, Dee's shoulders stiffened. How she dreaded these meetings—and all because of the language used by a few people. Dee colored at the off-color jokes, and cringed each time someone cursed using the name of God or Jesus. She'd thought of speaking up, but worried about how the others would respond. Would she be ridiculed? Would she lose her chance to chair the committee in the future? *But I have to put God first*, Dee decided. She cleared her throat . . .

Eli failed to put God first when it came to his sons. Hophni and Phinehas violated the priesthood established by God each time they stole the people's offerings or had sex near the tent of meeting. Their actions made a mockery of God. As a father, Eli had the responsibility to discipline them when he first heard of their wrongdoing. As a priest, he should have discharged them.

By not stopping the abuse, Eli shared the guilt. God confronted him on the issue: "Why do you honor your sons more than me by making yourselves fat on the best of all the sacrifices offered by my people Israel?" Because Eli had not put God first, the priesthood would be removed from Eli's family line and given to another of Aaron's descendants. Because of their sins, Hophni and Phinehas would both be killed on the same day.

Chances are, we'll eventually be exposed to someone who makes a mockery of God through their words or actions. Whether it involves our family, friends, or neighbors, we have a choice to make. Will we avoid confronting the person or will we put God's honor first, regardless of the possible consequences?

But now the Lord declares: I promise that
I will honor those who honor me.

1 Samuel 2:30

Ask yourself: **Am I dishonoring God by allowing someone within my sphere of influence to make a mockery of God?**

“A person breathes his last breath, and where is he?”

Job 14:1–10

Sierra sat down by her father’s hospital bed and reached for his limp hand. He’d been unresponsive for a couple of hours; the nurse said it wouldn’t be much longer. Sierra’s head jerked up as she felt a slight pressure. Her father’s eyes were open, but not looking at her. He seemed to be gazing at some distant point. His lips formed a hint of a smile; he took one last breath, and was gone. Sierra’s sadness at losing her father mingled with the joy of knowing where he had gone.

Job struggled with fluctuating emotions after he suddenly lost his children, his possessions, and his health. Job described earthly life as short and full of trouble. While a tree can sprout and grow again after being cut down, he questioned whether a person had such a hope. “A person breathes his last breath, and where is he?” Job asked. At other times, Job expressed confidence in life after death; in his depressed condition, life seemed futile and death final.

We have an advantage over Job, who lived before Jesus demonstrated by his resurrection that he had conquered death. Even so, death still represents the unknown, in a sense. It’s something we’ve never experienced, and we don’t know the details of how we’ll die. The prospect can be frightening to anyone.

If we’ve placed our faith in Christ, we know *where* we’ll be after we draw our last breath. The instant we leave our earthly body, we enter the presence of God. Our Savior and our deceased loved ones who were believers will be waiting for us. From our current perspective, we might seem to be a long way from our heavenly home and those who have already gone there; in reality we’re just a single breath away.

We would rather be away from these earthly bodies,
for then we will be at home with the Lord.

2 Corinthians 5:8 NLT

Ask God **to remind you that your loved ones who have gone home are not really far away from you.**

NOVEMBER

18

"How long will you lie there, you lazy bum?"

Proverbs 6:6–11

My first-grade music teacher taught us a song about an ant that spent the summer working to store up food for the coming winter. Nearby, a grasshopper squandered the warm months in idle play. When winter hit, the grasshopper found itself in deep trouble. I can still remember what the illustrations of the ant and the grasshopper looked like—and that was more than fifty years ago.

Solomon also thought the ant was a perfect illustration of industriousness. He challenged lazy, irresponsible people to "consider the ant" and become wise by watching its ways. Even though the ant has no overseer telling it what to do, it takes the initiative to provide for its future needs.

Solomon contrasted such diligence with the tendency of some people to rest when they should be working. "How long will you lie there, you lazy bum?" he asked. "When will you get up from your sleep?" Solomon pictured the end of such a man as poverty and need pouncing on him like robbers.

We all need to guard against spiritual laziness as well as the physical kind. The Bible makes it clear that our salvation is not something we work to earn; it's a gift from God. But the proper response to this gift is a life of service dedicated to performing the good works God planned ahead of time for us to do (see Eph. 2:8–10).

The New Testament describes the Christian life with active words like "run," "pursue," "flee from," and "fight." Our lifestyle is to be characterized by discipline, training, and working hard on behalf of God's kingdom. God wants us to live a balanced life and meet our need for rest, but our life should resemble the ant more than the grasshopper.

We do not want you to become lazy, but to imitate those who through faith and patience inherit what has been promised.

Hebrews 6:12 NIV

Ask yourself: **In what areas have I become spiritually lazy?**

"Did you begin in a spiritual way only to end up doing things in a human way?"

Galatians 3:1–12

Manuel was beginning to think that cross-country might not be the right sport for him. Of course, it didn't help that he'd ignored the advice his coach gave about getting a good night's sleep before the race. And what did Coach say about pacing? Manuel had started out strong but soon fell behind the pack. But the worst part was the confusing, poorly marked course. After letting his attention be drawn to a squirrel in the woods, now Manuel wasn't sure if he was still on the right track.

Paul warned the Christians in Galatia that listening to false teachers had pulled them off track in their spiritual growth. Some people were teaching that believers needed to keep the Jewish laws in order to have a complete salvation experience. Paul reminded the Galatians they hadn't received God's Spirit by following rules but by believing in Christ. In the same way, their growth would come from God's power at work in them, not by turning back to the law. "Did you begin in a spiritual way only to end up doing things in a human way?" he asked.

The history of Israel's and Judah's rulers in 1 Kings lists many kings who started out strong, with a desire to serve God, but allowed sin to sidetrack them. Instead of finishing well, their reigns ended in shame and degradation. Their lives serve to warn us that starting out with good intentions doesn't guarantee a successful ending.

Only the power of Christ can save us and only his power can enable us to live a godly life. When we depend on following rules, traditions, or manmade philosophies for our spiritual growth, we can get seriously sidetracked. If we keep our eyes on God and his pure truth, he will help us stay on course, finish our race, and finish it strong.

I want to finish the race I'm running.

Acts 20:24

Ask yourself: **What influences threaten to pull me off course and keep me from finishing my race strong?**

NOVEMBER
20

"What makes you so confident?"

Isaiah 36:1–20

The Assyrian field commander scoffed at the representatives King Hezekiah had sent. The besieged city of Jerusalem would prove to be no match for Sennacherib's massive army, but he hoped to convince Hezekiah to surrender without fighting. "Tell Hezekiah," the commander said, sneering, "'this is what the great king, the king of Assyria, says: What makes you so confident?'"

The commander ridiculed Hezekiah's hope of receiving aid from Egypt and their hope that God would rescue them. He claimed that God had turned against Judah. In a further effort to demoralize the starving inhabitants of Jerusalem, he shouted an offer to take them to a land where they would have plenty of food. He ended by listing other nations whose gods had proven ineffective against the power of Assyria. "Could the Lord then rescue Jerusalem from my control?" he mocked.

A crisis has a way of revealing where we place our confidence. Do we trust in our own wisdom and strength to handle tough problems? Is our first instinct to give up and surrender? Do we run to other people for advice and help? Or do we first drop to our knees and ask God to come to our aid? In the face of a situation that looked hopeless, Hezekiah beseeched God to rescue his people. Shortly afterward, God miraculously rescued Judah as he had promised.

Even when we face daunting problems, we can have unshakeable confidence in God if we trust his character and his promises. Rather than being self-confident or depending on others to help us, we can draw on the strength that comes from belonging to him. What makes us confident? A Savior who has promised to never leave us.

"Look! God is my Savior. I am confident and unafraid, because the Lord is my strength and my song. He is my Savior."

Isaiah 12:2

Ask yourself: **How does my life reflect confidence in my Savior?**

"How can you evil people say anything good?"

Matthew 12:33–37

As Austin drove home from his brother's house, he listened to his wife rave about Garrett's new car and the recent remodeling job on his house. Austin listened quietly for a few minutes, then he pulled onto the shoulder of the road and stopped the car. Yelling at the top of his lungs, Austin announced that he was sick and tired of hearing how great Garrett was—and could he please just have some peace and quiet the rest of the way home? The look on his speechless wife's face stopped him. "I'm so sorry," he said. "I have no idea where that came from."

People's words never surprised Jesus, because he knew their thoughts. When the Pharisees accused him of healing demon-possessed people by Satan's power, he knew their words came from their unbelieving hearts. "You poisonous snakes!" he said. "How can you evil people say anything good?" Jesus explained that a person's mouth speaks on the basis of what's inside a person, whether good or bad. He also warned that everyone will have to give an account for every careless word they speak.

Sometimes we may shock other people and even ourselves with the words that come out of our mouth. Many people get in the habit of hiding their true feelings; some people are so good at it they even fool themselves. We might be unaware of emotions like resentment, jealousy, anger, or contempt buried deep in our heart. But our language will eventually expose what's inside us.

We can't deal with the issue by simply cleaning up our language or working on our conversation. Real change requires yielding to the Holy Spirit's examination, confessing and repenting of sinful attitudes, and letting God's Word transform us from the inside. With the help of God's "speech therapy," we won't be embarrassed—or shocked—by the words that come out of our mouth.

Your mouth says what comes from inside you.

Matthew 12:34

Ask yourself: **What does my speech indicate about the condition of my heart?**

NOVEMBER

22

"Why did you give us only one region for an inheritance?"

Joshua 17:14–18

No one can deny that a sense of entitlement pervades American culture. Many people expect to be given things without having to work for them, and take for granted that if they want something, they should have it. As a result of this mindset, millions of people are drowning in debt incurred by living beyond their means. Also, some people choose to take advantage of the welfare system rather than do work they consider too menial.

The tribes of Ephraim and Manasseh displayed a sense of entitlement when they complained that their allotted land was too small. "Why did you give us only one region for an inheritance?" they demanded. Joshua told them to clear the forest in the hill country if they wanted more land. When the leaders continued to complain, Joshua challenged their unwillingness to put forth the effort to drive the powerful Canaanites out from their allotted land.

An undue sense of entitlement has no place in a believer's thinking. We know that whatever we have comes from God's hand, so being constantly dissatisfied is an insult to him. We are called to a life of loving service, not to treat other people as if they owe us something. If we're always feeling like we deserve more, we're probably being influenced by cultural attitudes.

On the other hand, our relationship with God entitles us to rich spiritual blessings, but to possess them requires effort. Are we willing to do the work to nurture our faith? Are we ready to move to a new level of trusting God if it will cost us something? Rather than complain that our inheritance is too small, we are challenged by God to move out and take hold of all that he offers us.

Not everything that the world offers—physical gratification, greed, and extravagant lifestyles—comes from the Father. It comes from the world.

1 John 2:16

Ask yourself: Have I allowed a sense of entitlement to creep into my thinking?

NOVEMBER
23

"What are mere mortals that you should think about them?"

Psalms 8; 144:1–4

When most people are asked "How are you doing?" they automatically answer with a standard "Good" or "Great" without giving it much thought. Author, speaker, and financial expert Dave Ramsey answers the question in a way that reflects his faith. When callers on his syndicated radio program ask that question, Dave answers, "Better than I deserve to be."

Another David also had a keen sense of gratitude for what God had done. In Psalm 8 he expressed wonder at how God displays his majesty in the heavens. When David saw the splendor of the moon and stars, he marveled that God could care so much for human beings, who seemed so tiny in comparison to the rest of creation. "What is a mortal that you remember him?" he asked.

In Psalm 144 David marveled at how God helped him in battle. "O LORD, what are humans that you should care about them?" he wrote. "What are mere mortals that you should think about them?" David felt awed that his Creator wanted to be so intimately involved in the details of his life.

When we contemplate the vastness of space or the beauty and magnificence found in nature, we can start to feel insignificant. That sense of smallness vanishes when we remember what a special place we have in God's creation. To think God would even be interested in us is amazing enough, but his concern took him all the way to the cross to pay for our sins. When we meditate on all God has done for us, we have more than enough to fill us with gratitude for the rest of our life. And to remind us that, despite our problems, we *are* doing better than we deserve.

> *I will give thanks to you with all my heart, O Lord my God. I will honor you forever because your mercy toward me is great.*
>
> Psalm 86:12–13

Ask yourself: **How can I keep my sense of gratitude to God alive?**

NOVEMBER
24

"Where are the other nine?"

Luke 17:11–19

Recent research has indicated that being thankful improves both our physical and emotional health. Holding on to feelings of thankfulness boosts our immune system and increases blood supply to our heart. Daily, guided exercises or the habit of keeping a weekly gratitude journal can increase our alertness, enthusiasm, and energy, and can improve our sleep. People who describe themselves as feeling grateful tend to suffer less stress and depression than the rest of the population.

For all its benefits, gratitude doesn't come naturally to us. As Jesus passed through a village, he was spotted by ten lepers who desperately longed to be healed. They stood at a distance, as required by law, and cried out, "Jesus, Teacher, have mercy on us!" Jesus told them to go and show themselves to the priest. As they walked off to obey, their skin disease disappeared.

One of the men turned back to praise God and thank Jesus for healing him. Jesus expressed amazement that only one man had thought to thank him. "Weren't ten men made clean?" he asked. "Where are the other nine?" He also pointed out that the only man who did respond was a Samaritan, a race looked down upon by the Jewish people.

Cultivating a spirit of thankfulness is more than a good idea; it's a direct command from God. He instructs us to give thanks to him regardless of our feelings or circumstances. When we focus on our blessings, it's easier to keep our problems and concerns in the right perspective. Our gratitude becomes the foundation of our worship of him.

Gratitude also strengthens our relationships with other people. We can't be in a right relationship with God or anyone else without a spirit of thankfulness. We don't want to be like the nine who forgot to say "thank you."

I will thank the LORD at all times.

Psalm 34:1

Ask yourself: **How often do I express gratitude to God or to other people?**

“What have we done wrong?”

Jeremiah 16:1–15

All eyes turned to watch the man in the orange jumpsuit shuffle into the courtroom, a public defender by his side. Police had gathered DNA evidence, fingerprints, and eyewitness accounts of the shooting. The accused man’s coworker had testified to incriminating remarks he’d overheard. Plus, the bank’s video camera had captured the entire incident. “How do you plead?” the judge asked the defendant. The man stiffened and glared at the judge. “Not guilty,” he muttered.

The people of Judah refused to admit their guilt when God confronted them about their sin. He warned that judgment was coming if they ignored his appeal to repent. But God knew they would feign innocence and say, “Why does the LORD threaten us with all these disasters? What have we done wrong? How have we sinned against the LORD our God?” Therefore, since the people clung to their idolatry instead of changing their ways, God sent the nation into a period of captivity.

Sometimes we don’t want to own up to our actions when we’ve done something wrong. So we pretend to be innocent and hope other people—and God—won’t notice. Then there are times when we don’t recognize the sin in our life. Whether we’re self-deceived or deceiving others, it’s dangerous to let sin slide without taking care of it.

That’s why it’s a good idea to consistently invite God to expose any sinfulness in our character, our attitudes, and our behavior. But we’d better be prepared to take the appropriate action. God will expect us to repent and turn away from any sin that he reveals. He wants to show us what we’ve done wrong, so we can make it right.

Examine me, O God, and know my mind. Test me, and know my thoughts. See whether I am on an evil path. Then lead me on the everlasting path.

Psalm 139:23–24

Ask God **to examine your lifestyle and your thoughts to reveal any areas of sin that you need to make right.**

NOVEMBER

26

"Don't you know that your body is a temple that belongs to the Holy Spirit?"

1 Corinthians 6:12–20

During the first century, the city of Corinth was a major trade route and one of the largest cities in the Roman Empire. Corruption and immorality abounded. Among the many heathen religions practiced, one stood out. Built on the most prominent point in the city, the temple of Aphrodite employed a thousand "priestesses." Sex played a major role in the worship of this goddess of love and beauty.

Christian converts from this pagan background found it hard to break old habits. Some of them considered sexual desire just another physical need that had to be met, like hunger. But in his letter to the Corinthian church, Paul blew that argument out of the water. "Don't you know that your body is a temple that belongs to the Holy Spirit?" he asked. Since their faith had made them one with Christ, uniting with someone in an immoral sexual relationship represented a grievous sin against God.

Paul also pointed out the unique nature of sexual sin. Besides offending God and hurting other people, an immoral sexual act is a sin against our own body. God laid down sexual boundaries for our protection; disregarding them exposes us to diseases that can leave permanent effects or end in death. Since what we do with our body affects our spirit, sexual immorality also damages our character and emotions.

Our society's casual attitude toward sex has influenced the thinking of many Christians. Regardless of what the culture condones, God says that any sexual expression outside of marriage is sin. He calls us to live a life of purity and to honor him in the way we dress, talk, and act toward the opposite sex. It should be obvious to everyone that our body is a temple of the Holy Spirit, not of Aphrodite.

For God wants you to be holy and pure,
and to keep clear of all sexual sin.

1 Thessalonians 4:3 TLB

Ask yourself: **How do I need to take a stand for God's view of sexual purity?**

"Now who will get what you've accumulated?"

Luke 12:13–21

Nancy surveyed the piles of books and boxes stacked almost to the ceiling. How would she ever organize all this stuff for the garage sale? A year had passed since her husband's death; she couldn't put this off any longer. As she worked, Nancy wondered how many hours Don had spent browsing flea markets and resale shops for books, baseball cards, and record albums. If only he'd devoted a fraction of that interest to spiritual matters. Would he have invested so much time in his various collections if he'd thought about how they would end up in the hands of strangers someday?

Jesus told about another man who thought more about his possessions than about his spiritual condition. A rich man blessed with good crops built bigger barns to hold his produce and goods. Thinking that he had "stored up a lot of good things for years to come," the man felt ready to take it easy and enjoy himself. God had a different perspective. "You fool!" he said. "I will demand your life from you tonight! Now who will get what you've accumulated?"

Many people enjoy collecting—everything from fine art to old bottle caps. Our challenge is to control the amount of time and money we invest in stuff we'll only have to leave behind someday. If loving God is our first priority, we'll be storing up things that will bring him glory and ensure our future rewards. We add to our eternal collection every time we perform an act of kindness in his name, encourage a fellow believer, share the gospel with someone, or invest our time and money in God's work. In the long run, what really matters is not how much we've accumulated down here but what we've stored in heaven.

[Jesus said] "That's how it is when a person has material riches but is not rich in his relationship with God."

Luke 12:21

Ask yourself: **Am I spending more time collecting things with eternal value, or things I'll have to leave behind someday?**

NOVEMBER
28

"What's happened to his promise to return?"

2 Peter 3:1–10

When I was growing up, the period between Thanksgiving and Christmas seemed like a long time. I remember how the days dragged by as I longed for Christmas morning to arrive. Now, those four weeks seem to zip by. With all the planning, preparations, and activities related to the holidays, it feels as though Christmas follows right on the heels of Thanksgiving. As an adult I have a totally different perspective on time than I had during my childhood.

Peter explained that God's perspective on time is not the same as ours. He warned about the prevalence of people who mock the Bible's prophecies about the future. "What's happened to his promise to return?" they ask. "Ever since our ancestors died, everything continues as it did from the beginning of the world." Such people will be shocked when the day of the Lord comes "like a thief," suddenly and without warning.

We live surrounded by people who ridicule us for believing that Jesus will return and that this world will end. They have no idea that God is holding back the end to give them a chance to receive his forgiveness and to escape judgment. God longs for every person to turn to him so they won't be destroyed.

God displays his patience toward the very people who hate him and mock his existence. Even though they deserve immediate judgment, God waits and hopes they will change their mind. Meditating on his example will motivate us to be patient with those who mock us for our beliefs. God wants us to use every means possible to show the world he's alive and well in us. Since God gives unbelievers every opportunity to accept him, the least we can do is use every opportunity to share our faith.

The Lord isn't slow to do what he promised, as some people think. Rather, he is patient for your sake.

2 Peter 3:9

Ask yourself: **Am I making use of God's patience to share the gospel with unbelievers?**

"Didn't we do miracles by the power of your name?"

Matthew 7:15–23

Charles enjoyed the private reception honoring his achievements at the university. But throughout the evening, his eyes wandered to the stranger who always seemed to be milling around on the edge of the crowd. When the last guest cleared the room, Charles approached the couple who had presided over the sign-in table. They admitted to being confused when the man's name didn't appear on the guest list, but his claim to be an old friend sounded convincing. "No," Charles shook his head. "I've never seen the guy before in my life."

Jesus warned about people who pretend to know him but really don't. He gave a sobering illustration to show that one day these impostors will be exposed. On judgment day, many will say to Jesus, "Lord, Lord, didn't we prophesy in your name? Didn't we force out demons and do many miracles by the power and authority of your name?" Jesus will answer simply, "I never knew you." These people had convinced others they were genuine disciples of Christ; they had even deceived themselves.

Just because someone claims to know Jesus doesn't necessarily mean they do. We can't assume people who perform supernatural miracles belong to God; they may be using trickery or demonic power. A person can look and sound like a Christian, but Jesus said a true believer will obey God's commands.

It's heartrending to think that churches include some people who have deceived themselves into thinking they're Christians but are sadly mistaken. Most believers will occasionally have doubts about their salvation, but we can assure ourselves with an obedience check. Does our life show an overall pattern of obedience to God's commands and a desire to do his will? We don't want to just know *about* Jesus; we want to know him personally.

We are sure that we know Christ if we obey his commandments.

1 John 2:3

Ask yourself: **Do I know that I know Jesus Christ?**

NOVEMBER
30

"Why are you standing out here?"

Genesis 24:28–32

In Conrad Reichter's novel *The Town*, the first settler of a wooded area in Ohio returns after an absence of forty years. In place of dense forest, Worth Luckett finds a bustling town. Instead of a one-room cabin, his oldest daughter, Sayward, lives in a three-story brick house as the richest person in town. Despite Sayward's pleas, Worth refuses to stay in her home and eat in her fancy dining room. He insists on staying in a shack by the river, sometimes ignoring the food she sends him.

Abraham's servant responded differently to an offer of hospitality. After he met Rebekah, he waited for an invitation to enter her family's home. As soon as her brother heard about her encounter with the stranger, he rushed out. "Come in, you whom the Lord has blessed," Laban said. "Why are you standing out here?" The servant gladly accepted Laban's provision for him, his men, and his animals.

Sometimes believers live like outsiders to the body of Christ. We may be struggling with personal problems we feel reluctant to share. We may think our lives are already too busy to get involved at church. It may be pride or past hurts that cause us to hold people at arm's length. Whatever the reason, we miss out on the fellowship, help, and encouragement God intended for us.

Pride, rebellion, or a flippant attitude toward sin can cause us to hold ourselves distant from God. He never forces himself on anyone, but we have a standing invitation to draw near to him in prayer. To accept his offer of hospitality requires us to trust him enough to be transparent before him. Why would we stand outside in the cold when we can bask in the warmth of his love and fellowship?

Come close to God, and he will come close to you.

James 4:8

Ask yourself: **Have I been holding myself at a distance from God or from other believers?**

DECEMBER

1

"Am I too weak to reclaim you?"

Isaiah 50:1–3

Russell paced the floor. *I can't do this*, he agonized. *I'm just not strong enough*. He'd been drug-free for a few months now, but the evening hours really tested his willpower. The weekly support group helped a lot but the next meeting was days away. Russell strained to remember what his leader said about relying on a higher power to get him through times like this. *Easier said than done*, he thought. Grabbing his phone, Russell used speed dial to call his group leader. He needed a reminder.

God reminded Israel that they should have relied on his strength to rescue them. Even though they had seen God's miraculous power used on their behalf in the past, this time Israel had turned to other countries for help instead of trusting in God. "Am I too weak to reclaim you?" God asked. "Don't I have the power to rescue you?" Because they had rejected him, God sent Israel into temporary captivity, comparing the event to a wife being sent away because of unfaithfulness.

We all have enemies we can't stand against without supernatural help. We may be dealing with an addiction that fights to regain control of our body. We may struggle with thought patterns that have taken root in our mind, or sinful habits that refuse to loosen their grip on us. Support groups, counselors, and friends can help us, but our best and ultimate resource is God's power.

Once we admit how helpless we are and acknowledge our need, God will step in and pour his strength into us through his Holy Spirit. Although some people experience a spontaneous deliverance, more often it's a lifelong process. As we learn to rely on him moment by moment, the awareness of how weak we are serves to remind us how strong he is.

Receive your power from the Lord and
from his mighty strength.

Ephesians 6:10

Ask yourself: **In what area do I most need God's strength and power today?**

DECEMBER
2

"Why are you so distant, Lord?"

Psalm 10

David wrote Psalm 10 as a prayer calling for God to help people oppressed by the wicked. He opened by asking God why he kept himself at a distance and hid his face during times of trouble. David freely expressed his feeling that God seemed disinterested and uninvolved when the wicked became powerful and exploited the weak. But David did not stop praying or pleading with God to arise and take action. He concluded the prayer by confirming his belief that God heard him and would correct the situation.

We can all relate to David's feeling of God holding himself at a distance. Sometimes we sense his presence in an almost tangible way; at other times he seems far away. Maybe we feel oppressed by the evil around us. Maybe we're suffering from the consequences of our own sinful choices. Or maybe our heart is breaking over trials God has allowed into our life to refine us and display his glory.

Many of the Psalms show us that it's okay to be honest with God. But it's not okay to stop praying. When we share our doubts with God and then meditate on his Word, it puts our focus where it should be: on God and his trustworthy character. Like David, we can turn our doubts over to God and declare our trust in him to act.

God is close to us when we're lonely, when we're terrified, when we're heartbroken, and when we're filled with doubts about him. Our emotions can crowd out the sense of his presence from our life just when we need him most. At those times, we have a choice to make: Will we focus on our feelings, or will we cling to his promise to be with us in times of trouble and heartache?

The Lord is near to those whose hearts are humble.
He saves those whose spirits are crushed.

Psalm 34:18

Ask yourself: **In tough times, do I focus on my emotions or on God's promises?**

DECEMBER
3

"Who is qualified to tell about Christ?"

2 Corinthians 2:12–17

At the sound of "Amen," Tyson bolted out the door like a hunted rabbit. *Too risky to hang around today*, he thought. Someone might try to talk him into signing up for the evangelism group going to the college campus tomorrow evening. It wasn't that Tyson didn't want to see people come to know Christ—he just wasn't any good at those types of discussions. Sharing the gospel seemed to come naturally to some people, but not to him. *That's just not my gift*, Tyson assured himself.

Paul considered himself to be a spokesman for Christ, and thanked God for using him wherever he went to spread the Good News like a fragrance. But he knew that his ministry's effectiveness didn't stem from any special credentials or skills on his part. "Who is qualified to tell about Christ?" he asked. Paul acknowledged that God alone made him qualified to tell the message of forgiveness through Christ.

Some people think that witnessing requires a specific spiritual gift, great speaking skills, or some kind of special training. But any believer is qualified to share God's message of love and forgiveness, whether we've known Christ for fifty years or one hour. It doesn't require a theological degree to share our own story or to outline the basics of God's offer of salvation.

God has appointed each one of us to be his ambassadors to a spiritually hungry world. Our witnessing techniques and styles may differ, but what counts is our willingness to be available. We already have the power of Scripture and the Holy Spirit. God will send us the people and situations and give us the right words. We need to concentrate on obedience, and let him take care of our "qualifications."

By ourselves we are not qualified in any way to claim that we can do anything. Rather, God makes us qualified.

2 Corinthians 3:5

Ask God **to give you more wisdom and boldness about sharing the Good News wherever you go.**

DECEMBER

4

"By what power did you do this?"

Acts 4:1–13

I squinted as the computer screen noticeably dimmed. The colors of the website didn't look as bright and the text seemed harder to read. But I knew the reason. The ports on my aging laptop had gone bad, and sometimes the computer failed to recognize the power cord. I checked the icon at the bottom of the screen and sure enough, it registered battery power. After I gently pushed the cord, the screen immediately brightened. What a world of difference switching from one power source to another made.

Peter and John found a new power source between the night of Jesus's arrest and their own trial. The two disciples were arrested after healing a lame man and preaching about resurrection through Jesus. As Peter and John stood before the Jewish council, the religious leaders demanded, "By what power or in whose name did you do this?"

The same men who ran away in the Garden of Gethsemane and hid after Jesus's death now openly testified to his resurrection and the salvation he made possible. The leaders were astonished by such courage and boldness coming from ordinary, uneducated fishermen. They took note that these men had been with Jesus.

As believers with the Holy Spirit living in us, we never have reason to feel intimidated or cowardly. God's supernatural power is available to us as we serve him and share his truth with others. We have to choose between operating in our human strength or staying connected to God's power through prayer, his Word, and an obedient lifestyle. When we ask God to fill us with his Spirit, we'll be astonished at what he enables us to do. And people will be able to tell that we, like the disciples, have been with Jesus.

God didn't give us a cowardly spirit but a spirit of power, love, and good judgment.

2 Timothy 1:7

Ask yourself: **Am I staying connected to the power source of God's Holy Spirit?**

DECEMBER

5

"Has Christ been divided?"

1 Corinthians 1:10–13

My parents live in a rural area that includes four small country churches. Once a year, the community has a week of special, combined services. Each night a different church hosts the service and provides the speaker. Members of different denominations and ethnic groups leave their familiar pews and come together to worship and praise God in a single service.

It seems as though Christians have always tended to divide into groups. Paul addressed the problem of division within the church at Corinth. The people had formed cliques on the basis of which preacher they preferred. Paul reminded them that their allegiance belonged to the One who was crucified for them, the One in whose name they were baptized. "Has Christ been divided?" he asked.

When Paul addressed this issue with the believers at Ephesus, he listed seven elements that form the basis of Christian unity: We're all members of the body of Christ, we have been given the same Holy Spirit, we all share the same hope of eternal life, we all received the Lord Jesus through the same act of faith and were baptized into his name, and we have the same heavenly Father over us all.

As believers, we have so many things that can divide us: music styles, worship postures, denominational or local church traditions, Bible translations, and scriptural interpretations. Unnecessary quarreling and divisiveness hurt the cause of Christ and make a mockery of his church. When believers stay focused on the gospel as the basis of our faith, we can join together to reach the world with the news of our Savior. We can accomplish so much more for God when we concentrate on what—and whom—we have in common.

There is one Lord, one faith, one baptism, one
God and Father of all, who is over everything,
through everything, and in everything.

Ephesians 4:5–6

Ask yourself: **Do I do anything that contributes to factions and divisions within the body of Christ?**

DECEMBER

6

"Do you resent my generosity towards others?"

Matthew 20:1–16

Well, my day's ruined, Carl thought. Something had just reminded him of his brother. Three years had passed since their father had died, dividing his estate among his three children. Carl had been able to set up college funds for his kids and buy the new car he needed. But it still galled him that Payton had gotten an equal share. Carl and his sister had been the ones caring for their father all those years, while Payton was off who-knows-where. He'd only reconnected with the family six months before his father's death.

Jesus told a story about some men with similar attitudes. After working all day in a vineyard, they received the agreed-upon wage. But they protested because the owner had given the same amount to others who had worked shorter periods of time, some only an hour. The owner denied treating the workers unfairly. "Can't I do what I want with my own money?" he asked. "Or do you resent my generosity towards others?"

We may not consider envy a serious issue, but God often includes it in lists of sins to avoid (such as Rom. 13:13). When we're jealous of what God has given someone else, we can't appreciate his generosity toward us. Envy hinders our relationships with other people and breaks our fellowship with God. If not checked, it can lead us into sinful behaviors we never dreamed we were capable of committing.

Besides the spiritual consequences, an envious disposition negatively affects our emotional and physical health. It steals our joy and peace as it crowds out other positive emotions from our mind. We can suffer physical symptoms without realizing the root cause. If we think we might be suffering from the effects of envy, we need to ask the Great Physician to diagnose and cure our sickness.

A tranquil heart makes for a healthy body,
but jealousy is like bone cancer.

Proverbs 14:30

Ask God **to examine your attitudes and reveal any jealousy you're not aware of.**

"Which of the two sons did what the father wanted?"

Matthew 21:28–32

I sure hope this works, Brooke thought as she tried to maneuver her English bulldog into the pet store. She'd grown tired of Rocky's tendency to go opposite the way she wanted him to, and his fondness for jumping on people wasn't funny anymore. But the store promised that nine classes using "proven techniques" would make a new dog out of Rocky. Just outside the door, Rocky plopped down on the pavement. *And I hope he doesn't flunk out of obedience class*, Brooke added.

Jesus told a story about a father and two sons to show that the Pharisees and religious leaders needed lessons in obedience. When a father asked one of his sons to work in the vineyard, the son said, "I don't want to!" Later, he changed his mind and did what his father had asked. When the father made the same request of the second son, the son replied, "I will, sir." But he never went to the vineyard. Jesus asked, "Which of the two sons did what the father wanted?"

Jesus accused the religious leaders of being like the second son, pretending to be interested in obeying God but refusing to do his will. Could he make the same accusation against us? Do our actions prove our willingness to obey, or do we merely give lip service to God, like the second son in the story?

God doesn't call it obedience when we have good intentions but put off doing something that he asks. He's also not pleased when we obey with a sour, grudging attitude. Long ago, I had a neighbor who taught her children the full definition of obedience: doing *what* you're told to do, *when* you're told to do it, *with* a happy face. What a worthy goal for all of God's children.

Without any hesitation I hurry to obey your commandments.

Psalm 119:60

Ask yourself: **How do I need to improve my level of obedience to God's commands?**

DECEMBER

8

"Why are you saying such things to me?"

1 Samuel 9:6–24

Several years ago at a writers' conference, author and speaker Cecil Murphey led us in a prayer that had a startling ending. "God, show me the truth about myself," we repeated, "no matter how beautiful it may be." Cecil later explained the basis for the prayer. "We often know our weaknesses. We probably have a few people around who gladly help us stay aware of our faults. *But what about our good qualities?* Too often we focus on what we're not—not spiritual enough, not loving enough, or not sensitive enough."

Saul focused on what he "was not" when Samuel confided that God had chosen him as Israel's first king. "Who will have all that is desirable in Israel?" Samuel said to him. "Won't it be you and your father's family?" The prophet's words astounded Saul. He protested that he came from an insignificant family in the smallest tribe of Israel. "So why are you saying such things to me?" Saul asked.

As we read the Bible, many of us concentrate on our flaws, failures, and shortcomings. We find it difficult to absorb the parts where God calls us co-heirs with Christ and promises we'll share in his glory. We struggle to take in the description of the heavenly future God has planned for us. We feel like asking, "Why are you saying such things to me?"

God knows we're not perfect, but when he looks at us he sees a dearly loved child cleansed of all sin through Christ's death. God also sees the Christlike person we'll grow to be with the Holy Spirit's help. How different our life would be if we could glimpse ourselves through the Father's eyes. Then we'd see that the truth about us really is a beautiful thing.

How great is the love the Father has lavished on us, that we should be called children of God!

1 John 3:1 NIV

Ask God **to help you accept the beautiful truth of the way he sees you.**

"Can a person cheat God?"

Malachi 3:8–12

Suzanne rushed to the door and felt sick as she saw the customer pulling onto the highway. The woman at the drive-through window had cashed a check, but Suzanne had misread the amount. If the woman had counted the money in the envelope, she would have seen that Suzanne only gave her a tenth of what she should have received. Asking someone to cover for her, Suzanne knocked on her supervisor's door. *I just hope the woman doesn't think I tried to rob her*, she thought.

Through the prophet Malachi, God accused the Israelites of robbing him. "Can a person cheat God?" he asked them. "Yet, you are cheating me!" The tithing system required the people to give a tenth of their produce and livestock. Since Levites didn't own land, part of this was stored in the temple to provide for the priests so they could focus on their service and ministry. God complained that the people had withheld these tithes.

Jesus's death fulfilled what the Old Testament animal sacrifices represented; we no longer live under a strict system of tithes. But God still expects us to support our church and other ministries. He also calls for a different kind of sacrifice. Paul explained that the only reasonable response to God's mercy and forgiveness is to offer ourselves as a living sacrifice. God asks us to willingly lay down our desires and dedicate every area of our life to him. Day by day, moment by moment, our goal is to offer it all to his control. It's not an easy lifestyle, and it's impossible without his help, but anything less than our all is cheating God.

> *Brothers and sisters, in view of all we have just shared about God's compassion, I encourage you to offer your bodies as living sacrifices, dedicated to God and pleasing to him.*
>
> Romans 12:1

Ask yourself: **Do I daily offer every part of my life as a sacrifice to God?**

DECEMBER

10

"How can we return?"

Malachi 3:6–7

The man sat in his hotel room and stared at his cell phone. How many times had he started to push the speed dial number for his house, only to chicken out again? And how many times had he regretted his stupid delusion that he was in love with his younger coworker? Only five months had passed, but it felt like another lifetime to him. With all his heart, he wanted to believe his wife would forgive him. But why would she take him back after he'd hurt her so badly? He knew he didn't deserve it.

Throughout Israel's history, the people repeatedly rejected God, and he repeatedly offered to take them back if they repented. In Malachi's day, the people were attending services and halfheartedly following the rituals of worship, but their hearts had strayed. When God urged them to return to him, he imagined them saying, "How can we return?" Because of their spiritual callousness, they implied that they had never left God in the first place.

Sometimes we're like the Ephesian church in Revelation. Jesus commended them for their good works, but accused them of having lost their deep love and devotion for him. If we sense that our passion for God has cooled and our heart has strayed, we need to remember what he did for us, repent, and return to our first love.

If we've let sin lure us away from the Christian lifestyle, we may feel as though we've gone too far for God to take us back. Even though we don't deserve it, God still waits for us to come home. The prodigal son left a life of degradation to return to an anxious father who waited with loving arms held out. We can also repent and return to our heavenly Father. He'll be holding out arms with wrists scarred by cruel Roman spikes.

Return to me and change the way you think
and act, and do what you did at first.

Revelation 2:5

Ask yourself: **Do I need to return to God? If so, what's holding me back?**

"Where could anyone get enough to feed these people?"

Mark 8:1–9

The woman looked into her near-empty cupboards. Life had been tough since she'd lost her job. But at least she and her two children had food and clothing. The church down the street had a ministry that helped people in her shoes. Tomorrow she could go to the food pantry and get what she needed to see her through. She'd also pick up the winter coats the staff had waiting for her kids. Thank goodness she had somebody to count on until she found work again.

The disciples should have known they could count on Jesus to meet people's needs. They'd already seen him take five small loaves of bread and two fish, feed a crowd of more than five thousand, and have twelve baskets of leftovers. But when Jesus expressed a desire to feed another hungry crowd, the disciples asked him, "Where could anyone get enough bread to feed these people in this place where no one lives?" Once again, Jesus used a few loaves of bread to feed a crowd of thousands—with leftovers.

Like the disciples, we can be quick to forget the amazing things God has done in the past. When faced with a crisis, we tend to automatically focus on the difficulties of the situation. We'd be better off concentrating on God's track record of guiding, helping, protecting, and providing for us. When we deliberately choose to meditate on how he's worked in our life in the past, we won't have trouble believing he'll come through for us again. God has already brought us this far; it's safe to assume we can count on him to see us through whatever lies ahead.

You thrill me, Lord, *with all you have done for me!*
I sing for joy because of what you have done.

Psalm 92:4 NLT

Ask God **to remind you of the amazing things he's done for you in the past.**

DECEMBER

12

"Do you want us to call down fire from heaven to burn them up?"

Luke 9:51–56

Talk about getting hot under the collar. As Jesus traveled toward Jerusalem, he sent messengers ahead into a Samaritan village to arrange overnight housing. But the people there refused to welcome Jesus and his disciples. Earlier, Jesus had instructed his disciples to respond to this type of treatment with the symbolic gesture of shaking an inhospitable city's dust off their feet. This time, however, two of Jesus's disciples wanted to take a different approach.

James and John remembered how Elijah had called down fire from heaven to kill the soldiers sent by an evil king to bring him in (see 2 Kings 1:9–12). The two brothers thought this seemed like an appropriate response to the present situation. "Lord," they asked, "do you want us to call down fire from heaven to burn them up?" Jesus turned around and rebuked them. Some manuscripts add that Jesus reminded his disciples that the Son of Man didn't come to destroy lives but to save them.

The purpose of Jesus's first coming was to offer God's gift of salvation, not to bring judgment or to punish people who rejected him. Retribution will come later, at the appropriate time. During his years of ministry on earth, Jesus had more important things to focus on than getting even. And so do we.

When someone rejects us as we're serving God, our natural human response is to get a little hot under the collar. We might even hurl some scorching words at our offenders. But a desire for retaliation hurts our witness and distracts us from our purpose: to share God's truth that leads to salvation and a life lived for Christ. God will take care of those who continue to reject his message. Our job is not to call down fire from heaven but to help people escape the fire of judgment.

God sent his Son into the world, not to condemn the world, but to save the world.

John 3:17

Ask yourself: **How do I handle rejection when I discuss my faith?**

DECEMBER
13

“Can they finish it in a day?”

Nehemiah 4:1–12

In August 2009 the cast and crew of the ABC television show *Extreme Makeover: Home Edition* set up camp in my county. Hundreds of volunteers gathered to help build a new home for a family of four living in a small, dilapidated, hundred-year-old house. Within a week, the old house had been torn down and the new one built, furnished, and decorated on a landscaped lawn.

Things didn’t run as smoothly for the building project that Nehemiah supervised. When he returned to oversee the rebuilding of Jerusalem’s broken-down walls, he faced heavy opposition from the Jews’ enemies. One man came to ridicule the work, saying, “What do these miserable Jews think they’re doing? Can they rebuild it by themselves? Can they finish it in a day?”

Besides ongoing threats and intimidation from outsiders, Nehemiah faced opposition from his own people. His enemies bribed prophets to try to discredit and scare him. With each new assault, Nehemiah prayed to God. Amazingly, the volunteers completed the walls in 52 days. This feat made a huge impression on the surrounding nations. Everyone knew the work could only have been done with God’s help.

God often calls us to undertake a building project. He may want us to repair a broken relationship or build a bridge between other people. We may need to strengthen our prayer life or fill in gaps in our spiritual practices. Or God may assign us a specific task to help rebuild the foundations of our country.

Whether we’re working on a small project or an extreme makeover of our lifestyle, we can expect heavy opposition. Satan will do everything he can to stop us; others may ridicule our efforts and hinder our progress. The work may take 52 days or a lifetime, but if it’s God-ordained, we can count on his help to finish it.

They realized we had done this work
with the help of our God.
Nehemiah 6:16

Ask yourself: **What building project does God want me to begin?**

DECEMBER
14

"Why not let Ishmael be my heir?"

Genesis 17:1–22

As Elizabeth made a right turn, she tried not to look at the two-story colonial on the corner. But she still had the same thought: *That should have been ours*. Last year she and Robert heard that the house would be going on the market, and they prepared to pounce. But after waiting almost a year, Robert got impatient and they ended up buying another house on the same street. When the "For Sale" sign went up a month later, they felt like kicking themselves for settling for their second choice.

Abraham and Sarah got impatient while waiting for God to fulfill his promise of an heir, prompting Abraham to father a son by Sarah's maid. But thirteen years later, God told him Sarah would bear a son. As Abraham thought about a hundred-year-old man fathering a child by a ninety-year-old woman, he laughed to himself. "Why not let Ishmael be my heir?" he asked. God restated that his eternal covenant would be established with Abraham's son by Sarah, not with Ishmael.

Abraham and Sarah's impatient decision led to much grief and conflict that still continues today. Their example serves as a warning for us to guard against the temptation to take things into our own hands when we grow tired of waiting for God to act. Otherwise, we may find ourselves in a situation or relationship that God never intended for us.

Their story also offers us encouragement. No matter how impossible God's promises seem, we can trust him to bring them to fruition. But he will do it in his timing, not ours. We don't want to miss out on God's perfect plan by settling for something less. Whether we're looking for a job, a house, or a spouse, God's best is always worth waiting for.

Surrender yourself to the LORD, and wait patiently for him.

Psalm 37:7

Ask yourself: **Is there some area where I'm being tempted to settle for less than God's best for me?**

DECEMBER
15

"Why should I forgive you?"

Jeremiah 5:1–9

The man paused at the door and took one last look around the apartment. When his eyes fell on the wedding photo above the mantel, he felt as though his heart would break. He'd spent three years trying to be a good husband. Each time his wife had returned from one of her "flings," he'd taken her back. She always said the right words, but never really seemed to be sorry for what she did. This time would be different. Picking up his suitcase, he thought, *I can't think of any reason to take her back anymore.*

God told Jeremiah that he planned to judge the people of Judah for their unfaithfulness. All levels of society, including the leaders, had completely rejected God and his teachings. When he corrected them, they hardened their hearts even more and refused to repent of their sin. "Why should I forgive you?" God asked in exasperation. He would put an end to their spiritual adultery by sending them into captivity.

What if God were to ask us that question after we die? Many people are counting on being a "good person" to get themselves into heaven. But the Bible teaches that we can never earn God's approval. All our attempts to do so are like filthy, stained rags in his eyes (see Isa. 64:6). The only way to receive God's forgiveness is by accepting the free gift of salvation made possible by Christ's death.

Just as we can't earn our salvation, we can't do anything to make God love us more. He loves and accepts his children unconditionally. Once we grasp that, we're free to offer him our devotion and service out of gratitude. And we'll be motivated to stay faithful to our loving, heavenly Father instead of committing spiritual adultery.

When God our Savior made his kindness and love for humanity appear, he saved us, but not because of anything we had done to gain his approval.

Titus 3:4–5

Ask yourself: **Am I trying to earn God's approval, or have I accepted his unconditional love and forgiveness?**

DECEMBER

16

"Who is my neighbor?"

Luke 10:25–37

The video footage shown on the evening news was sad but all too familiar. Someone with road rage had followed another driver to a gas station and spent several minutes punching and kicking him. Although the attacker didn't have a weapon, the other customers did nothing to intervene; they simply continued pumping gas into their cars. After the attacker left, a woman finally knelt by the victim and called police from her cell phone.

Jesus told a story about people who didn't want to get involved. Referring to the command to "Love your neighbor as you love yourself," an expert in the law asked Jesus, "Who is my neighbor?" Jesus answered with a parable about a Jewish man who had been robbed, beaten, and left for dead. Later, a priest and a Levite both passed by but ignored the victim. Finally, a Samaritan came by. Although the Jews despised his race, the Samaritan went to great lengths to take care of the man. Jesus pointed out that the Samaritan was the only one who acted as a neighbor to the wounded man.

The foundation of Christian living is to love God with all our heart, mind, soul, and strength, and to love our neighbors as we love ourselves. Being a neighbor to someone means intervening to help, as far as it's within our power. It also means caring for those around us just as we take care of ourselves. God wants us to look out for the best interests of other people, not just our own. If we ask him, God will give us compassion for the needs of those he has placed around us. After all, Christians should make the best neighbors—to anyone we happen to meet.

The second most important commandment is this:
"Love your neighbor as you love yourself."

Mark 12:31

Ask yourself: **Is there someone around me right now who needs a good neighbor?**

"Why do you forget our suffering and misery?"

Psalm 44:9–26

Carol drove to her office with a heavy heart. She still couldn't believe that her boss had only given her half a day off for the funeral. Carol's coworkers greeted her, seemingly oblivious to her black dress and red eyes. All afternoon, Carol tried to concentrate amid the usual joking and laughter. During the break, her supervisor talked only about her own crazy workload, even when Carol burst into tears and rushed to the ladies' room. *How can they be so cold and heartless*? Carol thought. *They know I just lost both my parents.*

No one would treat a hurting friend in such a coldhearted way, but sometimes people accuse God of being like that. Psalm 44 was written during a time when Israel had suffered a painful defeat in spite of their faithfulness to God. "Why do you hide your face?" the writer called out to God. "Why do you forget our suffering and misery?" Still, even though it looked like God ignored their sufferings, the people trusted God to deliver them on the basis of his past actions and their relationship with him.

David experienced much grief and suffering in his life, some caused by his own sin and some undeserved. He reminded himself that God was well aware of his misery, with an image of God collecting his tears in a bottle as though they were something of value. Whenever we hurt, God sees it—and he uses it for our good.

If we suffer for God's sake, he'll reward us someday. When our foolish actions cause us grief, he'll use it to help us mature spiritually. As long as we trust God, suffering will refine and strengthen our faith and make us more compassionate toward others. God doesn't ignore a single tear we shed, and he never lets it go to waste.

> *You have kept a record of my wanderings. Put my tears in your bottle. They are already in your book.*
>
> Psalm 56:8

Ask yourself: **Have I ever felt that God was indifferent to my suffering? Why did I feel that way?**

DECEMBER
18

"You don't mean me, do you?"

Mark 14:18–21

As Jesus and his twelve closest disciples celebrated the Passover meal, they began by dipping pieces of bread into a bowl. Suddenly, Jesus dropped a bombshell. "I can guarantee this truth," he told them. "One of you is going to betray me, one who is eating with me!" His words shocked and grieved the disciples. To share food with a person and then betray them was considered especially heinous.

One by one, the disciples asked Jesus, "You don't mean me, do you?" The wording indicates that the men expected a negative answer. Still, they asked for reassurance from Jesus about their personal innocence. Jesus repeated that his betrayer was someone dipping his hand into the bowl with him. (His affirmative answer to Judas's question recorded in Matthew 26:25 must have been spoken in private.)

People often read the Bible with the same attitude expressed by the disciples. Instead of looking for ways to apply the Scriptures personally, we think, *Surely this doesn't apply to me, does it? God couldn't be talking about me here, could he?* We expect a negative answer, and as a result, we miss out on the power of God's Word to correct our thinking, convict us of sinful habits or attitudes, and advise us on how to live a life that pleases God.

The best way to read the Bible is to expect God to speak to us personally through his words. Each time we open the Bible, we have an opportunity to grow in understanding of God and ourselves. He uses the Scriptures to transform our thoughts, our attitudes, and our behavior. But we have to be willing to accept the Holy Spirit's conviction and leading. It all begins by reading God's Word with an attitude of *Do you mean me, Lord?*

> *Every Scripture passage is inspired by God. All of them are useful for teaching, pointing out errors, correcting people, and training them for a life that has God's approval.*
>
> 2 Timothy 3:16

Ask yourself: **Do I read the Bible with an attitude that's receptive to the Holy Spirit's leading?**

"Why can't I follow you now?"

John 13:33–14:4

"Why can't I come with you now, Daddy?" Montel knelt down and saw his son's eyes welling up with tears. "Don't you remember how we talked about this?" he gently chided. Montel explained that he had to start his new job on Monday. He assured Corey that once he found a good place for them to live, he would come back and move the whole family. Feeling the little arms tighten around his neck, Montel wondered how to help Corey understand.

Peter didn't understand when Jesus said he was going away and the disciples couldn't follow him yet. "Lord," Peter said, "why can't I follow you now?" Jesus explained that he had to go and prepare a place for his followers. Peter had no idea of the vital work he would do for God's kingdom before he joined Jesus in that new place.

During the apostle Paul's imprisonment in Rome, he knew he would either be released or executed. He felt okay with either outcome. If his life was spared, that meant more opportunity to do God's work. Personally, Paul felt dying would be better, because then he would join Christ. But his main goal was to honor Christ through his life or his death.

Being a Christian means that we're pulled in opposite directions. A part of us longs to leave sin and earthly troubles behind and be united with our Savior. But staying on earth means more opportunities to be used by God, and more time to pray for lost loved ones. Some days the first option is especially appealing, but if our goal is to honor Christ, then either outcome will be okay with us.

> *I find it hard to choose between the two. I would like to leave this life and be with Christ. That's by far the better choice. But for your sake it's better that I remain in this life.*
>
> Philippians 1:23–24

Ask yourself: **Am I prepared to honor Christ through my life or my death?**

DECEMBER
20

"Why do you criticize other Christians?"

Romans 14:1–13

Darius was beginning to regret his decision to visit his coworker's church. The people seemed friendly, and Jerry made it a point to introduce him to those around him. But each time someone walked away, Jerry whispered some derogatory remark. That woman was "dressed like a hussy," the other one "cried during every service," that man "liked to raise his hands during the singing," that couple "allowed their teen to do things he shouldn't," the pastor "used the wrong translation," and so on. After the service, Darius didn't remember the sermon as much as he recalled Jerry's running commentary.

Paul addressed the problem of believers criticizing each other in the church at Corinth. Those who believed they shouldn't eat meat condemned those who did; the people who ate everything looked down on the vegetarians. Church members also disparaged each other on the basis of whether or not they observed certain days as holy. "Why do you criticize or despise other Christians?" Paul asked them. He emphasized that since all believers are servants of Christ, he alone has the right to judge them.

We can't compromise when it comes to major doctrines of the faith. But God wants us to resist the temptation to pass judgment on believers who think differently from us on minor issues. We never have an excuse to make derogatory remarks about a fellow believer in matters dictated by personal opinion. Whether we're pointing out people's faults or condemning them for their views on spiritual matters, we're dishonoring God.

Some people seem to naturally have a critical spirit; others put people down to build themselves up. We can overcome such tendencies by remembering that Jesus accepted us when we were a sinner and God's enemy. Since he did that for us, surely we can accept other believers.

Accept each other in the same way that Christ accepted you.

Romans 15:7

Ask yourself: **Do I have a critical spirit toward other believers?**

DECEMBER
21

"Is he slow to help them?"

Luke 18:1–8

I can't believe it's finally over, Monica thought as she walked out of the state attorney's office. For several weeks Monica had been trying to get the charges against her son changed. The other two store employees had been caught on the video camera actually stealing but had received only misdemeanor charges. Monica's son appeared on the video simply standing nearby—and faced a felony charge. Testimony by other employees only accused the other two teens. Finally, the charges against her son had been changed. It had been a long haul, but Monica was glad she hadn't given up.

Jesus told a story about another woman who refused to give up. A widow kept going to a judge to present her case and ask for justice. Since the judge didn't care about people or about serving God, he ignored her for a while. Finally, however, he decided to resolve her case so she would stop bothering him. Jesus contrasted the example of the uncaring judge with God. "Won't God give his chosen people justice when they cry out to him for help day and night?" he asked. "Is he slow to help them?"

Jesus used the example of the persistent widow to show his disciples they should always pray and never give up, especially in matters that called for justice to be done. It's hard to keep praying for the same request over a long period of time without getting discouraged. We may start to feel like God is ignoring us. But we know God loves us and cares for our needs. If we feel certain that what we're asking is within God's will, we can persevere, knowing he will help us. It may seem like a long haul, but God's answers are always right on time.

Keep on asking, and you will receive what you ask for. Keep on seeking, and you will find. Keep on knocking, and the door will be opened to you.

Matthew 7:7 NLT

Ask yourself: **Am I struggling with the temptation to give up on a prayer request that's close to my heart?**

DECEMBER

22

"What proof is there for this?"

Luke 1:5–25

Tammy looked across the kitchen table at her son. How many years had she prayed for this? Could it finally be coming true? After being involved with drugs since high school, her son claimed he had turned over a new leaf and started rehab. Tammy longed to believe his words, but part of her remained skeptical. It seemed too good to be true.

After praying for a son for so many years, Zechariah found the angel Gabriel's news too good to be true. Not only would Zechariah and Elizabeth have a son, but John would be a great man who would turn many people back to God. He would be filled with the Holy Spirit even before his birth and have the same power as Elijah. Zechariah's son would prepare people for the Messiah.

In spite of the detailed description that Gabriel gave, part of Zechariah remained skeptical. "What proof is there for this?" he asked. "I'm an old man, and my wife is beyond her childbearing years." Gabriel told Zechariah he would be unable to speak until John's birth since he didn't believe the message that God had sent him.

When we've had the same request for so long, our faith may weaken even as we continue to pray. We know God can heal, restore, and redeem in any situation. But after so much time passes, prayers for our heart's longing can become more of a habit. We've lost that sense of expectancy of seeing God act. When the answer does finally arrive, we may have trouble recognizing or believing it. If we've grown weary in prayer, we can ask God to examine our attitudes and help us overcome any traces of skepticism. And we can ask him to help us remember that, with him, nothing is too good to be true.

When you ask for something, don't have any doubts.

James 1:6

Ask God to give you the faith to believe in answers to prayers that would seem too good to be true.

DECEMBER
23

"How can this be?"

Luke 1:26–38

The angel Gabriel paid two visits to Daniel, a Hebrew serving in a prominent position in Babylon, to explain future events. He also appeared to Zechariah, a priest ministering at the altar of incense in the temple in Jerusalem. But his most important mission involved a poor young girl in the small village of Nazareth. God sent Gabriel to Mary to announce the event that would change all of history.

"You are favored by the Lord!" Gabriel's appearance and greeting startled and confused Mary. While she tried to figure out what he meant, Gabriel delivered his message. His words left no doubt in Mary's mind: she would give birth to the Messiah, which was every Jewish woman's dream. But Mary couldn't help wondering how this would happen, since she was a virgin.

"How can this be?" she asked. It's safe to assume that Mary didn't fully comprehend Gabriel's answer that the Holy Spirit would come and the "power of the Most High would overshadow" her. But without hesitating, she called herself "the Lord's servant," and submitted to whatever God asked of her.

When God asks us to do something, we may want to weigh the pros and cons before we commit. Sometimes we act like he owes us all the details of his plan—especially when his assignment seems frightening, implausible, or downright impossible. But God is looking for people with an attitude like Mary's.

We don't have to be an extraordinary person for God to do something special through us. But we do have to be willing to trust his character and his power. And we have to submit to his plan, even when we don't understand how everything will work out.

Mary answered, "I am the Lord's servant. Let everything you've said happen to me."

Luke 1:38

Ask yourself: **Am I ready and willing to accept God's plan for me, even when I don't fully understand it?**

DECEMBER

24

"Who brings out the stars one by one?"

Isaiah 40:26

Isaiah invites us to look up at the sky and see God's handiwork. He urges us to meditate on God's intimate involvement with his creation. "Who brings out the stars one by one?" he asks. With billions of stars in our galaxy, and billions of galaxies in the universe, who could imagine the total number? Yet God has given each one a name and makes sure not a single one is missing.

One dark night long ago, God lit up the sky with his glory as angels told shepherds about a birth that signaled the dawning of a bright new day. Jesus was the promised bright Morning Star that would come from the nation of Israel (see Num. 24:17; Rev. 22:16). He fulfilled the prophecy that "the people who walk in darkness will see a bright light" (Isa. 9:2).

Jesus brought light into a world darkened by sin and the shadow of death. "I am the light of the world," he told the Pharisees. Sometimes we feel oppressed by the darkness of the world around us; other times our circumstances make our personal world seem dark. We can always look to Jesus and his promise to light up our life with his peace and joy.

God has given us another source of light: his written Word. The Bible serves as a lamp for our feet and a light for our path (see Ps. 119:105). It illuminates our way so we don't stumble or stray from the right path. When we can't see our way clear to make a decision, the Word sheds light by offering direction and guidance. With Jesus to light up our life and the Bible to light our path, there's no reason for us to ever be in the dark.

He said, "I am the light of the world. Whoever follows me will have a life filled with light and will never live in the dark."

John 8:12

Ask yourself: **In what specific way do I need God to shed his light on my life today?**

“Does God really live on earth with people?”

2 Chronicles 6:1–21

There’s no way we can picture the excitement on that special day. The magnificent temple in Jerusalem had finally been completed and furnished. After priests brought the ark of the covenant to the Holy Place, trumpets blared while musicians played a variety of instruments and sang praises to God. Then a cloud filled the Temple and interrupted the activities. God’s glory had come to live in his house.

King Solomon knelt before the people to offer a prayer of dedication. He felt humbled that God had allowed him to build the temple, but he acknowledged that no structure could ever truly contain God. “Does God really live on earth with people?” Solomon asked. “If heaven itself, the highest heaven, cannot hold you, then how can this temple that I have built?” Although God is spirit (see John 4:24), he had made the temple a point of contact and communication with his people.

The sight of the Lord’s glory filling the splendid temple pales in comparison to the picture of a newborn baby lying in a manger a thousand years later. While the temple symbolized God’s spiritual presence, at Jesus’s birth God came down to earth in human form. Long before his birth, Isaiah had named the baby Immanuel, “God is with us” (see Isa. 7:14).

Jesus’s death, resurrection, and ascension paved the way for a new point of contact and communication between God and his people. As believers we have God’s Holy Spirit living inside us, making a personal relationship possible. We also have the promise of enjoying a new level of intimacy with God in heaven, where we can live together with him unhindered by the presence of sin. God is with us, in us, around us—and someday it will get even better. That’s more than enough reason to come and adore him.

A virgin will become pregnant and give birth to a son,
and she will name him Immanuel [God Is With Us].

Isaiah 7:14

Ask yourself: **How can I be more aware of God’s presence every moment of every day?**

DECEMBER

26

"Where is the one who was born to be the king of the Jews?"

Matthew 2:1–12

After driving around confused for almost an hour, the man finally gave in to his wife's nagging and stopped for directions at a gas station. It surprised him to learn how close he'd been to the house. If only that unmarked road hadn't thrown him off! Checking the time, the couple decided to forget it and head home. They argued all the way. She said they missed the party because he was too stubborn to ask for directions. He said they missed it because their friends' new house was hidden in the woods.

We don't know much about the wise men or the source of their information about Jesus. We do know that they didn't mind stopping to ask for directions. Arriving in Jerusalem from their country in the east, they asked Herod, "Where is the one who was born to be the king of the Jews?" The priests and scribes told Herod that the Messiah would be born in Bethlehem. A star led the wise men to a specific house, where they found Mary and Jesus. With great joy they worshiped the child and offered him precious gifts.

God never hides himself from people. He doesn't lay out a maze that we have to work through in order to reach him. God has displayed his glory in the heavens and all of creation. His written Word tells us what we need to know to find him and how to live a godly life. But we have to be willing to ask for help when we need it, and we must be willing to follow directions. Pride or aloofness on our part can cause us to overlook God's presence in our life. If we want to find him, we're expected to put our whole heart into the search. When we do that, God promises we'll find what we're looking for.

When you look for me, you will find me.
When you wholeheartedly seek me, I will
let you find me, declares the Lord.

Jeremiah 29:13–14

Ask yourself: **Am I wholeheartedly seeking God's will?**

DECEMBER
27

"Isn't this the carpenter's son?"

Matthew 13:54–58

The man smiled and waved at the crowd lining Main Street. *This town sure knows how to throw a celebration*, he thought. He only had a minor role in the television series, but the people didn't seem to mind. They'd given him the star treatment all week long—luncheons, receptions, a key to the city, and now he was leading the parade. *I should have come back to my hometown sooner*, he thought.

Jesus got a different kind of reception when he returned to his hometown. But his story wasn't "local boy makes good," it was a local boy growing up and claiming to be God. The people of Nazareth took offense at his claims; after all, they'd known Jesus since his childhood. "Isn't this the carpenter's son?" they asked. "Isn't his mother's name Mary?" Because of their familiarity with Jesus's family, the people couldn't see his true identity. Their lack of faith limited his miracles and healing ministry there.

As time passes, we can let our familiarity with Christianity dull the sense of wonder that knowing God inspires. We're especially vulnerable if we've been involved in church activities since our birth. We can reach the point of rattling off familiar songs, verses, or spiritual truths without being affected by their meaning. When this happens, we stop learning and growing as our attitude hinders the Spirit's work in our life.

One way to keep our faith fresh is to meditate on the mysteries of our faith—things our human mind can't fully understand, such as Jesus being God and man at the same time. The Bible gives us more than enough to ponder for a lifetime. Jesus *is* a carpenter's son, but we won't fully nail down who he is until we meet him face-to-face.

In the beginning the Word already existed. The Word was with God, and the Word was God. . . . The Word became human and lived among us.

John 1:1, 14

Ask yourself: **Have I let familiarity with the Bible cause my faith to grow stale?**

DECEMBER
28

"Who is this king of glory?"

Psalm 24:7–10

The procession marched up to the gates and called for admittance so that "the king of glory may come in." The gatekeeper called out, "Who is this king of glory?" A chorus of voices answered in unison, "The LORD, strong and mighty!" Again the gatekeeper inquired, "Who, then, is this king of glory?" The chorus responded, "The LORD of Armies is the king of glory!"

Many scholars think David wrote this psalm to celebrate bringing the ark of the covenant back to Jerusalem. The words were often used in worship services, sometimes set to music. The psalm pictures God as a glorious king about to enter the city, showing us who leads the church in battle against her enemies. It also foreshadows Christ's future return to earth.

In Revelation 19:11–19, John saw a vision of the final battle between God and evil. With most of the world worshiping the Antichrist, the armies of the world gather to fight against God. Suddenly Jesus rides out on a white horse with eyes like fire and many crowns on his head. In his mouth is a sharp sword, and behind him are the armies of heaven.

What a world of difference between Jesus's first and second comings to the earth! The first time he arrived as a newborn baby in humble surroundings; he'll return as a warrior king. Before, Jesus submitted to humiliation, torture, and execution on a cross. Next time, he will come to execute judgment on God's enemies and rule the nations.

Although the final battle is yet to come, Jesus already reigns in the hearts of believers. We have the King of kings fighting for us, the Lord of lords guiding us. As we learn to open our heart and mind to him more fully, each day we'll get a clearer picture of his glory.

On his clothes and his thigh he has a name
written: King of kings and Lord of lords.

Revelation 19:16

Ask yourself: **Should anything intimidate me today as I go about serving the King of kings?**

"Who deserves to open the scroll and break the seals on it?"

Revelation 5

John's vision of heaven included a moment of unbearable tension. He saw a long scroll rolled up and sealed with seven seals that would have to be broken one by one as someone read the contents. A powerful angel cried out in a loud voice, "Who deserves to open the scroll and break the seals on it?" But no one was found in heaven, on the earth, or under the earth who deserved to open the scroll. Overcome by a sense of hopelessness, John wept bitterly.

Then one of the leaders told John, "Stop crying! The Lion from the tribe of Judah, the Root of David, has won the victory. He can open the scroll and the seven seals on it." When John looked near the throne, he saw a Lamb who had been slaughtered take the scroll from God's hand. Immediately, the inhabitants of heaven began singing praises to Jesus. Soon, thousands upon thousands of angels joined in, declaring that the Lamb "deserves to receive power, wealth, wisdom, strength, honor, glory, and praise."

Today the name of Jesus Christ is often mocked, despised, and even hated. But one day Jesus will get all the honor he rightly deserves. Jesus redeemed the world by living a sinless life, dying for the sins of the human race, and rising from the grave. Because of the victory Jesus won, he alone has the authority and the credentials to oversee the completion of human history. We can take comfort in knowing that our future and the world's future are in his hands. In the meantime, we are free to concentrate on giving Jesus more of the praise and honor he so richly deserves.

The Lion from the tribe of Judah, the Root of David, has won the victory. He can open the scroll and the seven seals on it.

Revelation 5:5

Ask yourself: **What changes can I make in my life to bring Jesus more glory, honor, and praise?**

DECEMBER
30

"Won't the judge of the whole earth do what is fair?"

Genesis 18:16–33

Vivian started to enter the teachers' lounge, but did an about-face when she heard the topic of conversation. The entire faculty was buzzing about the students expelled from school last Friday. Everyone seemed to think the principal had been too harsh, but Vivian knew details the others didn't. She hated not being at liberty to talk about the case, especially when people seemed so quick to condemn her boss. *They'll change their opinion when the whole story comes out*, Vivian told herself.

People are often quick to condemn God's decisions without realizing they don't know the full story. Abraham knew better. When God confided his plans to destroy the wicked cities of Sodom and Gomorrah, Abraham felt comfortable interceding on the basis of God's character. "Are you really going to sweep away the innocent with the guilty?" he asked. "That would be unthinkable! Won't the judge of the whole earth do what is fair?" God agreed to spare the entire city of Sodom if he found ten righteous people there.

Some people view God's punishment of wicked people in the Old Testament as cruel. Others question what the Bible says about future judgment of unbelievers. Many people use current events as proof of God's unfairness. But whenever we see God as unjust, it's because we don't have all the details.

As Creator, God is the only one with the right to judge the world. Since he's omniscient, he's the only one with the ability to judge fairly. We need to remember that our perspective of what's fair is shaped by our changeable emotions, personal experiences, prejudices, and our sinful nature. We can't expect to understand all of God's actions, but we can depend on his character. And we can trust him to be a fair Judge.

What he does is perfect. All his ways are fair. He is a faithful God, who does no wrong. He is honorable and reliable.

Deuteronomy 32:4

Ask yourself: **How do I handle circumstances that cause me to doubt God's fairness?**

DECEMBER

31

"When will this happen?"

Matthew 24

Many people over the centuries have tried to calculate the dates for end-time events. In 1988, a booklet entitled *88 Reasons Why the Rapture Will Be in 1988* sold more than four million copies. The author predicted that Jesus would return for believers between September 11 and 13. He later revised the date to September 15, then October 3. The author continued to publish booklets predicting the date for several years.

People have always been curious about God's timetable. After Jesus taught about future events, his disciples privately requested more details. "Tell us, when will this happen?" they asked. "What will be the sign that you are coming again, and when will the world come to an end?"

Jesus warned them not to be deceived by the many false teachers who would come, some displaying counterfeit signs and claiming to be the Messiah. Then he described end-time events that would take place, but emphasized that only God the Father knows the dates and hours for their fulfillment.

God wants us to be aware of signs of the times without getting caught up in someone's opinions and calculations. Since only God knows the timetable for history's final events, it's a waste of time to try to figure out specific dates. What God tells us is more than enough to motivate us to pray for unbelievers, witness about him, and live a godly life so we won't be ashamed when we meet him. Instead of asking "when," a better question would be, "How would I live my life differently if I knew that Jesus would come today?"

So think of the kind of holy and godly lives
you must live as you look forward to the day
of God and eagerly wait for it to come.

2 Peter 3:11–12

Ask yourself: **If Jesus returned for his church today, would I be prepared to meet him?**

Dianne Neal Matthews has written numerous devotionals, magazine articles, and newspaper features. Her work has appeared in *Focus on the Family*, *The Quiet Hour*, *LIVE*, *The Christian Communicator*, and on websites including CBN.com. She is the author of *The One Year On This Day* and *The One Year Women of the Bible* (Tyndale House), and has contributed to several compilation books including *Pearl Girls: Encountering Grit, Experiencing Grace* (Moody Press).

A mother and grandmother, Dianne also teaches at writers' conferences and speaks to women's groups. She is a member of the Christian Authors Network, Advanced Writers & Speakers Association, and Toastmasters International. Dianne and her husband, Richard, live in Utah. For more information, please visit www.DianneNealMatthews.com.